# CIVIL RIGHTS
# AND LIBERTIES

# CIVIL RIGHTS AND LIBERTIES

## Provocative Questions and Evolving Answers

Harold J. Sullivan

*John Jay College/The City University of New York*

Prentice Hall

Upper Saddle River, New Jersey 07458

*Library of Congress Cataloging-in-Publication Data*

SULLIVAN, HAROLD J. (HAROLD JOSEPH)
    Civil rights and liberties: provocative questions and evolving answers / HAROLD J. SULLIVAN.
        p.   cm.
    Includes bibliographical references and index.
    ISBN 0-13-084514-0
    1. Civil rights—United States.   I. Title.
    KF4749.S85    2001
    342,73'085—dc21        00-059837

VP, Editorial Director: *Laura Pearson*
Director of Marketing: *Beth Gillett Mejia*
Editorial Assistant: *Jessica Drew*
Editorial/Production Supervision: *Edie Riker*
Prepress and Manufacturing Buyer: *Benjamin D. Smith*
Cover Director: *Jayne Conte*
Cover Designer: *Joseph Sengotta*
Cover Art: *Reza Estakhrian / Tony Stone Images*

This book was set in 10/12 New Century Schoolbook by East End Publishing
Services, Inc., and was printed and bound by Courier Companies, Inc. The cover
was printed by Phoenix Color Corp.

© 2001 by Prentice-Hall, Inc.
A Division of Pearson Education
Upper Saddle River, New Jersey 07458

Printed in the United States of America

10   9   8   7   6   5   4   3   2   1

ISBN    0-13-084514-0

Prentice-Hall International (UK) Limited, *London*
Prentice-Hall of Australia Pty. Limited, *Sydney*
Prentice-Hall Canada Inc., *Toronto*
Prentice-Hall Hispanoamericana, S.A., *Mexico*
Prentice-Hall of India Private Limited, *New Delhi*
Prentice-Hall of Japan, Inc., *Tokyo*
Pearson Education Asia Pte. Ltd., *Singapore*
Editora Prentice-Hall do Brasil, Ltda., *Rio de Janeiro*

*To my wife Joan,*
*my love and best friend*
*who makes all things better.*

# Contents

# Contents

### CHAPTER 4

## Equality Under the Constitution   89

### CHAPTER 5

## Privacy and Individual Autonomy   121

## Contemporary Issue of Equality and Freedom    143

## Conclusion: What Is the Future of Civil Rights and Civil Liberties in America?    161

## Appendix: The Constitution of the United States    165

## Index    187

# Preface

Most of us have been exposed at some level to controversies concerning abortion, affirmative action, hate speech, obscenity, and the like. Many are puzzled and/or angered by what they have heard about such issues but have little or no understanding of what such issues are about and how and why the courts have dealt with them. In this book I hope to stimulate readers into thinking critically about such controversial issues in the civil rights/civil liberties field.

In order to stimulate such thinking, each section of this book is introduced with a question. The questions are followed by responses which present the variety of "answers" justices on the Supreme Court have given to such questions in actual cases which have come before the United States Supreme Court. The questions are phrased simply and directly, and each answer is an essay designed to make constitutional interpretation accessible to readers even if they have no background in constitutional law. I expect that when such readers see many of the questions, they will think to themselves: "I've always wondered about that." When they read the "answers," they will be exposed to various constitutional tests and doctrines. I also hope that when they read the questions and the variety of answers to them, they will be stimulated to explore in greater detail the U. S. Supreme Court decisions from which these answers were derived.

The subtitle of this book refers to "provocative questions and evolving answers." The answers provided by the United States Supreme Court justices have in fact been constantly evolving as the Justices have sought to apply the principles of the Constitution to changing circumstances and new questions, some of which could not have been anticipated by the authors of the Constitution.

By discussing both traditional and new issues throughout, in the end I hope to provoke readers into thinking about some questions that may become increasingly important in the future. These are issues with which the U. S. Supreme Court has only begun to grapple. I hope my discussion of them will stimulate readers to help evolve some new solutions on their own.

## ACKNOWLEDGMENTS

Any author, if he is honest with himself, must acknowledge that his work is largely a product of the inspiration, encouragement, and support of many beyond himself. I know I owe much to my family, many friends, and colleagues. My wife Joan Kross and I have been together less than four years, but as I said in the dedication, she has changed my life in all things for the better. As soon as she learned I was working on this project, she provided an essential push. . . . My mother Margaret Shine Sullivan, the other woman in my life, has from the beginning always believed in me and encouraged me. I thank as well the rest of my family, including especially my late sister Evelyn, who always supported me in everything I did as my brother Kenneth does today. My stepsons John and Edward asked intelligent questions, engaged me in spirited arguments, and provided encouragement (including Edward's insistence that I change the working title of this book). They sometimes seemed puzzled by the flexibility of my academic schedule; I hope my completion of this work will convince them that I do indeed really work for a living! My wife's mother Irene Kross, has also provided encouragement. I cannot acknowledge family support, however, without acknowledging my unofficial family, my closest friend for over 30 years, Stephen Devaux, and his wife Deb. Stephen goaded me almost daily as I completed this work. Most importantly he and Deb introduced me to my wife Joan. But the most unusual gift he could ever have given me is the opportunity to know and love his two awe-inspiring children, A.J. and Eric. Having been allowed to share close up in watching A. J. grow into the impressive young teenager he is now and to see his younger brother Eric blossom into his own has been one of the greatest sources of pleasure I have had.

Colleagues at the City University and other friends over the years have provided ideas and encouragement as this project has gone forward. I think in particular of all of my colleagues in the Government Department at John Jay College, especially Bob Sullivan, Barry Latzer, and

Roger McDonald, who provided useful suggestions. Other John Jay colleagues whose friendship and encouragement have been invaluable include Jim Cohen, Anna Goldoff, Karen Kaplowitz, and Basil Wilson. Outside of CUNY, Stephen White, with whom I first discussed the idea for this project two decades ago; Inez Smith Reid, who first introduced me to Constitutional law; Glenn Tinder whose book *Political Thinking* gave me the idea for the question and answer format of this book; and my mentor and friend from college, George Goodwin, Jr., deserve acknowledgment and thanks as do Beth Gillett Mejia, Jayme Heffler, and the editorial staff and the Prentice Hall reviewers: Richard Hardy, University of Missouri, Columbia; and Gregory M. Scott, University of Central Oklahoma.

Finally, I acknowledge two very different contributors to all of my work, my close friends over three decades in "the Group" and my students at John Jay College. I have maintained very strong friendships over three decades with a collection of University of Massachusetts at Boston classmates, known collectively as "the Group"; they, together with their spouses, friends, and significant others, as well as other friends in Boston and New York have helped make life fun as well as intellectually stimulating. With a little help from the U.S. Supreme Court (see p. 65), Grendel's Den in Harvard Square has often served as our preferred rendezvous for nearly two decades. I have had the privilege of teaching a wonderfully diverse array of students, many of whom have struggled against incredible odds to succeed. Many of them have done as well as the best anywhere. So I close thanking them for providing inspiration to all of their professors.

### CHAPTER 1

# Introduction: Judicial Defense of Civil Liberties and Civil Rights

The proper relationship of the individual to the state and society has always been a central question to political thinkers. The question becomes still more complicated in a society that claims to be governed by democratic principles. Probably the principal element in all the many competing definitions of democracy is the notion of majority rule. If, indeed, the government represents the will of the majority of the citizens, then perhaps we need not worry so much about protecting individuals from government. If we choose the government, what do we have to fear?

Most of us, however, are uneasy about giving power over our lives to others—even others like ourselves. Most of us often feel we want to be left alone. On the other hand, most of us do readily conform to societal norms with little complaint, and we may have little patience for people who insist on being different. Especially in this complex modern world in which we are forced to live close to each other and to interact with others on a daily basis, many may long for order.

In America the Constitution determines the rules for the relationship of the individual to the state. Broadly speaking, it defines the areas in which government may act and places restrictions on the power of government to interfere with or restrain our individual or collective choices. When we speak of constitutional protections for us as individuals, we are speaking broadly of **civil liberties** and **civil rights.** Although many of us use the terms interchangeably, they really define two somewhat distinct aspects of our relationship to the state and society. *Civil liberties* *refer to those restrictions on government which leave the individual free to think and sometimes to act as he or she chooses without interference from government. Civil rights,* on the other hand, refer to *those affirmative protections that government owes to each individual as a citizen or participant in the society.*

A classic example of a civil liberty is freedom of religion. In its most elemental sense we understand this to be our right to believe (or disbelieve) whatever we want without the threat of retaliation from government. Government is restricted from interfering with our religious beliefs. When we think of civil rights, the first example that comes to mind is our expectation that we must be free from discrimination based on our race. The realization of civil rights, however, can often require government action on our behalf, preventing other citizens from disadvantaging us solely because of our race. While civil liberties usually require that government leave us alone or keep its hands off, civil rights often require government action to protect our interests or rights from interference from others. Protection of civil rights, then, often requires government to act; protection of civil liberties usually just requires that government do nothing.

Even when we understand the differences between the terms civil rights and civil liberties, we have barely begun to come to some understanding of civil rights and liberties in the United States. The practical meaning of these terms here is determined first of all by the Constitution. But what is the Constitution? The Constitution is the legal document that assigns and distributes government powers. In assigning power, however, it both explicitly and implicitly limits government powers. Once a society decides to have a constitutional government, by giving some powers it implicitly withholds those not given or assigned. The purpose of the Bill of Rights in our Constitution was to put additional explicit limits on the powers of the national (or federal government) and the purpose of the Fourteenth and Fifteenth Amendments was to place additional restrictions on the powers of the individual states which collectively make up the United States.

Every liberty we may want may not be protected by the Constitution; every right upon which many of us might want to depend may not have been a concern of those who drafted and approved those sections of the Constitution that restrict government powers or give government a command to protect our rights. The principal sources of our constitutional rights and liberties are the first ten amendments to the Constitution, usually referred to as the Bill of Rights, and the Thirteenth, Fourteenth, and Fifteenth Amendments. It is important to notice that it was in the amendments or changes to the Constitution as originally drafted by the framers that our rights and liberties are most explicitly addressed. When the Constitution was submitted to the original 13 states for ratification or acceptance as the governing charter of the United States, many felt it did not protect civil liberties enough. As a condition for agreeing to ratify or accept the Constitution, many states insisted on more explicit limitations on federal government power. These were added by constitutional amendment almost immediately following ratification of the Constitution. Constitutional protections for civil rights really came only after the Civil War.

Any understanding of civil rights and liberties in America, then, begins with an understanding of the Constitution. But an understanding of the meaning of the Constitution requires an understanding of the role and significance of the courts, especially the United States Supreme Court. Although many sections of the Bill of Rights seem clear on the surface, for example, the First Amendment command that "Congress shall make no law . . . abridging the freedom of speech, or of the press," on reflection we may realize that this may not be as clear as it first appears. What does "abridge" mean? Is a law that regulates the places where we may speak, a law "abridging" our freedom of speech? What is encompassed by the phrase "the freedom of speech"? Does the freedom of speech include the freedom to interrupt others while they are speaking? Does it mean we may speak about the relative merits of the New York Yankees or the Boston Red Sox, about any subject we please, while a court of law is considering a tax case? Does it mean we may deliberately lie so as to damage the reputation of others? Does it mean we may make unwanted verbal sexual advances to an employee?

In the United States answers to question such as these, as well as answers to the questions that make up the body of this book, are provided by the courts. To understand the role of the courts in defining civil rights and liberties we must begin by trying to understand the concept known as **judicial review**. *Judicial review is the power that American courts claim to decide on the constitutionality of actions of other parts of government.* It is the power they exercise to declare actions of other branches and levels of government unconstitutional and therefore not binding on the courts. When a court rules that a law or other government action is unconstitutional, generally all it is really saying is that the court will refuse to apply that law in the cases before it. If the courts consistently refuse to follow a law as they adjudicate disputes, then the law will cease to have practical effect.

Although there is substantial evidence that the framers of the Constitution intended the courts to exercise the power of judicial review, the Constitution does not explicitly and unambiguously give this power to the courts. All who exercise power under the U.S. Constitution are sworn to uphold and defend it. When the courts claim an action of another branch of government violates the constitution, they are in effect second-guessing other government officials and challenging their fidelity to their oaths. In trying to understand the courts' exercise of the power of judicial review, we must view their claim in the context of an understanding of the nature of the judicial process.

## WHAT COURTS DO

It is the responsibility of courts to resolve disputes by applying the law in individual cases or controversies. The case in which the U.S. Supreme Court first expressly claimed the right to refuse to give effect to the actions of another branch of government was *Marbury v. Madison,* in 1803. The actual dispute in *Marbury* was rather trivial, involving a dispute over a presidential appointment to a relatively insignificant judgeship. Marbury was a judicial candidate; Madison, in his capacity of secretary of state, in effect represented the president. But as has often been true historically, cases which in the immediate sense seem trivial become the vehicle for important legal rulings and interpretations of the Constitution.

In *Marbury v. Madison* the U.S. Supreme Court was confronted with the question of what happens if in making laws the Congress of the United States, *in the view of the Court*, disregards the distribution of powers established by the Constitution and substitutes its own judgment for how governmental powers should be allocated. The Court recognized that in the ordinary course of deciding cases, courts virtually everywhere are required to apply general laws passed by legislatures to individual cases. The first task before a court is to discover which laws are relevant to the case, in other words which laws provide guidance.

In a country with a constitution a court would naturally look to it to see if it provides guidance. Then it would look to statutes, laws passed by legislatures carrying out powers given to them by the Constitution. Of necessity, however, in applying these laws, courts have to interpret their meaning.

In *Marbury v. Madison,* however, the Supreme Court confronted an additional question that has proved pivotal: What if there are two laws which both give guidance for deciding a case and those two laws appear to the court in question to be in conflict? If you follow one law, you would decide the case one way. If you follow the second law, you would decide the case differently. What is a court to do? Which law should the court apply to the case before it?

According to Chief Justice John Marshall writing for a unanimous Supreme Court in *Marbury v. Madison,* because the courts owe their very existence to the Constitution, because all government power in the United States is limited by the Constitution, when the Court determined in *Marbury v. Madison* that the Constitution was at odds with a law passed by Congress, they determined that it is only natural that in the case of such conflict they should follow the Constitution and disregard the law approved by Congress. In support of this position, Chief Justice Marshall cited the language of the Constitution itself. Article III gives to the federal courts the responsibility to decide cases or controversies arising under the Constitution and the laws of the United States. Article VI or the Supremacy clause says: "This Constitution and the laws of the United States which shall be made in pursuance thereof are the Supreme law of the land, And the judges in every state shall be bound thereby, anything in the laws of any state to the contrary notwithstanding."

Chief Justice Marshall argued that the Supremacy clause means only laws of the United States passed in *pursuance of the constitution* are "supreme." From this he concluded that in deciding cases to which a provision of the Constitution and a law both apply, the courts must determine if the law is "in pursuance of the Constitution" or contrary to it. If the courts are bound in deciding cases to laws made "in pursuance" of the constitution, they are then not bound by those contrary to the Constitution. If they must decide a case by applying a law contrary to the Constitution or by applying the Constitution itself, the Supremacy clause, in listing the Constitution first, means they must follow the Constitution.

Although the Court's justification for its power of judicial review was not always universally supported, it has today become a fundamental element of American life. How is the power of judicial review exercised in the ordinary course of adjudication?

When any case is brought before a court, the parties to the case expect the court to apply existing law to their dispute in order to determine whose claim will succeed. In a criminal case, for example, a prosecutor representing the government seeks to persuade a judge and/or jury to decide that the accused has violated a criminal statute, a law passed by some state legislature or by Congress. In order to decide whether an accused is guilty a judge must first decide what the law means before either he or she or the jury decides whether the accused has violated the law. Any time a law is applied in an individual's case, the meaning and scope of the law must be understood. This requires interpretation.

When in the course of adjudication a party to the case contends that the law being applied to him or her violates the Constitution, the court must decide on the legitimacy of that claim. This requires the judge to interpret the law in question and the relevant section of the Constitution to determine whether there is a conflict. If in the judge's view the conflict exists he or she will declare the law or government action in question "unconstitutional" and refuse to give it effect.

Consider a hypothetical example. What if Congress in response to the controversy aroused by the scandal surrounding President Clinton's relationship with Monica Lewinsky, were to pass a criminal law making it a crime punishable by a year in prison for anyone to discuss in word or print the personal life of the president or any other high government official. Suppose that a reporter, subsequent to the law's enactment, were to learn that the majority leader of the Senate had, himself, had an illicit sexual liaison with an administrative aide. The reporter decides to publish an article in the *New York Post* detailing this relationship, including lurid details obtained from interviews with the now dismissed aide. Following the publication, the United States Attorney for New York prosecutes the author of the article, and a trial is scheduled for the U.S. District Court for the Southern District of New York.

It is clear from the facts of this fictional case that the author in question has violated the statute passed by Congress. He has openly published an article including intimate details of a sexual relationship involving a high official in the U.S. government. What would the reporter's lawyers do? Clearly, they would ask the federal district court judge to throw out the case and dismiss the indictment on the grounds that the law in question violates the First Amendment to the Constitution which states in part that "Congress shall make no laws abridging the freedom of speech or of the press. . . ." What would the federal district court judge do? No doubt she would review the precedents, prior Supreme Court rulings interpreting the First Amendment, to decide whether she could apply the law in question against the accused without violating the First Amendment. She would, in other words, have to decide whether two laws, which both seem to apply to the case before her, are in conflict. If so, following *Marbury v. Madison*, she would decide to disregard the law passed by Congress.

Although there would probably be little doubt today that such a law violates the First Amendment, one can imagine another result. The court would first have to ask itself whether commentary on the personal lives of politicians is part of "the freedom of speech." We are so accustomed to such exposés today that we may think the answer to this question is obvious, but certainly this has not always been the case. Is such reporting one of the great purposes for which the Amendment was added to the Constitution in the first place? Would banning such reporting seriously jeopardize the values intended to be protected by the First Amendment? In many other countries where freedom of speech is also highly valued, articles like the one described here would clearly not be permitted.

We might ask ourselves if the likely result in this hypothetical case would be different in the United States had the law in question banned only "false" reporting on the personal lives of high public officials. If so, the result would clearly not have been as obvious. (See Chapter 2, Question 7.)

## HOW DO WE KNOW WHAT THE CONSTITUTION MEANS?

Whenever a court declares the action of some government agency unconstitutional, the judge explains his or her decision. The government agency in question will almost invariably appeal such an action to an **appellate court**. An *appellate court* is a *court that reviews the actions of trial courts to determine whether they have properly interpreted and applied applicable law in an individual case.* Appellate court judges issue "opinions" or *written explanations of their rulings or interpretations of the law.* Those interpretations in turn serve as **precedents**, *court decisions in prior cases which provide guidance to other courts called upon to decide similar cases in the future.* Generally court decisions overturning laws passed by Congress or a state legislature on constitutional grounds will be appealed by the government all the way to the United States Supreme Court. Usually, the Supreme Court is considered obligated to make the ultimate determination as to the constitutionality of state legislative or Congressional actions which have been overturned by a lower court. When the U.S. Supreme Court interprets the Constitution in the course of coming to a decision in a case in which a law has been challenged on constitutional grounds, its decisions interpreting the Constitution are considered controlling on lower courts. Those decisions provide precedents to guide the lower courts in similar cases. The parties in similar cases which arise in the future will know that if the trial court in their case disregards the Supreme Court interpretations, they too can appeal the decision up to the Supreme Court and, barring some change of mind, the Court will interpret the Constitution the same way again.

If we want to know what a specific provision of the Constitution means in practice, we must look to U.S. Supreme Court decisions interpreting the Constitution. By reading the Court opinions in cases that have previously arisen, we can usually determine what the Court is likely to do in a future case raising similar issues. Courts generally consider themselves bound by precedents. The rule of precedents, or *stare decisis*, however, in cases interpreting the Constitution is not considered as important as in cases interpreting ordinary statutes. Changing the constitution itself is very difficult. If a court misinterprets an ordinary statute or law, a legislature can correct the decision simply by changing the law. A change in the Constitution, however, is much more difficult. Generally a Constitutional amendment requires a two-thirds majority of both houses of Congress and the ratification of the legislatures of three-fourths of the states. A misinterpretation of the Constitution by the courts, then, is very difficult to correct or change. Because of this, courts are more willing to reinterpret the Constitution to correct perceived errors themselves. Such overturning of constitutional interpretations by the courts, however, although not exceptionally rare, is still unusual.

Often the Supreme Court itself is divided in its interpretation of the Constitution in the cases it decides. The very fact that a case reaches the Supreme Court tells us that it involves controversy. Different justices on the Court can have very different views concerning what a constitutional provision means, and even when they agree concerning its basic meaning, they may disagree concerning its application to the controversy before the Court.

The Supreme Court, like most appellate courts, makes its decisions by majority vote. A justice representing the majority view of the Court is designated to write an **Opinion of the Court**, which sets forth the legal rationale behind the majority's decision in the case. The opinion of the Court explains to the parties in the case, to concerned others, and to future courts hearing comparable cases why the Court ruled as it did and what that ruling means. When the chief justice votes with the majority, he or she either writes the Opinion of the Court or decides who will draft the Opinion of the Court. When the chief justice disagrees with the decision of the majority in the case, the senior associate justice voting with the majority decides who is to draft the Opinion of the Court. When justices on the Court disagree with the Opinion of the Court, they often express their disagreements by writing what are known as **Separate Opinions.** If a justice approves of the decision in the specific case but disagrees with the reasoning justifying it used by the author of the Court's opinion (or simply wants to add something), he or she may write what is know as a **concurring opinion**, an opinion that explains the rationale used by the concurring justice or justices to justify their agreement with the action of the majority but their differences, if any, concerning the rationale behind that action. A justice or justices who disagree(s) with the decision made by the Court will often write **dissenting opinions**, opinions which explain the grounds for their disagreement with the majority's decision.

Although the reasoning in court opinions not attracting the support of an actual majority of the Court are not considered precedents binding future cases and lower courts, they often point the way to other litigants in the future who are looking for grounds to challenge existing interpretations of the Constitution. Sometimes dissents ultimately serve as the foundation for new interpretations of the Constitution. Some dissents in the end have more lasting significance in American constitutional interpretation than opinions of the Court which society comes to reject on reflection.

Together, opinions of the Court, concurring opinions and dissents provide authoritative views as to the meaning of the Constitution. Because the variety of opinions also alert us to the variety of possible interpretations of the meaning of various constitutional provisions, they can provide a window to the controversies arising over civil rights and civil liberties in American life. Judicial opinions in actual cases will then provide the raw material for discussing controversial questions relating to civil rights and liberties throughout this book. As the reader will soon see, there are a variety of interpretations of most sections of the Constitution, especially those sections of the Constitution pertaining to civil rights and liberties.

## THE FOURTEENTH AMENDMENT AND THE "INCORPORATION" OF THE BILL OF RIGHTS

Because the United States has a federal system of government which divides government authority between a strong central government (usually referred to as the federal government) and the 50 state governments, potential and actual threats to civil rights and liberties can come from either or both levels of government. Today, according to contemporary interpretation by the U.S. Supreme Court, the United States Constitution restrains both the federal government and the states in precisely the same way with regard to almost all the civil liberties recognized by the Bill of Rights of the United States Constitution. The application of the same standards to both state and federal government, however, is largely a twentieth-century development. In order to understand United States Constitutional standards for contemporary issues in civil rights and liberties it is, therefore, no longer important to distinguish between threats to those rights and liberties emanating from state or federal government. Nonetheless it is useful briefly to survey how, in spite of the federal system, the states came to be covered by constitutional guidelines initially developed to restrain principally the national government.

The Bill of Rights, as noted above, was added to the Constitution because some feared that the Constitution as drafted might enable the national government to interfere with important liberties. The Bill of Rights was not intended to bind the states. Each of the original states had its own constitution which to varying degrees limited the state's powers to interfere with individual liberties. When some sought the protection of the federal Bill of Rights from claimed invasion of individual liberties by state governments, the Supreme Court, emphasizing the framer's original purpose, concluded in *Barron v. Baltimore,* 1833 that the Bill of Rights restricted only Congress and the national government. The state governments were restrained only by their own constitutions and by the few limited restrictions on them included in the body of the unamended Constitution of 1787.

Following the Civil War, however, in order principally to assure protections for African-Americans from hostile legislation within the former "slave states," additional protections for rights and liberties were added to the Constitution through the Thirteenth, Fourteenth, and Fifteenth Amendments. These restrictions, especially the Fourteenth and Fifteenth Amendments, provided a basis for forcing the state governments to conform to some national constitutional standards for civil rights and liberties and served to alter somewhat the relationship between state and national governments. Very quickly, however, conflict arose within the Supreme Court over whether the Fourteenth Amendment subjected state governments to the national standard of the Bill of Rights in the same way as the national government or whether the scope of its protections for individual liberties in the states was far more limited.

Today, as a result of many court decisions spread over decades, virtually all the protections for individual liberties included in the Bill of Rights restrict state and local governments in the same way they restrict the national government. Because the focus of this book is on central substantive issues concerning fundamental civil rights and civil liberties, we will not survey in detail the complex arguments for and against applying the protections for civil liberties included in the Bill of Rights to state governments through the Fourteenth Amendment. We will, however, briefly explore how the Bill of Rights became substantially "incorporated" under into the Fourteenth Amendment as restrictions on the powers of state and local government.

Because the Fourteenth Amendment does not explicitly provide that state governments be subject to the protection for civil liberties included in the Bill of Rights, the case for their inclusion required interpretation of two sections of Section 1 of the Fourteenth Amendment. Section 1 of the Fourteenth Amendment states that

> All persons born or naturalized in the United States and subject
> to the jurisdiction thereof, are citizens of the United States and
> of the State wherein they reside. No State shall make or enforce
> any law which shall abridge the privileges or immunities of citizens
> of the United States; nor shall any State deprive any person of life,
> liberty, or property, without due process of law; nor deny to any
> person within its jurisdiction the equal protection of the laws.

When the U.S. Supreme Court was called upon to interpret the meaning of the Privileges and Immunities clause in the *Slaughterhouse Cases* of 1873 , it rejected by a 5 to 4 vote the argument that that clause was designed to apply the Bill of Rights to the states. Instead the Court confined the interpretation of this clause to rights, such as the right to travel from state to state—rights of a national character—which had existed before the adoption of the Fourteenth Amendment. The Court came to this conclusion in part through its determination that the primary purpose of the amendment was to extend existing constitutional protections to African-Americans who had previously been granted no rights by the states of the Confederacy and few rights even by states that had long banned slavery. Though the Amendment declared that all, including formerly enslaved African-Americans, were to be both citizens of the United States and of the state where they resided, the Court argued that they must be accorded all the rights held by other citizens but only those grounded in their national citizenship. Such national rights, according to the Supreme Court decision in *Barron v. Baltimore,* never included protection from state government infringements of rights protected by the Bill of Rights against infringement by the national government.

The Court majority's narrow interpretation of the Privileges or Immunities clause was challenged by four of the nine justices on the Court, who argued in dissents that privileges and immunities of citizens of the United States included all the protections for fundamental liberties included in the Bill of Rights. Despite the dissents, the U.S. Supreme Court has never yet overturned its initial narrow interpretation of the Privileges or Immunities clause. The protections for individual liberties which now apply to the states as well as the federal government were applied to them through the Due Process clause of the Fourteenth Amendment. In effect the Court has gradually come to interpret the word "liberty," which is protected against state infringement "without due process of law," to include most of the liberties encompassed by the Bill of Rights and more.

This process of "incorporation" of the protections of the Bill of Rights into the liberties protected by the Fourteenth Amendment against infringement by the states has been gradual, selective, and the subject of great controversy on the Court. First of all it is important to remember that almost any liberty or right, including even the right to life, can be restricted by government as a punishment for crimes. So initially when we read that "life, liberty, or property" may not be taken away without "due process of law," we understand that following proper procedural protections included under the concept "due process of law," liberty, or property, or even life may be taken away. But liberty means more than simply being free from imprisonment or other physical constraint. The term "liberty" must be given content or meaning through interpretation.

In interpreting the Fourteenth Amendment Due Process clause, then, the Court has had many occasions when it has had to define what "liberty" means. To some this term means simply and exclusively the specific liberties outlined in the Bill of Rights (referred to in constitutional interpretation as "total incorporation"); to others it has meant only those liberties included in the Bill of Rights which are fundamental liberties traditionally respected within Anglo-American legal-political traditions ("selective incorporation"); to others it has been an evolving concept including even more rights and liberties than those expressly recognized in the Bill of Rights ("total incorporation plus" or "selective incorporation plus"). Finally, to some the meaning of "liberty" and of "due process" in the Due Process clause of the Fourteenth Amendment is not directly tied to any of the specific provisions of the federal Bill of Rights

In the twentieth century the argument in support of incorporation of the Bill of Right has been best exemplified by Justice Hugo Black. Justice Black argued that the history of the enactment of the Fourteenth Amendment made it clear that its authors and principal supporters intended that the Privileges or Immunities clause would itself apply the Bill of Rights to the states (see the Appendix to his dissent in *Adamson v. California,* at 93–123 (1946). But recognizing that this interpretation had been rejected by the Court in the *Slaughterhouse* cases, he for a time supported the applications of the Bill of Rights to the states through the Due Process clause, arguing that the liberties protected by the Fourteenth Amendment were nothing more, or nothing less, than those included in the Bill of Rights. Justice Black argued against those (discussed below) who would substitute some other standard for determining which liberties are to be protected:

> I cannot consider the Bill of Rights to be an outworn 18th century "straight jacket." . . . Its provisions may be thought outdated abstractions by some. And it is true they were designed to meet ancient evils. But they are the same kind of human evils that have emerged from century to century whenever excessive power is sought by the few at the expense of the many. . . . I fear to see the consequences of the Court's practice of substituting its own concepts of decency and fundamental justice for the language of the Bill of Rights. . . . If the choice must be between the selective process of the *Palko* decision applying some of the Bill of Rights to the states or the *Twining* rule applying none of them, I would choose the *Palko* selective process. But rather than accept either of these choices, I would follow what I believe was the original purpose of the Fourteenth Amendment—to extend to all people of the nation the complete protection of the Bill of Rights (*Adamson v California* (1946), Black, J. dissenting, at 89).

According to Justice Black, any other interpretation of the Fourteenth Amendment allows Supreme Court justices to substitute their own judgments for those of the framers of the Bill of Rights and the Fourteenth Amendment.

One of the chief proponents of viewing the Due Process clause of the Fourteenth Amendment as being entirely independent and distinct from the Bill of Rights was Justice Felix Frankfurter, a contemporary of Justice

Black on the Court. In the same case, *Adamson v. California,* he rejected both Black's "total incorporation" and the Court standard of "selective incorporation," derived in part from Justice Benjamin Cardozo in *Palko v. Connecticut.* Instead he would substitute a case-by-case approach for determining whether state actions challenged under the Fourteenth Amendment adequately protect liberties on the whole.

The *Adamson* case concerned the question of whether the privilege against self-incrimination from the Fifth Amendment precluded a comment within a trial on a defendant's failure to respond at trial to charges against him. Had this been a federal criminal case, this practice would have been prohibited by the Fifth Amendment. The question then was whether the Fourteenth Amendment Due Process clause imposed this same restriction upon the states. In interpreting the Fourteenth Amendment Due Process clause, Justice Frankfurter, in direct contradiction to Justice Black, argued:

> The [Fourteenth] Amendment neither comprehends the specific provisions by which the founders deemed it appropriate to restrict the Federal government nor is it confined to them. . . . And so, when, as in a case like the present, a conviction in a State court is here for review under a claim that a right protected by the Due Process clause of the Fourteenth Amendment has been denied, the issue is not whether an infraction of the specific provisions of the first eight Amendments is disclosed in the record. The relevant question is whether the criminal proceedings which resulted in conviction deprived the accused of the due process of laws which the United States Constitution entitled him. Judicial review of the guaranty of the Fourteenth Amendment inescapably imposes upon this Court an exercise of judgment upon the whole course of the proceeding in order to ascertain whether they offend those canons of decency and fairness which express the notions of justice of English-speaking peoples even toward those charged with the most heinous offenses (*Adamson v California* (1946), Frankfurter, J., concurring at 66–68).

In reply to the position of Justice Black, who argued that the Bill of Rights alone provides the meaning of liberty and due process under the Fourteenth Amendment, Justice Frankfurter argued:

> These standards of Justice are not authoritatively formulated anywhere as though they were prescriptions in a pharmacopoeia. But neither does the application of the Due Process clause imply that judges are wholly at large. The judicial judgment in applying the Due Process clause must move within the limits of accepted notions

of justice and is not to be based upon the the idiosyncrasies of a merely personal judgment (at 66–68).

When there is any doubt that a state action contradicts such "accepted notions of justice," Justice Frankfurter argued that respect for federalism and the state courts required the Supreme Court to defer to their judgments (at 67–68).

In effect the middle ground on whether the protections accorded by the Bill of Rights applies to the states is provided by those justices who adopt what is termed "selective incorporation" of the Bill of Rights under the umbrella of the Fourteenth Amendment. In this view some of the provisions of the Bill of Rights are more central to the preservation of liberty than others. Where the line is to be drawn between rights and liberties encompassed by the Due Process clause of the Fourteenth Amendment has been a moving target throughout the twentieth century. The movement, however, has been toward increasing the breadth of coverage as more and more provisions of the Bill of Rights have been viewed as "fundamental."

Justice Benjamin Cardozo's opinion in *Palko v. Connecticut,* 1937, has provided a principal rationale for selectively applying particular provisions of the Bill of Rights to the states through the Due Process clause of the Fourteenth Amendment. Although he rejected the argument that the "liberty" protected by the Fourteenth Amendment was precisely tied to the specific liberties listed in the Bill of Rights, Justice Cardoza did argue that some of those "liberties" were of such fundamental importance to a free society that, in effect, we would not have "liberty" if they were to be disregarded.

The question before the Court in *Palko* was whether granting the state a new trial of a defendant because of errors, detrimental to the prosecution at a first criminal trial, amounted to unconstitutional "double jeopardy." Under the Fifth Amendment it was clear that a second trial would not be permitted in federal cases. Because this case involved a state prosecution, the question became whether subjecting a defendant to punishment following conviction at a second trial, or "double jeopardy," would deprive him of "liberty without due process of law" contrary to the Fourteenth Amendment.

In determining which rights and liberties derived from the Bill of Rights are applicable to the states through the Due Process clause of the Fourteenth Amendment, Justice Cardozo in effect asks whether the specific liberties in question ". . . have been found to be implicit in the concept of ordered liberty." According to this view and summarizing Court precedents established at the time of the *Palko* decision, Justice Cardoza found that, for example, the right of free speech is included under the liberties protected by the Fourteenth Amendment. On the other hand, "[t]he right to trial by jury and the immunity from prosecution except as a result of an indictment [although they] may have value and importance . . . are not of the very essence of a scheme of ordered liberty. To abolish them is not to violate a 'principle of justice so rooted in the traditions and conscience of our people as to be ranked as fundamental" (at 324–325).

The justices who have in effect supported selective application of the Bill of Rights to the states through the Fourteenth Amendment have not relied on the specific provisions of the Bill of Rights in determining the outer limits of the "liberty" protected by the Due Process clause of the Fourteenth Amendment. Both in drawing lines to include some provisions of the Bill of Rights and not others, and in discovering and defining liberties nowhere specifically mentioned in the Constitution (see discussion of right to privacy in Chapter 5), these justices have demonstrated the crucial role played by the Supreme Court in defining the meaning of civil liberties and civil rights in America. They not only interpret for us what specific provisions of the Constitution mean, they also decide which provisions are more "fundamental" than others and which liberties, nowhere specifically mentioned in the Constitution, are nonetheless part of constitutional protected liberty.

As a result of Court decisions interpreting the scope of Fourteenth Amendment protections for civil rights and liberties against state governments, all rights and liberties discussed in this book restrict the national (federal) and state governments in the same ways and to the same degree. It will therefore not be necessary generally for us to distinguish between the levels of government involved as we discuss the varying interpretations found in Court decisions of our rights and liberties.

## THE CHECKERED HISTORY OF JUDICIAL DEFENSE OF RIGHTS AND LIBERTIES

Before beginning our exploration of the Supreme Court's protections for our rights and liberties and of the great variety in interpretation given even some of our more fundamental freedoms, it is important to recognize that the Supreme Court through much of our history has not been in the forefront of extending protection of our civil liberties and civil rights. In part because the selection process for Supreme Court justices is itself part of the political process, the same pressures that can from time to time influence democratically elected leaders to give inadequate protection to civil rights and liberties can influence our unelected, yet politically appointed, Supreme Court justices to reflect the dominant views of their times. If society is in a repressive mood, so too can be the U.S. Supreme Court. If politicians can sometimes be dismissive of individual liberties or the rights of minorities, so too can Supreme Court justices, who tend to be selected from among the more privileged sectors of society.

It is important to remember as we survey the variety of views on the Court concerning some of the more important rights and liberties that the Court has from time to time provided the Constitutional cover for what many consider some of our government's more regrettable actions.

A few examples might help us keep the Court in perspective. It took the U.S. Supreme Court to state explicitly what the founders of our country no doubt intended but nonetheless left unstated: America as founded rested on profoundly racist ideas of white supremacy. In *Dred Scott v. Sandford,* 1857 Chief Justice Roger Taney argued that even "freed slaves" had "no rights which the white man was bound to respect." African-Americans, according to Taney's Opinion for the Court, could, under the Constitution of 1789, never be citizens. Only the Civil War and a Constitution revised by the Thirteenth, Fourteenth, and Fifteenth Amendments could change the results of the Court's interpretation. Subsequently later Court interpretations, even of these amendments, had for generations permitted federal and state governments to disregard their clear purpose of mandating racial equality under the law.

In the periods following both the First and Second World Wars the U.S. Supreme Court gave judicial sanction to constitutional interpretations of our free speech protections which permitted punishment of people espousing views that the majority found threatening. In cases such as *Gitlow v. New York* (1925) and *Dennis v. United States* (1951), the Court read into the First Amendment exceptions to our free speech protections that are today widely rejected. In ruling as it did, the Court reflected the fears of its time.

On the other hand there have been moments in our history where the Supreme Court has taken positions that extended rights and liberties. At some of these moments the Court has been well ahead of the political leadership of society and probably the desires of most citizens, but it has taken stands that it felt were dictated by its duty to interpret the Constitution. In *Brown v. Board of Education,* the U.S. Supreme Court in effect overturned its own ruling in *Plessy v. Ferguson* 56 years earlier which had said that the Equal Protection clause of the Fourteenth Amendment permitted state-imposed separation of citizens in public places on the basis of race. In declaring state-imposed racial segregation in the schools unconstitutional in *Brown,* the Court set in motion a legal and political struggle that would last a generation or more to undo the entrenched system of racial segregation found in the American South. In this decision the Court was ahead of much of society. In the area of free speech in the later part of the twentieth century the Court has protected free expression even of those despised by society.

In reviewing the performance of the Court on pivotal civil liberties and civil rights issues, it is important to keep a sense of perspective. The Court rarely speaks with one voice; the Court can sometimes be a conscience for the nation and at other times merely a temporary legitimizer of its more selfish and destructive instincts.

## LEGISLATIVE PROTECTIONS FOR RIGHTS AND LIBERTIES

This book explores civil rights and civil liberties issues through judicial decisions and opinions enforcing constitutional provisions; it is important, however, to remember that judicial decisions are not the only source of protection for our rights and liberties. Both the Congress and the state legislatures can, and do, approve laws that provide protections beyond those required by the Constitution. Through its Article 1, Section 8 powers to "regulate commerce among the states . . ." for example, Congress has chosen to prohibit private persons from interfering with the ability of people to participate in the economic life of the country on account of race, color, creed, national origins, or disability.

The ability of Congress in particular to pass laws such as the Civil Rights Act of 1964 and the Americans with Disabilities Act depends on the reach of its commerce power. Supreme Court interpretations of this power of Congress have shifted dramatically over the course of American history. The question of the limit of Congress' Commerce power is, however, beyond the scope of this book. Our focus is on Constitutional provisions that in and of themselves directly define and give meaning to constitutional safeguards for civil rights and liberties.

Because the Constitution, itself, restricts only government action however, (see Chapter 6, Question 4) these additional statutory protections for civil rights are not a matter of constitutional "right." They are given to us largely at the discretion of Congress and the state legislatures as they exercise their regulatory power over commercial activity and other private conduct. We do not discuss the specific provisions of these federal and state laws except where necessary to explain how the Constitution places limitations upon them. (See discussion of Affirmative action, Chapter 4, Question 4.)

## CONTINUING CONTROVERSY: WHY SO MANY QUESTIONS?

Any book that seeks to explore the rich territory of civil liberties and civil rights in America cannot avoid being selective in its coverage. This book is no different. Our focus is on those fundamental rights and liberties that have been at the core of controversy in American constitutional history and politics. These are rights and liberties at the core of the American political system—those which determine most centrally the nature of our political institutions. First of all, we explore core First Amendment issues relating to freedom of thought and expression. The ability of citizens to be part of the political process requires their ability to become informed concerning options available to society and the ability to make themselves heard in decision-making counsels. In selecting questions I have attempted to highlight core First Amendment principles and explore continuing controversies concerning the limits, if any are appropriate, on the expression of ideas.

Freedom of religion has long been considered a core value in American political life. Because of the nation's increasing diversity and the history of persecution of peoples throughout the world over issues of conscience, the definition of this freedom and any limits to it will no doubt continue to be one of the leading agenda items for the Supreme Court. In selecting questions, here, too, we attempt to highlight basic principles guiding freedom of religion litigation and to explore ongoing controversies in this field.

No issue has divided American society more than the question of race. Slavery and racial discrimination marked America from its very beginnings and have had a direct impact on the original design of the Constitution and its revision. Conflict over race has led us to decide how important equality is and what equality demands—even beyond race to issues of gender and unequal distribution of wealth and opportunity. Developing an understanding of how the justices of the U.S. Supreme Court in the contemporary era have addressed these issues through interpretation of the Fourteenth Amendment is the purpose of Chapter 4.

The most controversial decisions of the Supreme Court in the latter part of the twentieth century have no doubt been those concerning the right to privacy—especially issues related to abortion rights, homosexual rights, and the right to die. None of these rights are explicitly discussed in the Constitution, yet all are crucial to determining the fate of individuals and individual autonomy in contemporary society. All too have been the subject of some of the more heated and emotional political controversy that has engaged the United States Supreme Court. Each of these issues will be explored as well as the core question behind all of them: How does the Court identify rights and liberties which are not explicitly mentioned in the Constitution?

Finally in Chapter 6 we move away from what have historically been core issues of civil liberties and civil rights to an exploration of emerging new issues. The contemporary communications environment presents some newer threats to what Justice Oliver Wendell Holmes termed the "free marketplace of ideas." Are First Amendment standards which were designed to keep that marketplace of ideas open and competitive threatened by new technologies and/or by concentrated economic power? Another issue is the government's ceding increasing aspects of our lives to private groups. Are our constitutional protections adequate to deal with possible new threats from some private sources?

Finally in Chapter 7 we will explore some of the implications of current court interpretations of core constitutional issues for the future in an effort to invite the readers to think about possible emerging threats to civil rights and liberties.

Throughout, questions are posed that should help the reader think through historic and continuing controversies that have engaged the attention of American courts as they attempt to give practical meaning to the relatively few words included in the Constitution of the United States.

## REFERENCES

*Adamson v. California*, 332 U.S. 469 (1946).

*Barron v. Baltimore*, 32 U.S. 243 (1833).

*Brown v. Board of Education*, 347 U.S. 483 (1954).

*Dennis v. United States*, 341 U.S. 494 (1951).

*Dred Scott v. Sandford*, 60 U.S. 393 (1856).

*Gitlow v. New York*, 268 U.S. 652 (1925).

*Marbury v. Madison*, 5 U.S. 137 (1803).

*Palko v. Connecticut*, 302 U.S. 319 (1937).

*Plessy v. Ferguson*, 163 U.S. 597 (1896).

*The Slaughterhouse Cases*, 83 U.S. 36 (1873).

# The First Amendment and Freedom of Expression

## INTRODUCTION

Freedom of speech and freedom of the press are core constitutional values in American democracy. Without open public debate and discussion over issues that touch at the foundations of society, it is impossible for the people effectively to control the direction of our political institutions. This chapter begins, therefore, with a basic question: *What is freedom of speech?* It introduces the idea that from its inception the idea of freedom of speech may have included some limits on our ability to say what we want when we want. It seeks to explain the difference between censorship or "prior restraint," the stopping of speech or publication deemed threatening to some important societal value, and punishment for speech after it has occurred.

The second question addressed in this chapter is: *How has the Court justified limits on the expression of ideas?* Despite the clear command of the First Amendment that "Congress make no law . . . abridging the freedom of speech and of the press," the United States Supreme Court throughout our history has to varying degrees and under varying circumstances argued that the Constitution does permit punishment for speech and publication. This section reviews some of the central "doctrines" of First Amendment adjudication such as "clear and present danger," "balancing," "preferred position," and "bad tendency." It begins, however, with a discussion of Justice Hugo Black's "absolutist" position, which argues that no limits on speech are justifiable.

Because to all of us from time to time some speech seems clearly offensive and even dangerous, the third question addressed in this chapter is: *Shouldn't we ban dangerous ideas?* This section focuses on the difference between mere advocacy and action. It assesses the often-cited example of dangerous speech, "falsely shouting fire in a crowded theater and causing a panic," in order to see when, if ever, mere words are dangerous. It will investigate the possible value of even "dangerous" speech.

One particular form of speech that many find extremely disturbing is the phenomenon known as "hate speech." In light of America's troubled history of racial tension and conflict, "racist speech" seems particularly dangerous. This section, then, seeks to answer Question 4: *May the government punish those who engage in hate speech?*

As the discussion following Question 1 should make clear, the Supreme Court has long held the view that obscenity is not included in the categories of expression protected by the First Amendment. Nonetheless what many people consider obscene still exists. This section therefore seeks to answer the question: *Why must society tolerate obscenity?* Question 5 explores the difficulty which the Court has faced in trying to define obscenity. We discuss the various standards the Court has used to distinguish obscenity from "protected" expression. Finally, we will discuss the efforts by some feminists to ban obscenity as "sex discrimination."

The development of the Internet which brings all kinds of expression into the homes of citizens who own a computer and modem raises a new issue for those concerned about obscenity. Question 6 asks: *Why does government permit sexually explicit material to invade our homes over the Internet?* In exploring the Court's approach to the issues raised by this question, we will begin our exploration of the implications of the Internet for freedom of expression, a topic to which we will return in Chapter 6, Question 2.

Many citizens are justifiably disturbed by the tenor of our public discussion and debate. There seems to be little concern for truth as charges are hurled back and forth and as the lives of public officials and celebrities are dissected in the media. This section, therefore, seeks answers to Question 7: *Why not require that people in public debate tell the truth?* This section discusses issues surrounding libel and slander cases. It will focus on the *New York Times* standard, the conflict between protecting individual reputations and robust public debate, the different treatment given by the courts to public figures and private citizens, and the question of upon whom should the burden of proving "truth" fall.

A form of expression which has stirred much political controversy has been "flag burning." Because of the reverence which most Americans hold for the flag, people react, sometimes violently, to its desecration.

This section, therefore, seeks to answer Question 8: *How is burning the American flag a form of free speech?* In answering this question, this section reviews the Court's approach to so-called symbolic speech and introduces the First Amendment requirement that regulations of speech must be "content neutral."

Finally, although freedom of speech is widely held to be an essential precondition for democracy, some find it hard to understand why a democratic society should tolerate free speech for enemies of democracy and even of free speech itself. This section, then seeks to answer Question 9: *Why should a democratic society tolerate the expression of views that are offensive to the majority?* This section discusses the fundamental role of free debate in a democratic society. It discusses difficult cases, such as that of the Nazis in Skokie, Illinois. Finally, the topic of this section should allow for a summing up and conclusion to the entire chapter, providing an assessment of the role played by free speech in a society that considers itself to be democratic.

### Question 1    *What is "freedom of speech"?*

The First Amendment to the United States Constitution commands that "Congress shall make no laws . . . abridging the freedom of speech or freedom of the press." Since the U.S. Supreme Court decision in *Gitlow v. New York* in 1925, the Fourteenth Amendment has been interpreted as applying this same restriction to the states. Although the language of the First Amendment is more direct and emphatic than probably in any other part of the Constitution, there has always been considerable debate concerning precisely what the First Amendment free speech/free press clause protects.

When children speak in class out of turn or when they are expected to be silent, limits are placed on their freedom *to* speak. When a member of the United States House of Representatives speaks without having been recognized by the presiding officer, he is silenced. If you visit a courtroom to watch a trial and decide to tell the court you don't like what you see, you will at best be removed and more likely, if you refuse to be silent, found in contempt of court and sent to jail. None of these examples is thought to raise any First Amendment problems. No reputable First Amendment scholar or Supreme Court justice has ever seriously argued that freedom of speech means you can say whatever you want wherever or whenever you please.

The First Amendment really concerns open debate, the ability to express and to hear a variety of points of view. Although on the surface the First Amendment would seem to prohibit any governmental interference with the verbal or written expression of ideas, most Supreme Court justices have argued that certain forms of expression are completely out-side Constitutional protection. They would argue that the First Amend-ment does not protect all speech; rather it protects what has been understood historically as "the freedom of speech." Certain categories of speech are included in that phrase; others are not included (see Meikeljohn, pp.16–19).

In a famous passage from his decision in *Chaplinsky v. New Hamp-shire* (1942), Justice Frank Murphy argued:

> There are certain well-defined and narrowly limited classes of speech, the prevention and punishment of which have never been thought to raise any Constitutional problem. These include the lewd and obscene, the profane, the libelous, and insulting or "fight-ing" words—those which by their very utterance inflict injury or tend to incite an immediate breach of the peace. It has been well observed that such utterances are no essential part of any exposi-tion of ideas, and are of such slight social value as a step to truth that any benefit that may be derived from them is clearly out-weighed by the social interest in order and morality. "Resort to epi-thets or personal abuse is not in any proper sense communication of information or opinion safeguarded by the[Constitution]. *Cantwell v. Connecticut*, 310 U.S. 296 (1940)."

Although this passage might appear to provide clear guidance to any-one seeking to understand the limits of freedom of speech, in reality it has not held up under scrutiny. Even those who generally accept the premise that the First Amendment protects only those expressions that contribute to the "exposition of ideas" and "the search for truth" have had to confront the questions concerning, for example, precisely what is "obscene" or "libelous." Attempts to limit either can in some circumstances spill over into limits of the exposition of ideas and the search for truth.

### Prior Restraint

Demand for the protection of freedom of speech emerged against a historical backdrop of censorship, the need to obtain prior approval of some government agency before speaking or publishing. The historical rejection of any right of government to silence us *before* we speak or write has led to a broad consensus among Supreme Court justices that "prior restraint" on the press is the least acceptable form of government inter-ference with free expression. As the British legal philosopher William Blackstone put it: "Every freeman has the undoubted right to lay what sentiments he pleases before the public; to forbid this, is to destroy the freedom of the press" (*Near v. Minnesota*, at 713).

The consensus against prior restraint, however, does not extend to a belief that no one should be or can be punished for what they say or print. Although you generally do not need prior government approval to express any ideas you desire, should what you say or print offend some important government interest, you may be subject to some form of punishment *after* you speak.

The distinction between prior restraint and punishment after you speak could be stated as follows: The First Amendment protects your right to say what you feel you must, but it does not always free you from suffering adverse consequences for what you say. Obviously fear of seriously negative consequences would keep most people quiet, but, at least in the absence of prior restraint, the ultimate decision concerning what the public may hear is left to potential speakers and not to the government. The fear of the consequences will certainly discourage most from expressing ideas punishable by law, but in the absence of effective prior restraint, it is at least possible that someone will inform society about information which the government might want suppressed.

As Chief Justice Warren Burger observed in *Nebraska Press Association v. Stuart* (1976), before one can be punished for something he has already said or written, they have the opportunity to appeal to the highest courts to protect First Amendment values. "A prior restraint . . . [however,] has an immediate and irreversible sanction." Even if the censor's order is ultimately lifted, while it remains in effect, society is denied information. Contrasting prior restraint with the threat of punishment after speech, Chief Justice Burger went on to argue: "If it can be said that the threat of criminal or civil sanctions after publications 'chills' speech, prior restraint 'freezes' it at least for a time" (at 559).

Although the U.S. Supreme Court has never upheld a government attempt at prior restraint, most on the Court have claimed that there are limited circumstances in which even prior restraint would be approved. The Supreme Court decision in which the broad prohibition against "prior restraints," *Near v. Minnesota*, 1931, was first proclaimed recognized certain potential "exceptional cases" relating to protecting the public from obscenity and incitement to riot. In the area of what today we term "national security," the *Near* Court argued that "[No] one would question but that a government might prevent actual obstruction of its recruiting service or the publication of sailing dates of transports or the number and location of troops" (at 716). It was this "national security" exception that provided the focus of the debate within the Supreme Court in the famous Pentagon Papers cases, *New York Times Co. v. United States*, 1971.

Beginning June 13, 1971, the *New York Times* published an until-then secret government study, "History of U.S. Decision-Making Process on Viet Nam Policy," better known as the Pentagon Papers. Almost immediately the U.S. government went to court and obtained an injunction blocking further publication of the classified study. Within a matter of days the U.S. Supreme Court heard the arguments of the parties in the case, and on a 6 to 3 vote overturned the injunction. The Court's action reflected the "heavy presumption against . . . [the] constitutional validity" of prior restraints (*per curium,* at 714). Simply, the government did not come up with a sufficiently weighty justification for overcoming the presumed right of the press to print whatever it wants.

Although the justices on both sides differed concerning the details of the appropriate standard to be applied in a case such as this, there was broad agreement that if the government could ever win, it must show that publication would result in ". . . direct, immediate, and irreparable damage to our Nation or its people" (Stewart P., concurring at 1088). Most of the justices referred to the troopship example from *Near* as providing the standard. In the words of Justice William Brennan, "only government allegation and proof that publication must inevitably, directly and immediately cause . . . " harm comparable to that which would flow from publishing the location of troopships in time of war and thus aiding enemy submarines to sink the ships and kill the men would be of sufficient weight to justify prior censorship of the press (at 726–27).

Perhaps because he doubted that such an extreme example would ever arise or perhaps out of deeply held principle, Justice Black argued that prior restraint was never constitutionally permissible. In assessing the very limited circumstances when most justices would permit a prior restraint, Black wrote: "In my view it is unfortunate that some of my Brethren are apparently willing to hold that publication of the news may ever be enjoined. Such a holding would make a shambles of the First Amendment" (at 715).

Generally where the Court divided in this case was over the question of the actual severity of the danger posed by the publication of the Pentagon Papers. While the dissenters in the case were more willing to trust the executive's assessment of the danger, doubting the Court's ability to weigh and understand foreign policy matters, Justices William Brennan, Byron White, and Potter Stewart argued that the government had not sufficiently proved that the harm caused by publication would be irreparable. Justice Hugo Black, one of the justices in the majority, however, argued that prior restraint was never permissible arguing that the First Amendment protected the press precisely " . . . so that it could bare the secrets of government and inform the people."

As a result of the *New York Times* decision, the secret government history of the Vietnam war was published. This report certainly embarrassed the government because it revealed that the war from its beginning had its foundation in misjudgments and a general pattern of deception.

The government did attempt to prosecute Daniel Elsberg, a former defense department official, for turning the classified report over to the press, but his prosecution was thrown out on the grounds of government misconduct unrelated to the First Amendment's free speech protections. Although we cannot know how Elsberg's prosecution would have been received by a trial jury or by the appellate courts had he been convicted, we are free to speculate. Would a jury have been willing to convict him knowing what his action revealed? Wouldn't some jurors have voted not guilty simply because they were pleased that someone had at last provided them with the "truth" about a war which many found either unjust or stupid?

Had the government's attempt at prior restraint been successful, we might have waited many years to learn what the publication of the Pentagon Papers revealed. The threat of prosecution did not deter Elsberg or suppress the truth. Even had the prosecution run its course, Elsberg's apparent law violations might have been excused by jurors or his conviction could have been overturned on appeal. If you doubt that prior restraint is any greater a threat to free speech than the threat of criminal prosecution after publication, consider that Elsberg was willing to risk prosecution in order to tell his story, and in the end he was not punished. Had the government won in *New York Times v. United States,* to this date the true story about the Vietnam War might not be known.

Although there are some who historically have argued that the First Amendment does no more than to forbid censorship and the routine resort to prior restraint, the consensus today is that the First Amendment also limits the government's power to punish people for what they say or print. Particularly in the twentieth century the Supreme Court has struggled constantly to identify the limited circumstances when people may be punished merely for what they say or print.

## Question 2   *How has the Court justified limits on the expression of ideas?*

Although the justices on the Court have sometimes been willing to permit the punishment of speech simply because the words themselves were false or offensive and contributed nothing to the "exchange of ideas," often when the Court has permitted government limits on speech, it has been precisely because the words might stimulate thoughts that will (or might) produce unacceptable actions.

Generally in free speech cases we must understand the distinction between mere words and actions. No one, for example, seriously argues that the First Amendment protects your right to *do* anything you want. Some, however, argue that it does protect your right to *say* anything you want. The majority on the Supreme Court, however, have justified sometimes punishing words that could lead people to engage in illegal actions.

The speaker then is being punished not simply for what he says but rather for the acts that his speech could produce.

On the other hand, one Supreme Court justice, Hugo Black, argued that a sharp line should be drawn between speech and action. In effect he argued that the First Amendment protects your right to say anything you please. The government may never punish you for your words or for the ideas you express. Should you or someone else act on those words, the government may then step in. But until the line between speech and action is actually crossed, the government must keep hands off.

This view of Justice Black is known as First Amendment "absolutism." To the absolutist, the First Amendment means exactly what it says: Congress shall make *no* law abridging freedom of speech . . . . *No* means *none,* not *some.* As long as all one does is speak or write, the government may not step in to restrain or punish. If one acts, however, the First Amendment provides no protection.

Most on the Court have not accepted Black's absolutist interpretation of the First Amendment. Although today the justices on the Supreme Court find little room under the First Amendment for limits on speech, the Court generally holds to the view that under some circumstances even mere words are not constitutionally protected from punishment. Over the years however, there has been much difference of opinion concerning precisely under what circumstances speech loses its constitutional protection.

To begin to understand why most of the Court argues that sometimes speech or press is not protected even by the emphatic words of the First Amendment, we must understand, in the words of Justice Blackmun, that the "First Amendment, after all, is only one part of an entire Constitution" (*New York Times v. United States*, at 761). Articles I and II of the Constitution give to the government much power to accomplish many important and sometimes vital ends. Clearly the First Amendment is meant to restrict the exercise of those powers. Those who reject First Amendment absolutism ask, however, whether speech should be allowed to defeat the purposes of legitimate exercises of government power.

Government officials take oaths to "preserve, protect and defend the Constitution." What if someone or some group advocates the violent overthrow of that Constitution? Does the Constitution protect the speaker's right to try to convince others to destroy it? Local authorities have the plain duty to protect the public safety. What if a speaker attempts to incite to riot? Clearly, sometimes a speaker's unlimited right to speak can threaten legitimate government concerns.

When should a speaker's First Amendment rights give way in the face of a government's claim for the necessity of regulation? In answering a question such as this, some justices have argued for a "balancing" of First Amendment rights on the one hand against the government interests calling for limiting speech or press on the other. Such justices

would themselves attempt to measure the relative value of each claim in light of the specific circumstances in which the case arose. They attempt to measure the potential costs to government or society in leaving a particular speech unpunished against the benefits derived from allowing it. Other justices argue that such weighing of competing "interests" is best left to the democratic process. Trust legislatures elected by the people and not judges isolated from the people.

A problem that some observers find in such balancing is that it can produce inconsistent results. Different judges (or legislators) will judge the significance of competing claims differently. Some will give great weight to the values served by free speech; others will see order and security as more important.

Beginning in the early part of this century, the Court began the effort to identify standards to be used to judge circumstances when protections for speech and press give way to protections for other governmental interests or social values. In several important cases, Supreme Court justices attempted to develop standards which they could use to decide when a speaker's free expression can be limited by government.

During World War I some were prosecuted for distributing pamphlets and making speeches in apparent violation of laws meant to forbid obstruction of military recruitment, interference with war production, or inciting insubordination within the armed forces. In one such case which reached the Supreme Court, *Schenck v. United States* (1919), Justice Oliver Wendell Holmes developed a standard for judging when speech might be punished. According to Holmes:

> [the] question in every case is whether the words used are used in such circumstances and are of such a nature as to create a *clear and present danger* [emphasis added] that they will bring about the substantive evils that Congress has right to prevent. It is a question of proximity and degree. When a nation is at war many things that might be said in time of peace are such a hindrance to its effort that their utterance will not be endured so long as men fight (at 52).

The "clear and present danger" doctrine, which emerged from this case, has survived several decades and a variety of interpretations (see Question 3 below). What in essence it amounts to is a statement that under some circumstances government interests can outweigh First Amendment freedoms. Because only a "clear and present danger" that speech will actually precipitate illegal action justifies limiting speech, however, the doctrine gives some priority to First Amendment rights over routine government interests.

The reasoning behind the Court's decision in *Gitlow v. New York,* (1925), six years after *Schenck,* provided even less protection to speech than that seemingly provided by the "clear and present danger doctrine." While the "clear and present danger doctrine" seemed to require a court to measure carefully the seriousness of a threat and its "proximity" or closeness in time, the so-called "bad tendency" standard announced by the Court's majority in *Gitlow* explicitly rejected judicial calculation of dangers posed by speech. In discussing the potential consequences of a publication advocating "revolutionary mass action" as a prelude to the establishment a "Communist" regime, Justice Edward Sanford for the Court majority wrote: "The State cannot reasonably be required to measure the danger from every such utterance in the nice balance of a jewelers scale" (at 669). Once the legislature itself has determined that such revolutionary advocacy poses a danger, all the courts are permitted to do is determine if a specific statement's "natural tendency and probable effect was to bring about the substantive evil which the legislative body might prevent"(at 671).

Although debate over the adequacy of the the "clear and present danger doctrine" continues to this day, the "bad tendency" standard announced in *Gitlow* has generally been rejected as providing too little protection for speech. Today almost any government effort to punish political speech is presumed unconstitutional. Since *Brandenburg v. Ohio,* 1968, when the Supreme Court unanimously struck down the convictions of Ku Klux Klan members for advocating violence, the Court has held that the First Amendment does not permit "a State to forbid or proscribe advocacy of the use of force or of law violation except where such advocacy is directed to inciting or producing imminent lawless action *and* [emphasis added] is likely to incite or produce such action" (at 447).

In his concurring opinion in *Brandenburg* Justice William O. Douglas joined ranks with Justice Black in attacking even this version of "clear and present danger doctrine" and rejecting virtually any limits on speech:

> I see no place in the regime of the First Amendment for any "clear and present danger" test, whether strict and tight as some would make it, or free-wheeling as the Court . . . [has sometimes] rephrased it. When one reads the opinions closely and sees when and how the "clear and present danger" test has been applied, great misgivings are aroused. . . . [T]he threats were often loud but always puny and made serious only by judges so wedded to the status quo that critical analysis made them nervous. (at 454)

When one reviews the periods in history when cases reached the Court and when the Court upheld government restrictions on speech, it does appear that a factor present was near public hysteria over threats that in retrospect appear much more imaginary than real. Fears that speeches or pamphlets by little known people during World War I would lead to the crippling of our war effort or fears of Communist subversion or revolution in the periods following both world wars seem rather silly now. These fears, however, were enough to lead legislatures and the Supreme Court to justify repression of open public debate.

Today, and even during the tense period of the Vietnam War, the Court appears much more vigilant in its protection of the free speech rights of even generally despised groups. Although all justices have not adopted the specific language, most now view the First Amendment and the values it protects as warranting special judicial protection. The justices seem to recognize what some have termed the "preferred position" of First Amendment rights. While in most areas of constitutional adjudication deference is shown to legislative judgments, and those challenging a law carry the burden to demonstrate its unconstitutionality, in First Amendment adjudication the Court subjects legislation limiting free expression to very careful scrutiny. Before approving any limit on speech or press the Court generally demands evidence that some "compelling governmental interest" requires restrictions on free expression. This special treatment for the First Amendment is justified in part because of the emphatic language of the Amendment itself and in part because of the vital role free debate plays in the democratic political process.

## Question 3    *Shouldn't we ban dangerous ideas?*

When arguing that "dangerous" speech should be limited, people often bring up the example of shouting "fire" in a crowded theater. According to Justice Holmes in *Schenck v. United States*, (1919), "The most stringent protection of free speech would not protect a man in falsely shouting fire in a crowded theatre and causing a panic." It might be useful to analyze the reasons why this example is so frequently mentioned as a justification for punishing dangerous speech. What is it about falsely shouting "fire" that causes us to recoil?

To falsely shout "fire" can directly and immediately produce physical injury as a result of panic. Almost inevitably, it produces an immediate reaction, flight, without occasion for thoughtful reflection.

In deciding whether we should punish or restrict "dangerous" ideas, shouldn't we first ask if there are really any ideas that have an effect comparable to falsely shouting "fire"?

In the Supreme Court decision from which the fire example and the "clear and present danger" doctrine comes [see Question 2 above], the expression punished was a pamphlet that urged resistance to military conscription during World War I. Might the response to such a pamphlet have been comparable to the response to shouting "fire", that is, one that is immediate and possibly catastrophic?

How might we distinguish the circumstances in *Schenck* and other cases in which the clear and present danger doctrine has been applied, from the circumstances surrounding shouting "fire" in a crowded theatre? First, although the danger might arguably be real, the danger was not immediate in the sense that some instantaneous and irreversible response would result. To put it simply, there was time for people to reflect on the consequences of their actions. Having heard or read the words, the audience had time to weigh engaging in illegal actions in light of the likely consequences, that is, going to jail for violating the law.

Indeed, Justices Oliver Wendell Holmes and Louis Brandeis eventually attempted to restrict the clear and present danger doctrine to circumstances where the danger was both real and immediate. In their dissent in *Abrams v. United States* (1919), they wrote: "Only the emergency that makes it immediately dangerous to leave correction of evil counsels to time warrants making any exception to the sweeping command, 'Congress shall make no law . . . abridging freedom of speech.' (at 630). To the argument that some ideas might incite others to commit illegal acts, Holmes responded in *Gitlow* v. *New York* (1925): "Every idea is an incitement. It offers itself for belief and if believed it is acted on unless some other belief outweighs it or some failure of energy stifles it at birth" (at 673).

Fear of going to jail is not the only thing that might outweigh dangerous ideas and prevent us from acting in response to them. Far more important is the fact that we are all subject to arguments on the other side. Certainly the dominant opinions in society that we hear everyday do not support "dangerous" ideas. If they did, no law restricting the actions advocated would be passed in the first place. In sum, we are not just victims of dangerous ideas. We are also able to weigh alternatives and consequences. Such weighing of alternatives by citizens is at the heart of freedom of speech and of democracy.

When we consider how society should deal with those who advocate ideas that to us appear dangerous, perhaps we should ask what causes them to speak as they do. Before we would condemn someone for shouting fire in a crowded theater wouldn't we first ask whether he felt there really was a fire? If you are in a theater and you think there is a fire, should you wait until you actually see flames before you alert others? If signs of fire are not apparent to most in the audience, they might panic simply because you say there is a fire. They might instead, however, take prudent precautions without running headlong toward the exit.

Hearing a speaker say that a "war is evil," "the draft is unjust," "the police are your enemies," or that "the government should be overthrown"—

hearing any "dangerous" idea—will not cause most of us to act. It may, however, cause some of us to consider why others feel that way. Although we will shun the illegal course of action advocated, our attention may be drawn to the grievances that cause others to speak angrily or forcefully.

The value, then, of extreme or "dangerous" speech is that it can rivet our attention far better than measured scholarly dissertations on injustice. It does not force us to act, but it can entice us to listen to the grievances of those who speak "dangerous" words. If it does that, it can contribute to the free exchange of ideas.

In the "free marketplace of ideas," just as in a supermarket, a new product may have to be garishly displayed to attract our attention. If the consequences of a mistaken judgment are slight (i.e., the product is inexpensive), we may sample it. If the product is expensive, however, we are likely to read the label carefully and ask others for advice before risking too much of our hard-earned money. The same is true with new ideas. We are not likely to follow ideas that pose risks. Knowledge that certain actions that may be advocated are illegal will cause us to hold back. It is one thing to talk, to listen, and to think; it is quite something else to act. The distinction between mere speech and action is essential to understanding the role of speech and freedom of the press.

**Question 4**    *May the government punish those who engage in "hate speech"?*

In light of America's ongoing problem of racial division, hostility, and even racist violence, it seems perfectly natural for us to want to remove the idea of racial hatred at the root of such violence from public debate. Although for much of our early history notions of white racial supremacy had been in effect written into our Constitution, following the Civil War the Thirteenth, Fourteenth and Fifteenth amendments removed the constitutional foundations for racial discrimination. Nonetheless racial hostility and violence remain a problem and racial tensions periodically explode in our communities. In good faith efforts to remove racism from our society and to protect citizens from the emotional (and perhaps worse) harm caused by racist epithets, many states have enacted "hate speech" statutes. Many of these statutes also address crimes motivated by religious intolerance and gender discrimination as well. Some forbid crimes motivated by homophobia, or hatred of people because of their sexual orientation.

In 1992 the U.S. Supreme Court in *R.A.V. v. St. Paul* had to decide on the constitutionality of a St. Paul, Minnesota's Bias-Motivated Crime ordinance. The ordinance was challenged by one of several teenagers who were prosecuted for placing a burning cross on the lawn of a black family in their neighborhood. Burning crosses had long been a symbol of Klu Klux Klan intimidation of African-Americans. The ordinance provided:

> Whoever places on public or private property a symbol, object, appellation, characterization or graffiti, including, but not limited to, a burning cross or Nazi Swastika, which one knows or has reasonable grounds to know arouses anger, alarm or resentment in others on the basis of race, creed, religion, or gender commits disorderly conduct and shall be guilty of a misdemeanor. (at 580)

The teenager who challenged the statute did so on the basis that it violated his First Amendment rights. His assertion was that the statute was "substantially over broad and impermissably content based" (at 580). The "overbreadth" claim was founded on the argument that the statute's definition of punishable expression swept too broadly, encompassing speech that is in fact constitutionally protected. For example, the statute prohibited speech that "arouses to anger, alarm or resentment in others on the basis of race. . . ." The Supreme Court has long held that merely provoking "anger" in others cannot be sufficient grounds for punishing speech (see *Terminiello v. City of Chicago*) (1949). After all, almost any provocative idea can provoke someone to anger or resentment. Certainly many statements by conventional politicians cause the blood in some citizens to boil!

Justice Scalia's Opinion of the Court, however, found that the Minnesota courts had solved the obvious overbreadth problem in the statute by construing (or interpreting) it to apply only to speech addressing the prohibited subjects that amount to "fighting words." Ever since its decision in *Chaplinsky v. New York*, (1942), the U.S. Supreme Court has held that some categories of speech are simply outside First Amendment protection. In *Chaplinsky*, Justice Murphy wrote:

> There are certain well-defined and narrowly limited classes of speech, the prevention and punishment of which have never been thought to raise any Constitutional problem. These include the lewd and the obscene, the profane, the libelous, and the insulting or "fighting words"—those which by their very utterance inflict injury or tend to incite an immediate breach of the peace. It has been observed that such utterances are no essential part of any exposition of ideas, and are of such slight social value as a step to truth that any benefit that may be derived from them is clearly outweighed by the social interest in law and order."(at 572)

Although the definitions of each of these prohibitable categories of speech has been significantly refined since *Chaplinsky*, it remains true that these "categorical exceptions" to free speech protections cited remain today.

Justice Anton Scalia agreed that the Minnesota court's confining the speech prohibited by the ordinance to actual "fighting words" saved the ordinance from an overbreadth challenge. It did not, however, save the ordinance from a challenge on the grounds that it violated "content neutrality." According to Justice Scalia's opinion, "[t]he First Amendment generally prevents government from proscribing speech . . . because of disapproval of the ideas expressed. Content-based regulations are presumptively invalid" (at 382). The problem with the Minneapolis ordinance according to the opinion of Justice Scalia was that it selected certain "fighting words" for prohibition not solely because they were "fighting words," but also because they expressed viewpoints and attitudes that the majority of society rejects and condemns. The content "bias" that Justice Scalia found in the statute is that it prohibited "fighting words" directed at some favored targets, for example, race, or gender, but did not address "fighting words" directed toward others (homosexuals, union members, etc.). Although not explicitly stated, what may have troubled Justice Scalia and those who joined his opinion is that the ordinance in question appears to condemn those whose views are not "politically correct," views which many of society's opinion leaders find taboo.

Although under the "fighting words" doctrine and other categorical exceptions there is a presumption that they are not really included in the concept of "the freedom of speech," they are not wholly noncommunicative. They, like actions, can express ideas, or at least intensity of emotion associated with ideas. Like symbolic actions, they are not wholly protected by the First Amendment, but neither, according to Justice Scalia's interpretation, may they be restricted in particular instances because of government's or society's hostility to the underlying message they may rather crudely convey. As Justice Scalia himself wrote: "Fighting words are . . . analogous to a noisy sound truck: each is, as Justice Frankfurter recognized, a 'mode of speech' (citation omitted); both can be used to convey an idea; but neither has, in and of itself, a claim upon the First Amendment. As with the sound truck, however, so also with fighting words: the government may not regulate use based on hostility—or favoritism—towards the underlying message expressed" (at 386).

Other justices, while agreeing on "overbreadth" grounds that the ordinance was unconstitutional, contended that under Justice Scalia's approach, in order for Minneapolis to overcome Justice Scalia's constitutional objection to the ordinance, it would have had simply to ban all fighting words without exception. Since, however, in the words of Justice Byron White's concurring opinion "the government may proscribe an entire category of speech [fighting words,] because the content of that speech is evil," it may also ban only a subset of that category because "the content of that subset is, by definition, worthless and undeserving of constitutional protection" (at 401).

Justice White rejects Justice Scalia's contention that fighting words are "quite expressive indeed," arguing instead that "[f]ighting words are not means of exchanging views, rallying supporters, or registering a protest; they are directed against individuals to provoke violence or to inflict injury. *Chaplinsky,* 315 U.S., at 572. Therefore, a ban on all fighting words or a subset of the fighting words category would restrict only the social evil of hate speech, without creating the danger of driving viewpoints from the marketplace" (at 401).

Justice Scalia, in his opinion, rejected Justice White's characterization of his views. He responded that the state does remain free to prohibit some fighting words and not others, but that its basis for distinguishing between the prohibited and the permitted must be something other than hostility to the speaker or his underlying message or point of view. He argued, for example, that because obscenity is also a category of speech not protected by the Constitution, government may prohibit some obscenity while ignoring other obscene expressions.

> When the basis for the content discrimination consists entirely of the very reason the entire class of speech at issue is proscribable, no significant danger of viewpoint discrimination exists. Such a reason, having been adjudged neutral enough to support the exclusion of the entire class of speech from First Amendment protection, is also neutral enough to form the basis of distinction within the class. To illustrate: a State might choose to prohibit only that obscenity which is most patently offensive in its prurience—i.e., that which involves the most lascivious displays of sexual activity. But it may not prohibit, for example, only that obscenity which includes offensive political messages(citation omitted). (at 388)

Although Justice Scalia does not provide an example directly relating to "fighting words," we might wonder whether he would be willing to uphold a "hate speech" statute that forbade only speech calling for the death or extermination of any class of citizens. Such speech when addressed to a member of any particular group would no doubt satisfy the "fighting words" category. Such a statute would address a most extreme manifestation of "hate speech, " and it would not seem to favor any particular segment of society.

Although the Supreme Court was unanimous in condemning the Minneapolis ordinance, four of the nine Justices rejected at least in part Justice Scalia's approach. The other justices were not so troubled by Minneapolis' singling out only some "hate speech" for punishment. In light of the history of racial conflict in America and of the victimization of racial minorities, they felt that it was reasonable for the city to focus on this most damaging form of hate speech. In Justice White's words: "This selective regulation reflects the city's judgment that harms based on race, creed, religion, or gender are more pressing public concerns than the harm caused by other fighting words. In light of our Nation's long and painful experience with discrimination, this determination is plainly reasonable" (at 407).

Justice White did not, however, respond to an argument implicit in Justice Scalia's approach, that is, that others, not included in those mentioned in the Minneapolis statute, have been and are subjected to hate speech also. Homosexuals, for example, are frequently victimized by verbal assaults akin to those suffered by racial minorities, yet such "fighting words" were not covered by the ordinance's prohibitions. Could it be that homosexuals are not as favored by the majority of the Minneapolis city council or the majority of that city's population? Would their inclusion have stimulated the opposition of antigay religious conservatives to the hate speech ordinance? If the exclusion of antigay hate speech from the ordinance had been the result of the antigay bias of the majority, was Justice Scalia wrong to condemn the ordinance for failing to be "content neutral"?

Despite their vigorous disagreement with Justice Scalia's Opinion of the Court, the remaining four justices also found the ordinance unconstitutional. Their grounds, however, was "overbreadth." According to their reading of the Minnesota Supreme Court's construction of the ordinance, it permitted punishment of words "which inflict injury or tend to incite an immediate breach of the peace." Because that Court appeared to equate "injury" with words or displays "that one knows or should know will create anger, alarm or resentment based on racial, ethnic or religious bias," Justice White's concurrence found it still to suffer from "overbreadth." "Although the ordinance reaches conduct that is unprotected, it also makes criminal expressive conduct that causes only hurt feelings, offense, or resentment, and is protected by the First Amendment. . . . The ordinance is therefore fatally over broad and invalid on its face" (at 414).

Those who either have been or fear being victimized by racist or sexist speech may find the Court's refusal in this instance to permit punishment of that which causes them such discomfort disturbing, but to insulate all of us from expression that causes someone distress could at some point silence almost all of us. Most of us, however, can think of words or phrases which we know to be extremely hurtful and provocative to racial minorities, women, or homosexuals to name just a few. Could a statute be designed which would just single out those particularly offensive phrases or epithets which cause such obvious pain? If we think about such a potential statute, however, we might also recognize that sometimes members of the very groups "victimized" by such epithets use those same words themselves. Even others, who may not themselves be in the same racial group, might in fun or as part of good-natured banter use the same words without producing a hurtful reaction. Can the law fairly and clearly distinguish between what are "fighting words" if used by one person, but mere lighthearted banter if used by another? There is probably no offensive phrase or word in or out of the dictionary that has not been exchanged between teenage boys in the course of playful "conversation" without any participant taking offense. We may think we can discern the difference between "fighting words" and loose or vulgar talk, but can we safeguard free speech if the government tries to do so?

## Question 5    *Why must society tolerate obscenity?*

Ever since its decision in *Chaplinsky*, the Supreme Court majority has argued that obscenity is not protected by the First Amendment. Obscenity was included in those categories of speech given no constitutional protection because they ". . . are no essential part of any exposition of ideas, and are of such slight social value as a step to truth that any benefit that may be derived from them is clearly outweighed by social interest in order and morality" (571–72). When the question before the Court is obscenity, there is no need for the government to prove that a particular magazine or movie, for example, poses some "clear and present danger" of producing some unlawful action. Obscenity in itself is considered harmful enough to forfeit constitutional protection.

Then why does what many people consider obscenity survive?

The Supreme Court's claim that the Constitution does not protect obscenity does not help us identify what obscenity is. Over the years the Court has attempted time and time again to identify obscenity. After its decision in *Roth v. United States,* (1957), that "presumed obscenity to be '*utterly* without redeeming social value,' " a plurality on the Court argued that for material to be found obscene it must be proved to be "utterly without redeeming social value." This, according to the Court in *Miller v. California,* (1973), amounted to a burden that was "virtually impossible to . . . [prove]" (at 22).

The Court has been concerned that any limits on material that is obscene not "spill over" onto material that deserves constitutional protection. Many works considered obscene in the past, James Joyce's *Ulysses,* for example, are today considered great works of literature. Although their sexually explicit content may offend some, to others it is " central to the story." Scientific and even political information may include material that to some appears vulgar or even obscene. To forbid any material containing such content, however, could interfere with communication on matters central to society's interests.

In order to avoid punishing expression that is constitutionally protected, the Court has attempted to define obscenity as clearly as possible. If it fails to define obscenity precisely, a citizen could be punished for publishing material that he could not have known with certainty was obscene (and, therefore, not constitutionally protected). Or alternatively, a person might refrain from writing a story or showing a film that deserves constitutional protection because he or she fears prosecution.

*Miller v. California* (1973), represents the Court's most recent attempt to define obscenity. According to the Court, state obscenity statutes must limit only

> . . . works which depict or describe sexual conduct. That conduct must be specifically defined by the applicable state law, as written or authoritatively construed. A state offense must also be limited to works which, taken as a whole, appeal to the prurient interest in sex, which portray sexual conduct in a patently offensive way, and which, taken as a whole, do not have serious literary, artistic, political, or scientific value (at 24).

Of course, this *Miller* standard in defining obscenity does not automatically help us identify obscenity. What precisely appeals to "prurient interests"? What is "patently offensive"? Whose "prurient interests"? To deal with questions such as these, the majority of the Court in *Miller* would rely on the judges and juries ("triers of fact") within the states.

> The basic guidelines for the trier of fact must be:
> (a) whether " the average person, applying contemporary community standards" would find that the work, taken as a whole, appeals to the prurient interest . . . (b) whether the work depicts or describes, in a patently offensive way, sexual conduct specifically defined by the applicable state law, and (c) whether the work, taken as a whole, lacks serious literary, artistic, political, or scientific value (at 24).

According to Chief Justice Burger: "It is neither realistic nor constitutionally sound to read the First Amendment as requiring that the people of Maine or Mississippi accept public depiction of conduct found tolerable in Las Vegas, or New York City. . . . People in different States vary in their tastes and attitudes, and this diversity is not to be strangled by the absolutism of imposed uniformity" (at 33).

The standard for obscenity then depends on the values and standards that will vary from place to place. On its surface, however, the Court's guidelines do not leave communities free to suppress sexually explicit speech at will. Their discretion is constrained by the requirements of this *Miller* decision.

Did these *Miller* guidelines end the debate or resolve the uncertainty?

According to the dissenters in *Miller*, concepts such as "prurient interests," "patent offensiveness," and "serious literary value" are inherently vague. "The meaning of these concepts necessarily varies with experience, outlook, and even idiosyncrasies of the person defining them" (at 84). To permit the state to interfere with speech or press on the basis of such vague concepts seriously endangers First Amendment freedoms.

Although Justice Douglas, and earlier Justice Black, felt that the First Amendment permitted no interference with written, spoken, or filmed depiction of sexually oriented material, Justice Brennan would not go quite that far. In his dissent in *Paris Adult Theatre I v. Slaton,* (1973) he, however, weighed what possible interests might justify limiting such expression in the absence of any precise standard for distinguishing the obscene from the constitutionally protected. In the end he argued that only an interest in protecting children and unconsenting adults from exposure to such materials justified the risks posed by limits on expression that might inevitably sweep too broadly.

On this basis the state might regulate the distribution of sexually oriented material to only those who want such material and/or to adults who are mature enough to make the decision for themselves. As Chief Justice Burger, the author of the *Miller* standard, noted, however, Brennan's approach does not provide guidelines for distinguishing with any precision between sexually oriented materials that might be distributed to children or unconsenting adults from those that might not (at 27).

It is only on the question of withholding constitutional protection from "child pornography" that the Court has come close to unanimity on an issue relating to obscenity. In effect, in *New York v. Ferber,* (1982), the Court decided that sexually oriented material depicting children engaged in sexual acts deserves no constitutional protection. In identifying such material a majority of the Court did not feel constrained to weigh possible "serious" literary or scientific value of such material or to find that it appeals to the average person's prurient interests. The Court felt that the likely physiological and emotional harm inflicted on children who participate in production of such material far outweighs any interference with First Amendment freedoms. "The prevention of sexual exploitation and abuse of children constitutes a government objective of surpassing importance" (at 757).

Punishing distribution of such sexually explicit depictions of children is justified as the only effective means of preventing the harm caused by employing children in such production. To stop the exploitation of children, the state must "dry up" the market. To avoid long-term "emotional" harm the distribution of a "permanent record" of a child's participation in such production must be punished (at 759).

The Court's approach in *Ferber*, focusing as it did on the harm that making pornography has on participants (in that case children), seemed to some to open the door for an assault on pornography because of the harm it does to women.

Because many feminists believe that pornography contributes to male attitudes that demean women and foment sex discrimination and even violence, some have advocated banning pornography as a form of sex discrimination. In this effort they have sought to control sexually explicit materials not necessarily on the grounds of morality but rather in the interests of fighting sex discrimination. Under an ordinance adopted in Indianapolis, Indiana, pornography was defined in part as "the graphic sexually explicit subordination of women, whether in pictures or in words . . ." (*American Booksellers Association, Inc, v. Hudnut*, at 324).

When this statute was challenged in court, Circuit Judge Frank A. Easterbrook in effect accepted the argument put forward by its supporters that "men who see women depicted as subordinate are more likely to treat them so. Pornography is an aspect of dominance. . . . Depictions of subordination tend to perpetuate subordination" (at 328–29). Yet despite his listing of the doleful consequences for the status of women that may be attributed to men's attitudes shaped by pornography, Judge Easterbrook struck down the Indianapolis statute as violative of the First Amendment.

The problem which the statute attempted to address was the possibility, and even likelihood, that pornography might effectively persuade, that it might succeed in influencing the attitudes of men in particular and society in general. The statute clearly discriminated "on the grounds of the content of speech. Speech treating women in the approved way-in sexual encounters 'premised on equality'—is lawful no matter how sexually explicit. Speech treating women in the disapproved way—as submissive in matters sexual or as enjoying humiliation—is unlawful no matter how significant the literary, artistic, or political qualities of the work taken as a whole" (at 328). It was this preference for one point of view over another that led to the invalidation of the statute. In the words of Judge Easterbrook, "The Constitution forbids the state to declare one perspective right and silence opponents" (at 325, judgment affirmed *Hudnut v. American Booksellers Association Inc.* 1986).

While the lesson of the *Miller* decision is that efforts to restrict "hard core" pornography have sometimes withstood constitutional challenge, uneasiness remains. It is hard to believe that the Court has succeeded in defining obscenity in a manner that can readily be understood by all. Many believe that leaving the definition of such terms as "prurient interests" and "patently offensive" to varying community values violates the notion that the Constitution applies to all government conduct throughout the United States. While the rural South may well have different notions of what is acceptable than the streets of Manhattan, much of the press and film production today is for national and international audiences. A magazine that may be sold in New York under its "contemporary community standards" might lead to prosecution in Tuscaloosa under that community's standards. Can we, consistent with the First Amendment applicable throughout the United States, punish a publisher or distributor for selling in Alabama what the First Amendment protects in New York? On the other hand, unless we argue that the Constitution forbids all interference with obscenity, is it fair to subject the people of rural Maine to the standards of Las Vegas?

Perhaps many agree with Justice Stewart when he wrote: "I don't know what obscenity is, but I know it when I see it" (*Jacobellis v. Ohio*, 1964 Stewart, J., concurring at 197). Whether a government or a Supreme Court's acting on the basis of such an observation provides adequate protection for First Amendment freedoms is one of those questions that still needs to be answered.

## Question 6   *Why does the government permit sexually explicit material to invade our homes over the Internet?*

As most people are aware, today a vast computer network, the Internet, is available to bring an ever-growing stream of information and entertainment into the homes of all who possess a computer and access to the World Wide Web. Almost anyone has the capacity to disseminate information, ideas, and images to a worldwide audience. And as many parents know, an increasing number of children are even more adept than their parents at accessing that information at any time any day or night.

The Internet has created an entirely new communications environment, one never envisioned by the authors of the First Amendment. This new channel of communications has enormous potential for advancing the exchange of information and ideas. However, because it facilitates those of like mind reaching others who share particular ideas, it also opens up the possibility of the increasing fragmentation of communication. Rather than ideas clashing with ideas in the "free marketplace of ideas," like minds may speak only to like minds (for further discussion of this point, see Chapter 6, Question 2). One thing that is clear, however, is that the Internet offers us the opportunity to easily seek and obtain information on almost any topic.

Parents are naturally afraid of the potential influences that might reach their children. They are afraid of the many hours that children spend unsupervised at their computer monitors seeking out new information and cyber adventure. In an effort to protect children and in a natural response to parental concerns about their own ability to monitor everything their children might view, Congress passed the Communications Decency Act of 1996. The act was designed to punish "knowing" transmission of "obscene or indecent" messages to anyone under 18 years old (*Reno v. American Civil Liberties Union,* at 2338).

Promptly following the law's passage, the American Civil Liberties Union, joined by other interested parties, filed a law suit challenging the act's constitutionality under the First Amendment.

The Supreme Court has long held that obscenity is not protected by the Constitution (See Question 5 above). The Court has unanimously upheld laws that punish obscenity aimed at children. Adult entertainment, involving explicit sexual conduct, however, has received at least limited constitutional protection. The government is not permitted to censor all speech, movies, video, or other communication simply because it might inadvertently be encountered by sensitive audiences, including children. The Court has, however, allowed restrictions on the time, place, or manner of dissemination of sexually explicit adult entertainment in the interest of assuring that only mature audiences who seek to view or read such material are likely to come in contact with it.

In both *Young v. American Mini Theatres, Inc.* (1976) and *City of Renton v. Playtime Theatres, Inc.,* (1986) the Court upheld zoning ordinances that restricted the locations in which even adult entertainment facilities can be located. In these cases the Court claims to have upheld the ordinances in question not because of societal disapproval for the sexually explicit nature of the entertainment in question, but rather because of the "secondary effects of such theaters on the surrounding community." According to Justice Lewis Powell in *American Mini Theatres,* ". . . the ordinance by its terms is designed to prevent crime, protect the city's retail trade, maintain property values, and generally 'protec[t] and preserv[e] the quality of [the city's] neighborhoods, commercial districts, and the quality of urban life. . . .' If the City had been concerned with restricting the message purveyed by adult theaters, it would have tried to close them or restrict their number rather than circumscribe their choice as to location" (at 82, n. 4.).

In light of these precedents, proponents of keeping sexually explicit adult material off the Internet argued in effect that the Internet was an inappropriate location for the dissemination of sexually explicit materials. Because of ready access to the Internet by children, Congress felt justified in declaring the Internet in effect a nonadult entertainment zone, free of indecent materials which might fall into children's hands.

When the issue reached the United States Supreme Court, however, the justices found the government's position unpersuasive. The Court took note of the unique characteristics of the Internet, the difficulty that would be encountered by "speakers" who would legally be required to either remain "silent" or keep their messages exclusively in the hands of adults. The Court recognized that the Internet provided a new and promising forum for the exchange of ideas and was loathe to permit restrictions on this new public forum.

Unlike an adult entertainment theater or zone, Justice John Paul Stevens, writing for the Court in *Reno v. American Civil Liberties Union*, 1997, recognized that "[o]nce a provider posts its content on the Internet, it cannot prevent its content from entering any community." While a child entering an adult theater can easily be recognized and turned away, there is as yet no reliable technique for age identification of Internet users who may enter an adult "chat room." Realistically the only way an Internet provider can be sure his message will not reach a child is to refrain from speaking entirely. To punish one who posts a message on the Internet if his or her message reaches an underage user will lead only to child-appropriate messages being posted. The Court, however, has never permitted restricting adult communication to levels appropriate for children.

The Court came to its decision despite its ruling in *Federal Communications Commission v. Pacifica Foundation*, (1978) upholding a Federal Communications Commission (FCC) regulation of "indecent" material on the radio. In that case, George Carlin, a famous comedian, did a monologue using what he termed "filthy words," "the words you couldn't say on the public, ah, airwaves, um, the ones you definitely wouldn't say ever." (at 729). The broadcast of this monologue at 2 PM on October 30, 1973, led to a complaint being filed by the father of a young son. The commission in turn ruled that the station's conduct in broadcasting the "indecent" material "would be associated with the station's license file, and in the event that subsequent complaints are received, the Commission will then decide . . ." what punitive measures it might then take.

In deciding whether broadcast of "patently offensive words dealing with sex and excretion may be regulated because of its content," the Court argued that it had "long recognized that each medium of expression presents special First Amendment problems." Because broadcasting was considered by the Court at the time to have "established a uniquely pervasive presence in the lives of all Americans," the Court justified more restrictions on it than would be permitted for the print media, for example. "Patently offensive, indecent material presented over the airwaves confronts the citizen, not only in public, but also in the privacy of the home, where the individual's right to be left alone plainly outweighs the First Amendment rights of the intruder. . . . Because the broadcast audience is constantly tuning in and out [or channel surfing, to use a more contemporary phrase] prior warnings cannot completely protect the listener or viewer from unexpected program content" (at 748).

The Court in *Pacifica* also emphasized the fact that "broadcasting is uniquely accessible to children, even those too young to read. Although . . . an [indecent] written message might . . . [be] incomprehensible to a first grader, Pacifica's broadcast could have enlarged a child's vocabulary in an instant" (at 749).

The Court in *Reno v. American Civil Liberties Union* found the differences between the Internet and the CDU and broadcast media and FCC regulation to be significant enough to justify the apparently conflicting results in the two cases. First, the FCC order in *Pacifica* in effect regulated "when—rather than whether—it would be permissible to air such a program in that particular medium . . . Second, unlike the CDA, the [FCC] Commission's declaratory order was not punitive; . . . [the Court] expressly refused to decide whether the indecent broadcast 'would justify criminal prosecution.' Finally, the Commission's order applied to a medium which as a matter of history had 'received the most limited First Amendment protection' in large part because warnings could not adequately protect the listener from unexpected program content. The Internet, however, has no comparable history" (at 2342).

In contrast to the broadcast media, the Court concluded that the sexually explicit and/or indecent material on the Internet is usually accompanied by advanced notice of its nature and content. Those viewing, therefore, are generally only those who elect to see such material. According to the Court, [t]he district court specifically found that "communications over the Internet do not 'invade' an individual's home or appear on one's computer screen unbidden. Users seldom encounter content 'by accident' " (at 2343).

Although the Court's decision may leave parents feeling vulnerable, nothing in the Court's opinion appears to preclude Congress from passing less sweeping legislation that might in effect create "adult zones" on the Internet. As technology advances it will no doubt become increasingly possible to "tag" sexually explicit materials to enable parents to acquire software that will block access to it by their children. Until such a time comes, however, the Court's decision makes it clear that the government may not restrict adults taking advantage of the Internet to access only materials suitable for viewing by children.

## Question 7   *Why not require that people in public debate tell the truth?*

That people should not lie seems like a pretty simple proposition. That people should not attempt to influence the decisions of others with lies, especially when those decisions concern the future of a whole society, seems indisputable. But lies, or at least half-truths and exaggeration, are a common part of everyday political debate. Many media outlets, especially such tabloids as the *National Enquirer* or the *National Star*, are known for their wild stories. Reports of aliens from outer space landing in Detroit may do no harm, but stories about the private lives of politicians or other celebrities can damage reputations and potentially destroy careers. Because the tabloids are known for their unreliability, few take them seriously, but the same cannot necessarily be said for the more "responsible" press. When should First Amendment protections hinge on the truthfulness of the expression?

In 1964 in *New York Times Co. v. Sullivan,* (1964), the Supreme Court was called upon to decide whether the First Amendment protects a newspaper or citizens from libel actions brought by public officials. Libel is a written or published false statement damaging to the reputation of another. At the height of the civil rights movement in the South, an advertisement sponsored by supporters of the civil rights movement and Dr. Martin Luther King, Jr., appeared in the *New York Times*. The advertisement criticized actions of the Montgomery, Alabama police department in suppressing civil rights demonstrations and arresting Dr. King. The advertisement contained some factually inaccurate statements that were deemed by the Alabama courts to have damaged the reputation of the Montgomery, Alabama police commissioner.

The Supreme Court was confronted with the question of whether the First Amendment provides protection for libelous statements criticizing the official conduct of government officials. In approaching this question Justice Brennan's opinion of the Court noted our ". . . profound national commitment to the principle that debate on public issues should be uninhibited, robust, and wide-open, and that it may well include vehement, caustic, and sometimes unpleasantly sharp attacks on government and public officials" (at 270).

In political debate concerning emotionally charged issues, exaggeration and false statements are inevitable. To require that only statements that can be proved to be true be made would deny the freedom of expression essential "breathing space" (at 272). If defendants in libel suits were required to prove that all they have written is true, this might deter "would-be critics of official conduct . . . from voicing their criticism, even though it is believed to be true and even though it is in fact true, because of doubt whether it can be proved in court or fear of the expense of having to do so" (at 279).

To some these negative consequences flowing from insisting on the truth may not seem so terrible. What, you might ask, do we lose if people hold their tongues until they know for sure what they are saying? After all many of us are sick of the charges and countercharges and the "backbiting" that have become a central part of political debate today.

Perhaps a brief review of what happened during the Watergate scandal might put these ideas in perspective.

During the 1972 presidential election campaign, agents of the Nixon White House broke into the Democratic National Committee office apparently to install electronic listening devices. To this date we are uncertain about what they expected to learn, and we really do not know exactly who ordered the break-in. What did eventually become clear, however, was that high administration and campaign officials participated in a coverup. And several were eventually convicted of obstruction of justice and other serious offenses. Because of President Nixon's role in the coverup, impeachment proceedings were initiated against him. Nixon resigned from office shortly before an impeachment vote was scheduled to take place in the House of Representatives.

Public knowledge about the Watergate scandal emerged very slowly. When the charges first appeared in the press, no one had sufficient evidence to prove that either Nixon or his aides had participated in the planning of the breakin or, more importantly, in the obstruction of justice which followed it. To put it simply, many made charges and printed accusations which they could not then prove to be true. Those charges, however, brought denials from government officials. Subsequent debate about the credibility of those denials and continued press accusation led to investigations and the eventual emergence of evidence that would establish much of the truth.

If the slightest misstatement by the press could have led to a libel suit, would reporters have had the temerity to print accusations which they could not prove? If Nixon had not been forced by public opinion to respond to unproven accusations, would the obvious holes in his story and the subsequent damning evidence have ever emerged?

In its decision in *New York Times v. Sullivan* the Court in the end decided that the threats to free public debate posed by resort to libel actions by public officials were too great. Today, as a result of the *Times* decision, a public official may not recover ". . . damages for a defamatory falsehood relating to his official conduct unless he proves that the statement was made with 'actual malice'—that is, with knowledge that it was false or with a reckless disregard for whether it was false or not" (at 279–80). The public official in effect has to prove that the person making accusations against him was knowingly and deliberately telling a lie. This is a very difficult standard to meet.

At the beginning of the Watergate scandal, it is unlikely that those who accused Nixon and high officials in his administration with an illegal "coverup" could have proved their charges true. It is equally clear, however, that Nixon or his aides could not have met the standard for proving "actual malice" on the part of their accusers. Their grounds for suspicion were substantial enough to make any charge of a "reckless disregard for the truth" insupportable.

Public officials are, of course, not the only targets for damaging stories in the press. Celebrities, from sports figures to movie stars, are the constant subject of accusations and seemingly outrageous stories. While the *New York Times v. Sullivan* decision argued for the need for vigorous and uninhibited debate about the official conduct of public officials, what standard should apply to the activities of those who are famous but who are not part of government?

Sometimes, of course, the line between public officials and other celebrities gets quite blurred. Many celebrities, especially movie stars, involve themselves directly in public debate. One, Ronald Reagan, even got himself elected president!

During the early 1980s a freeze on the production and deployment of nuclear weapons as a first step toward arms reductions was advocated by many. When formal debates on this subject were held on television, however, it was not just politicians who participated. The actors Paul Newman (pro-"freeze") and Charlton Heston (anti-"freeze") debated each other on network TV. Similarly, during the Vietnam War actors and other participants in the performing arts often led protests both at home and abroad. Later in the mid-1990s Charlton Heston became a leader in the National Rifle Association, an organization that vigorously opposes most gun regulation.

Recognizing that "public figures," like "public officials," often play an influential role in ordering society, the Court in *Curtis Publishing Co. v. Butts* and *Associated Press v. Walker* (1967), decided that both should be treated alike when they attempted to sue for libel. According to then Chief Justice Earl Warren, ". . . 'public figures' have as ready access as 'public officials' to mass media . . . , both to influence policy and to counter criticism of their views and activities. Our citizenry has a legitimate and substantial interest in the conduct of such persons, and the freedom of the press to engage in uninhibited debate about their involvement in public issues and events is as crucial as it is in the case of 'public officials' "(at 164).

Usually when we think of politicians and celebrities, we assume that they have many more privileges than do ordinary citizens. We think of ourselves as vulnerable while they always get their way. In dealing with the question of how to treat libel of "ordinary" citizens, the Court has taken our relative vulnerability into account. When it comes to our ability to protect our reputations from unfair injury, the Court's interpretation of the First Amendment permits average citizens to use legal remedies now generally unavailable to the famous and powerful. In this area of law, at least, the greater your obscurity, the greater your legal protections.

The distinction made between public officials and figures on the one hand and private citizens on the other is based on two advantages public personalities have over the rest of us. First, because of being more accessible to the media, public figures are better able to respond to charges and accusations made against them; and second, public figures generally have sought notoriety and have benefited from their celebrity status. Public criticism, even unfair attacks, come with the territory. Since private citizens generally cannot easily command media attention to state their side of the story when they are attacked and because they have neither sought nor benefited from public notice, they are " . . . not only more vulnerable to injury than public officials and public figures; they are also," according to the Court, "more deserving of . . . [compensation for injury.]" (*Gertz v Robert Welch, Inc.* (1974), at 345).

The differences in the treatment of libel against public figures or officials and private citizens have not ended the debate concerning how the law should deal with untrue charges and statements. Are politicians and celebrities truly able to protect themselves from unfair and untrue attacks? Do private citizens need special protection?

Justice Brennan, the author of the *New York Times* decision that made it difficult for public officials to win libel suits, doubts that the distinction between people in public life and those in private life adequately protects legitimate public debate. The *New York Times, Curtis Publishing Co., and Walker* decisions all emphasized to varying degrees the roles played by public officials and public figures in "ordering society." The stress was on their "public" role. Today, however, many of the more damaging attacks on famous people concern their "private" lives rather than their public performance.

As the campaign for the 1988 presidential election began, Gary Hart was clearly the leading contender for the Democratic presidential nomination. He was forced to withdraw from the race, however, after allegations surfaced about alleged extramarital affairs. Although the charges against him did not concern his positions on political issues, his voting record in the Senate, the breaking of any laws, or using his political office for financial gain, his chances of becoming president evaporated.

In the end Mr. Hart came close to admitting that some of the charges of sexual misconduct were true, but in considering the significance of his case for the Court's position concerning libel, we might speculate about what might have happened had the charges been untrue. Because he was a public official, to win a libel judgment he would have had to have proved that those who made the charges told knowing lies or that they had shown a "reckless disregard for the truth." Even if the charges had been untrue, the likelihood that he could have won is slight indeed. The charges alone might well have been sufficient to have cast enough doubt on him to have fatally damaged his campaign. The time taken in publicly responding to such charges would surely have distracted his and the public's attention from real debate on vital political issues.

More recently, even before his involvement in the Lewinsky scandal, President Bill Clinton had to contend with a variety of charges and scurrilous attacks, many of which concerned his private life. Can anyone seriously say that he was less vulnerable to injury than a private citizen? Isn't it his very public status that invites damaging attacks, many of which are no doubt untrue.

Because in part he doubted that public officials and public figures can always command media attention to respond to reckless attacks on their purely private conduct, Justice Brennan argued that the heightened protection of First Amendment rights provided by the *New York Times* standard concerning libel should apply in all debate about matters of public interest whether or not the persons caught up in the debate were public officials or public figures. "The public's primary interest is in the event; the public focus is on the conduct of the participant and the content, effect, and significance of the conduct, not the participant's prior anonymity or notoriety" (*Rosenbloom v. Metromedia, Inc.*, 1971, at 43).

In its decision in *Chaplinsky* (see above) the Court argued that libel was among those limited categories of speech not protected by the First Amendment because ". . . such utterances are no essential part of any exposition of ideas, and are of such slight social value as a step to truth. . . ." The Court's decision in *New York Times*, however, recognized that the best method for finding the truth is to encourage free, open, and "robust" debate. Except in the instance of the deliberate lie designed purely to inflict injury, the Court in effect adopted the view expressed by Justice Holmes in a very different kind of case: "That the best test of truth is the power of the thought to get itself accepted in the competition of the market." (*Abrams v. United States*, 1919, Holmes, dissenting at 630).

Isn't the danger posed by silencing or punishing views and even offensive personal attacks greater than the damage potentially inflicted by such attacks?

## Question 8    *How is burning the American flag a form of free speech?*

Drawing a sharp line between speech and action can be difficult. Some, as we have seen, justify punishing people simply for advocating ideas that could possibly cause others to engage in illegal actions. Others are loathe to accept any limits on mere words, arguing instead that government should focus directly on actions. There is, however, another side to the sometimes fuzzy distinction between words and actions. Sometimes ideas are expressed not in speech, the press, or on film, but rather through actions; such nonverbal expression has been termed "symbolic speech." In symbolic speech cases, the question before the courts is: When do actions equal speech? When does punishing certain actions interfere with the exchange of ideas?

Although one might want to argue that the First Amendment protects any action designed to express an idea, on reflection no one could support such a position. For example, one might choose to express one's opposition to the president by burning down the White House. Some actually do burn or bomb abortion clinics to show their opposition to abortion. As the cliché goes: "Actions speak louder than words." Few miss the message in such actions, but virtually everyone recognizes that the framers of the First Amendment did not intend to authorize arson.

What if the target for burning is not the White House or an abortion clinic, but an American flag or a draft registration card? On such questions the courts are, sometimes, sharply divided.

In its decision upholding the constitutionality of a law punishing those who burned their draft registration cards, the Court devised a formula to aid it in deciding when the Constitution protects "symbolic speech."

During the Vietnam war, the law required men of draft age to carry their draft cards on which was listed their degree of eligibility for the draft. Burning these documents in public became a popular form of protest among those opposed to the War. In apparent response to such actions, Congress made destruction of such records a crime. Although the Court admitted that the First Amendment sometimes protected actions designed to express ideas, it upheld government regulation of such conduct under the following circumstances:

> . . . a government regulation is sufficiently justified if it is within the constitutional powers of the government; if it furthers an important or substantial governmental interest, if the governmental interest is unrelated to the suppression of free expression; and if the incidental restrictions on alleged First Amendment Freedoms is no greater than is essential to the furtherance of the interest. (*United States v. O'Brien,* 1968, at 377).

Since the government had the right to require draft registration, and since, the Court argued, the information printed on the registration cards facilitated communication between the draft board and the individual registrant permitting the "smooth and proper functioning of the system that Congress has established to raise armies" (at 381), the Court upheld the law.

Although it was obvious to any observers at the time that Congress passed the law primarily to punish a particular form of protest—to stifle this dramatic communication—the Court argued it was not its duty to assess the Congressional motives. In banning the burning of draft cards, Congress had successfully stifled one form of "symbolic speech," but as Justice Harlan's concurring opinion argued, other channels of communication involving "pure speech" remained open. People were still free to speak and write against the war.

Perhaps more than any other example of "symbolic speech" burning the American flag in protest elicits anger and controversy. To many the flag borders on a sacred symbol. They are profoundly offended when others treat it disrespectfully. The offense comes, however, not because a piece of striped cloth has been burned, but because the action expresses ideas that are offensive; for example, contempt for the country. However offensive this idea may be, few constitutional scholars would doubt that the First Amendment protects such ideas. The issue, then, is whether the First Amendment also protects this mode of expression.

Old flags are properly burned when they are being discarded or replaced by new flags. It is, therefore, not the act of burning but the thought behind it than offends.

In his dissent from a Court decision striking down the conviction of a flag burner, Justice Abe Fortas argued: "If a state statute provided that it is a misdemeanor to burn one's shirt or trousers on the public thoroughfare, it could hardly be asserted that the citizen's constitutional right is violated. . . . If as I submit it is permissible to prohibit burning of personal property on the public sidewalk, there is no basis for applying a different rule for flag burning" (*Street v. New York,* 1969, Fortas, dissenting, at 616).

Fortas seems to focus simply on the conduct in question. The problem with his approach, however, is that, generally, states do not pass laws carrying stiff penalties for burning your shirt. They do pass such laws for burning the American flag. Could it be that their fear is not arson or smoke pollution, but of ideas? If so, are such laws permissible under the First Amendment?

It was not until 1989 that the Supreme Court in *Texas v. Johnson* confronted this First Amendment question directly. Johnson was convicted for burning an American flag in protest outside the Republican national convention in Dallas in 1984. Under the Texas flag desecration statute he was sentenced to one year in prison.

In his opinion of the Court in *Texas v. Johnson,* Justice William Brennan, acknowledged the "expressive element in conduct relating to flags. . . . The very purpose of a national flag is to serve as a symbol of our country; it is, one might say, 'the one visible manifestation of two hundred years of nationhood' " (at 405). It is precisely because of its primarily expressive significance that conduct relating to the flag is in most instances protected by the First Amendment. As is the case with any exercise of free speech, the Constitution does not permit the state to "prohibit the expression of an idea simply because society finds the idea itself offensive or disagreeable. . . " (at 414). While acknowledging the fact that society in general is deeply offended by flag desecration, Justice Brennan and a majority of the Court concluded that if we were to punish those who desecrate the American flag, "we [would] dilute the freedom that this cherished symbol represents" (at 420).

The dissenters on the Court as well as the Court's critics in society focused on the flag's unique role in society. It is that role, they contend, that justifies limits on its physical desecration. While acknowledging that the Texas law did interfere with one form of symbolic expression, amounting, in Chief Justice William Rehnquist's words, to "an inarticulate grunt or roar that, it seems fair to say, is most likely to be indulged in not to express any particular idea, but to antagonize others. . . . ," it still left undisturbed "a full panoply of other symbols and every conceivable form of verbal expression to express . . . deep disapproval of national policy."

In response to the Court's decision striking down the Texas flag desecration statute, President George Bush and countless others called for a constitutional amendment to permit the states and the federal government to pass laws punishing flag desecration. In pressing their objections, the dissenters on the Court and the critics outside argued in effect that the flag symbolizes only good. In the words of Justice Stevens: "It is a symbol of freedom, of equal opportunity, of religious tolerance and good will for other people who share our aspirations." Others, however, might sometimes view the flag differently. To the Klu Klux Klan members and sometimes to African-Americans alike it has sometimes been a symbol of white supremacy and intolerance. The flag was carried by soldiers who liberated Europe from the Nazis, but it was also carried by soldiers who "exterminated" native Americans. Many of the loudest proponents of a constitutional amendment permitting bans on flag desecration to this day celebrate Civil War "rebel" heroes who fired cannon against it.

Whatever happens to proposals for constitutional amendments banning flag desecration or laws meant to circumvent the Supreme Court's decision upholding this form of free expression, those in society who are offended by flag burning still have the recourse provided by the First Amendment. In the words of Justice Brennan: "The way to preserve the flag's special role is not to punish those who feel differently about these matters. It is to persuade them that they are wrong."

***Why should a democratic society tolerate the expression of views that are offensive to the majority?***

Majority rule is the most fundamental tenet of democracy. Only the majority has the right to put its will into law, and all are expected to obey the majority's will expressed in law. In the United States there is a consensus on many fundamental ideas concerning how society should be ordered. There is, as well, very broad agreement that some philosophies and ideas are unacceptable. One need only think of the near universal condemnation of Nazism to understand this point. Yet despite the consensus opposed to Nazism, Nazis are still permitted to express their views. Similarly despite the fact that the civil rights revolution has produced widespread popular rejection of open racism, the Ku Klux Klan (KKK) still exists and still stages marches under the protection of the law.

If virtually all of us reject and despise the views espoused by such groups, why must we tolerate them? Isn't permitting them to continue publicly to express their opposition to the values the vast majority of us share contrary to the principal of majority rule? Isn't it a threat to democracy itself?

The answers to such questions are complex, but they concern the very heart of the values meant to be protected by the First Amendment. If the vast majority of us "know" that the Nazis and the KKK represent ideas that are evil, what possible purpose is served by giving them a chance to attract others to their cause? The answers involve an exploration of the meaning of democracy and the search for truth.

In his dissent in *Abrams v. United States* (1919), Justice Holmes confronted the issues raised by questions such as these:

> Persecution for the expression of opinions seems to me perfectly logical. If you have no doubt of your premises or your power and want a certain result with all your heart, you naturally express your wishes in law and sweep away all opposition. To allow opposition by speech seems to indicate that you think speech impotent, as when a man says that he has squared the circle, or that you do not care wholeheartedly for the result, or that you doubt either your power or your premises. *But when men have realized that time has upset many fighting faiths, they may come to believe even more than they believe the very foundations of their own conduct that the ultimate good desired is better reached by free trade in ideas—that the best test of truth is the power of the thought to get itself accepted in the competition of the market, and that truth is the only ground upon which their wishes safely may be carried out.* That at any rate is the

theory of our Constitution. It is an experiment, as all life is an experiment. Every year if not every day we have to wager our salvation upon some prophecy based upon imperfect knowledge. While the experiment is part of our system I think that we should be eternally vigilant against attempts to check the expression of opinions that we loathe and believe to be fraught with death, unless they so imminently threaten immediate interference with the lawful and pressing purposes of the law that an immediate check is required to save the country. [emphasis added]. (*Abrams v. U.S.* (1919), Holmes dissenting, at 630)

The idea expressed by Holmes was not new. It adopts a position previously taken by both John Milton's *Areopagitaca* and John Stuart Mill's *On Liberty*. Simply, we can only be confident that we have found the truth, that we know the truth, if we are willing to let our "truth" be tested in competition against other ideas. If our beliefs attract the support of society after being subjected to open challenge, then our ideas are probably correct. If, however, our ideas win out through silencing opposition, because other ideas are either not expressed or not heard, then we have no right to have confidence in them.

In a democratic society the decision-making process is like the search for truth. Obviously what the majority decides is what the majority believes is the best policy among the alternatives. If society is prevented by laws or by its own prejudices from hearing all possible alternatives, then it is acting out of at least partial ignorance.

Holmes, however, addresses the issue of whether a democratic society can tolerate the expression of views which directly challenge democratically made decisions. Isn't permitting defiant challenges the same as an admission of doubt, a belief that you have made an error? Isn't tolerance for rejected ideas a sign of weakness or uncertainty?

As Holmes argued, we can look back at history and see that "time has upset many fighting faiths." New information and experiences have often shown that beliefs firmly held by virtually all society were simply wrong. Witches were burned at the stake. Galileo was threatened with a similar fate when he denied that the earth was the center of the universe. Despite the firmly held beliefs of the vast majority for most of human history, the earth is not flat!

We can have little doubt that Milton, Mill, and Holmes are correct. Generally, acting on information is preferable to ignorance. But no doubt many of us are left uneasy when confronted by those who express beliefs we "know" are evil or at least just plain wrong. Don't we have to choose? Don't we have to sometimes make final decisions and simply reject outrageous alternatives?

When a group of American Nazis announced plans to march in Skokie, Illinois during the late 1970s even many long-time advocates of civil liberties and freedom of speech felt things had gone too far. Skokie was a town which had a large Jewish population, including a substantial number of survivors of World War II Nazi extermination camps. Permitting American Nazis to march in such a town would force many victims of Nazi atrocities to relive their horrible experiences and might as well cause them to fear that it could happen again.

To those who opposed permitting the Nazi march, the Nazis were not simply expressing an alternative point of view to those shared by most of society. The Nazi were not simply wrong; they were the personification of evil in the world. To tolerate even this small march could once again cause their hateful ideas to become acceptable. It is one thing to believe that the best way to find the truth is through the unrestricted competition of ideas, but most of us know that most people do not listen with an open mind. Some, possibly a majority, might hear the Nazi lies and for a time at least believe them and act on them. After all, even as Lincoln argued that "you can't fool all of the people all of the time," he acknowledged that "you can fool all of the people some of the time." Do we have enough confidence in the majority to take the chance that they might be seduced by Nazi ideology. Why take the risk?

If we could be certain that the majority would silence only those espousing genuinely evil ideas, perhaps little would be lost by silencing Nazis. But experience has shown that often the majority finds the "truth" sufficiently troubling to silence those who speak it. In the Skokie case the ideas expressed by the Nazis were profoundly shocking and frightening to the majority in that community. Because they found those ideas so terrible, they attempted to use the law to ban the public expression of Nazi beliefs. If, however, the measure of what can be said and what cannot be said is a function of the level of revulsion or hostility the potential "speaker" or marcher evokes in the community, then Martin Luther King, Jr., and other civil rights advocates could have been silenced in many American communities during the 1950s and 60s. Dr. King challenged the deeply ingrained beliefs and prejudices of a majority in many communities. A review of old television tapes and newsreels from that era would show the extreme emotion and hostility directed against King and other demonstrators by very average-looking white Americans. Perhaps they felt King challenged their whole way of life. When Dr. King led an open housing march in Cicero, Illinois in 1968, he and his fellow marchers had to be protected by National Guard troops from a mob determined to keep blacks from living in "their" community.

Although today we "know" that King was right and the Nazis are wrong, the majority clearly has not always known this. If the majority can silence opinions which they find intolerable, then at varying times in our history it would have been those who speak the truth who would have been silenced.

When free speech is vigorously safeguarded, will the truth always prevail? Certainly not. Without protection for freedom of speech, however, we have no right to expect that the truth will ever prevail. The best anecdote for bad speech is, in Justice Brandeis' words, "more speech, not enforced silence" (quoted in Meikeljohn, p. 56).

## REFERENCES

*Abrams v. United States*, 250 U.S. 616 (1919).

*American Booksellers Association, Inc. v. Hudnut*, 771 F.2d 323 (7th Cir., 1985).

*Association Press v. Walker*, 388 U.S. 130 (1967).

*Brandenburg v. Ohio*, 395 U.S. 444 (1969).

*Cantwell v. Connecticut*, 310 U.S. 296 (1940).

*Chaplinsky v. New Hampshire*, 315 U.S. 568 (1942).

*City of Renton v. Playtime Theaters, Inc.*, 476 U.S. 41 (1986).

*Curtis Publishing, Co. v. Butts & Associated Press v. Walker*, 388 U.S. 130 (1967).

*Federal Communications Commission v. Pacifica Foundation*, 483 U.S. 726 (1978).

*Gertz v. Robert Welch, Inc.*, 418 U.S. 323 (1974).

*Gitlow v. New York*, 268 U.S. 652 (1925).

*Jacobellis v. Ohio*, 378 U.S. 184 (1964).

Meikeljohn, Alexander, *Free Speech and Its Relation to Self-Government* (New York: Harper & Row, 1948).

*Miller v. California*, 413 U.S. 15 (1973).

*Near v. Minnesota*, 283 U.S. 697 (1931).

*Nebraska Press Association v. Stuart*, 427 U.S. 539 (1976).

*New York v. Ferber*, 485 U.S. 747 (1982).

*New York Times Co. v. Sullivan*, 376 U.S. 254 (1964).

*New York Times Co. v. United States*, 403 U.S. 713 (1971).

*Paris Adult Theatre I v. Slaton*, 413 U.S. 49 (1973).

*R. A. V. v. St. Paul*, 505 U.S. 377 (1992).

*Reno v. American Civil Liberties Union*, 117 S. Ct 2329 (1997).

*Rosenbloom v. Metromedia*, Inc. 403 U.S. 29 (1971).

*Roth v. United States*, 354 U.S. 479 (1947).

*Schenck v. United States*, 249 U.S. 47 (1919).

*Street v. New York*, 394 U.S. 576 (1969).

*Terminiello v. City of Chicago*, 337 U.S. 1 (1949).

*Texas v. Johnson*, 491 U.S. 397 (1989).

*United States v. O'Brien*, 391 U.S. 367 (1968).

*Young v. American Mini Theatres, Inc.*, 427 U.S. 50 (1976).

### CHAPTER 3

# Freedom of Religion

## INTRODUCTION

The ancesters of many Americans came here to escape religious persecution in their homelands. The quest for religious liberty, therefore, has always been an important element in American life. If public opinion surveys and the rhetoric of politicians are to be believed, today religion continues to play an important role in the lives of most Americans. In order to protect religious liberty and religious expression, the First Amendment to the Constitution provides for the separation of church and state. Over two centuries after the adoption of the First Amendment the Supreme Court's understanding of the requirements of the religion clauses continues to stir controversy and continues to evolve. Vigorous debate continues concerning what separation of church and state means. This chapter explores central questions relating to religion and the Constitution.

One of the core issues regarding the First Amendment is to what degree it demands strict separation of government from religion. Some argue for a "wall of separation" between church and state, while others assert the constitution mandates accomodation between church and state. Question 1 asks: *Why can't government help advance the religious values that the majority of Americans share?* This section begins with a brief description of the Establishment and Free Exercise clauses of the First Amendment and then explores in greater depth the variety of understandings on the Court of what in particular the Establishment clause forbids. It reviews the so-called *Lemon* test frequently used by justices on the Court in recent decades to judge the constitutionality of government programs which in some way affect religion or religious institutions.

While the Establishment clause focuses on the propriety of government support for religion, the Free Exercise clause concerns the freedom of people to practice their religion without government restriction. Question 2 asks: *Are there limits on a person's right to practice his or her religion?* Here we explore deep divisions within the Court in recent years concerning the degree to which government must provide exemption from laws and other regulations when compliance with them would conflict with a person's religious beliefs. The issue is whether the Free Exercise clause of the First Amendment protects merely one's right to believe or whether it protects as well one's right to act in accordance with his or her beliefs.

Sometimes the right to free exercise of religion appears to run into conflict with the prohibition against establishment of religion. The controversy over religion in the public schools highlights this conflict. Question 3 asks: *Doesn't banning "voluntary prayer" in the public schools interfere with children's freedom of religion?* Here we explore the highly controversial Supreme Court decisions concerning government-sponsored prayer in public schools. Concerning a related issue Question 4 asks: *If secular groups are allowed access to the schools, shouldn't religious groups have the same rights?* This question forces us to explore the issue of whether the Establishment clause forces government to discriminate against religious expression in our public institutions. The Court has been forced to weigh the relationship between free speech and religious expression and whether the Constitution mandates or forbids equal access by religious groups to public forums.

Controversy about the teaching of evolution in the public schools has existed since early in this century. In 1999 the curriculum guidelines for the state of Kansas removed discussion of evolution from the state's approved scientific curriculum. Fundamentalist religious groups have long denounced evolution as contrary to literal interpretation of the origins of the human species as described in Genesis. This section explores Question 5: *Doesn't teaching evolution in the public schools amount to the "establishment" of a secular religion?*

Finally, in light of all of the contemporary debate concerning the issue of religion in our public life, Question 6 asks: *Is the separation of church and state breaking down?* This section explores the evolution of Court interpretations of both the Establishment and Free Exercise clauses away from the strict separation philosophy adopted by the Court in the mid-twentieth century. Our discussion of this question will serve to summarize the current state of the church/state relationship in America.

### Question 1   *Why can't government help advance the religious values that the majority of Americans share?*

A larger proportion of the American population attends church on a regular basis than in most other countries, and surveys of the population show that most Americans consider themselves religious. When questions concerning religion and government arise, it is natural that many are confused. Even people who consider themselves tolerant of the feelings and beliefs of others have a difficult time understanding why prayer in the schools, for example, is controversial. Many when told that some object to school prayer respond: "It won't do them any harm, and it might do them some good." Whenever former President Ronald Reagan hit the campaign trail, he was always guaranteed cheers from the crowd when he called for the restoration of "voluntary prayer" in the public schools.

If we look beyond America, however, we can readily see the divisive role played by religion in many countries throughout the world. Calls are heard periodically in some "fundamentalist" Islamic countries for "holy war." Persecution of minority religious sects is found almost everywhere. Ancient nationalist political conflicts, such as those in the north of Ireland or Kosovo, take on religious overtones. Virtually every nation has at one time or another felt confident that "God is on our side."

The history of the relationship between church and state in America is often distorted and easily misunderstood. Many early Americans came here to escape religious persecution, but once here many practiced religious intolerance themselves. Most of the original colonies had an "established" state church or churches and/or provided tax support for favored churches. From the beginning there was dissent from minority religions and warnings from leaders like Jefferson and Madison of the dangers of links between church and state.

Today some churches still seek state support for religious schools and other sectarian institutions. Religious and political leaders frame the struggle for civil rights, for helping the poor, for and against capital punishment, or for laws forbidding abortion in religious terms. Clergy men sometimes endorse candidates for office, and in 1988 two Protestant ministers, Jesse Jackson and Pat Robertson, actually ran for president of the United States.

Legal debate concerning religion and the state in America revolves around the meaning of the First Amendment Free Exercise and Establishment clauses. The First Amendment religion clauses state: "Congress shall make no laws respecting an establishment of religion, or prohibiting the free exercise thereof." There is no doubt that the Establishment clause at minimum prohibits the government from setting up a single recognized state church. There has, however, been considerable controversy concerning whether this clause commands a complete separation between church and state. Some see the Establishment clause as mandating simply "no preference" on the part of government for one church over another. They rely on the historic understanding based on European experience that "establishment" refers to state support for a single recognized church. A respected constitutional scholar, Leonard Levy, has argued, however, that the "establishments of religion" found in most of the American colonies and original states involved state support for churches in general. In some of the first states citizens were forced to pay taxes to support their own churches. The state was in effect a collection agency for many churches. When Madison and Jefferson opposed established religions, they opposed not only state preference for particular religions, but also such state tax support for any religions. They considered religion to be a purely private matter.

Many, however, argue that the Constitution does permit accommodation between government and religion in general. Some would go so far as to argue that government's failure to aid all religion amounts to a preference for irreligion, or what some have termed "secular humanism."

The dominant view on the Supreme Court during much of the twentieth century had been, however, that the Constitution mandates a "wall of separation" between church and state. The Court majority generally in effect has argued that the First Amendment not only forbids a preference for any particular religion, but it also forbids a preference for religion in general over irreligion. It bans any entanglement between government and religion.

In a much quoted passage from the Supreme Court's decision in *Everson v. Bd. of Education* (1947) Justice Hugo Black summed up the meaning of the Establishment clause as follows:

> Neither a state nor the Federal Government can set up a church. Neither can pass laws which aid one religion, aid all religions, or prefer one religion over another. Neither can force or influence a person to go to or remain away from church against his will or force him to profess a belief or disbelief in any religion. No person can be punished for entertaining or professing religious beliefs or disbeliefs, for church attendance or non-attendance. No tax in any amount, large or small, can be levied to support any religious activities or institutions, whatever they may be called, or whatever form they may adopt to teach or practice religion. Neither a state nor the Federal Government can, openly or secretly, participate in the affairs of any religious organization or group and vice versa. In the

words of Jefferson, the clause against the establishment of religion by law was intended to erect a "wall of separation between church and state" . . . . (at 15–16)

When Justice Black wrote these words, he was writing for a Court majority which actually upheld a very limited government program to pay for transportation to schools for all students, including those attending religious schools. The four justices who dissented in *Everson* called for an even stricter and more total separation of church and state. Black's words endorsing a "wall of separation," however, clearly reflect the unanimous view of the Supreme Court at the time, one mandating a nearly complete separation of church and state.

The issue of the proper relationship between church and state will not, however, go away. Since the *Everson* decision, the Court has been forced to decide a number of cases, and its decisions have not always been consistent. In a decision upholding government support for the display of a Christmas creche on public land, Chief Justice Warren Burger dismissed the concept of a " 'wall' of separation" as "a useful figure of speech." But he went on to argue that ". . . the Constitution [does not ] require complete separation of church and state; it affirmatively mandates accommodation, not merely tolerance, of all religions, and forbids hostility toward any . . .". (*Lynch v. Donnelly* (1984).

In support of this position, Chief Justice Burger and other advocates of accommodation cite the long history of official recognition of religious themes and religious observances in American public life. Acts of Congress have placed "In God We Trust" on our coins and "one Nation, under God" in the pledge of allegiance. Presidents as far back as Washington have proclaimed Thanksgiving Day and days of prayer and fasting. Congress begins each session with prayers offered by chaplains on the public payroll, and chaplains are provided for the armed forces as well. The list could go on. Clearly, our practice has not always corresponded to the proclaimed principle of a "wall of separation."

Separation of church and state, however, cannot mean a total denial of the role of religious values in American life. Many who opposed America's sad history of racial oppression did so citing religious grounds. Prohibitions against murder, stealing, or lying are found both in secular law and in the Ten Commandments. Surely the prohibition against an "establishment of religion" found in the First Amendment does not mean that the state may not pursue policies that happen to be consistent with religious values.

The Supreme Court on a number of occasions has attempted to delineate when it is permissible for state or federal laws to parallel religious laws or commands. In *Lemon v. Kurtzman* (1971), Chief Justice Burger attempted to summarize the Court's evolving understanding of the Establishment clause. He argued that the framers of the Establishment clause

> did not simply prohibit the establishment of a state church or state religion. . . . Instead they commanded that there should be "no law *respecting* an establishment of religion." A law may be one "*respecting*" the forbidden objective while falling short of total realization. A law "respecting" the proscribed result, that is, the establishment of religion, is not always easily identifiable as one violative of the Clause. A given law might not *establish* a state religion but nevertheless be one "respecting" that end in the sense of being a step that could lead to such establishment and hence offend the First Amendment . . . (at 612).

From this analysis Chief Justice Burger went on to develop guidelines which have come to be known as the *Lemon* test:

> Every analysis in this area must begin with consideration of the cumulative criteria developed by the Court over many years. Three such tests may be learned from our cases. First, the statute must have a secular legislative purpose; second, its principal or primary effect must be one that neither advances or inhibits religion; finally, the statute must not foster "an excessive government Entanglement with religion" (at 612, 613).

Thinking about the "purpose prong" of the *Lemon* test, one can understand that although prohibitions against murder are found in the Bible, the state does not necessarily prohibit murder *because* it is prohibited in the Bible. People's natural instinct to live provides quite ample secular motivation in itself, even to those who have neither read nor even heard of the Bible.

On the other hand when the Supreme Court was confronted with a challenge to a Kentucky statute requiring the posting of the Ten Commandments in every public school classroom, the Court majority found no "secular purpose" behind the action, and therefore struck it down as a violation of the Establishment clause. In so ruling the Court dismissed the state's contention, noted in small print at the bottom of each display of the Ten Commandments in the schools, that "[t]he secular application of the Ten Commandments is clearly seen in its adoption as the fundamental legal code of western Civilization and the Common Law of the United States" [citations omitted,] (*Stone v. Graham,* (1980), at 41).

According to the per curium opinion in *Stone v. Graham,*

> The preeminent purpose for posting the Ten Commandments on schoolroom walls is plainly religious in nature. . . . The Commandments do not confine themselves to arguably secular matters, such as honoring one's parents, killing or murder. . . . Rather, the first part of the Commandments concerns the religious duties of believers: worshiping the Lord God alone, avoiding idolatry, not using the Lord's name in vain, and observing the Sabbath Day. . . (at 42).

When the Court was confronted with a constitutional challenge to "Sunday closing laws," however, it chose to downplay the fact that "[t]here is no dispute that the original laws which dealt with Sunday labor were motivated by religious forces" (*McGowan v. Maryland,* at 431), arguing instead that today such laws ". . . have become part and parcel" of the increased government concern in this century for "improvement of the health, safety, recreation and general well-being of our citizens." Today, then, according to the Chief Justice Warren's opinion of the Court, "[t]he present *purpose and effect* of most of them is to provide a uniform day of rest for all citizens; the fact that this day is Sunday, a day of particular significance for the dominant Christian sects, does not bar the State from achieving its secular goals" (at 445).

In applying the *Lemon* test to various state programs to aid parochial schools, the Court acknowledged the possibility, as asserted by the states, that their "purpose" was secular, that is, assuring that all children, including those in church schools, are provided with good educations in secular subjects. But in applying these principles to a particular Rhode Island program supplementing the salaries of teachers in certain secular subjects, the Court concluded that assuring that the teachers would *not* inculcate religious doctrines at state expense would require a level of state supervision of practices within church schools as to amount to "excessive entanglement" between church and state. In effect the chief justice argued that it is simply too difficult to keep religious teachings separate from secular in religious schools founded on religious principles. Because the Court majority believed that assuring that state funds would not be used for religious teaching would require an intrusive state regulatory supervision of the schools, there would inevitably be an "excessive entanglement" between church and state.

Another and somewhat different manifestation of what the *Lemon* test terms "excessive entanglement" can be found in *Larkin v. Grendel's Den, Inc,* (1982). Grendel's Den was a restaurant in Harvard Square in Cambridge, Massachusetts. Under Massachusetts law "[p]remises . . . located within a radius of five hundred feet of a church or school shall not be licensed for sale of alcoholic beverages if the governing body of such church or school files written objection thereto." Because of the objection by the adjoining Holy Cross Armenian Catholic parish, an application by Grendel's Den for a liquor license was denied. Although the courts below the U.S. Supreme Court did not deny the existence of a secular purpose behind limiting liquor establishments near churches or schools, they did find that the "veto" authority given to churches conferred "a direct and substantial benefit upon religions" (at 120). In other words it had in the words of Chief Justice Burger's opinion of the Court, "a 'primary' and 'principal' effect of advancing religion." In addition, however, the Court expressed concern about "the entanglement implications of a statute vesting significant government authority in churches." Chief Justice Burger concluded that "[t]his statute enmeshes churches in the exercise of substantial government powers contrary to our consistent interpretation of the Establishment Clause; '[t]he objective is to prevent, as far as possible, the intrusion of either [Church or State] into the precincts of the other.' *Lemon v. Kurtzman* 403 U. S., at 614" (at 126).

The Court's frequent reliance upon the *Lemon* test for determining when government actions violate the Establishment clause has produced considerable controversy on the Court. Justice Anton Scalia dismisses the *Lemon* test, arguing that "[o]ur religion-clause jurisprudence has become bedeviled (so to speak) by reliance upon formalistic abstractions that are not derived from, but positively conflict with, our long-accepted constitutional traditions" (*Lee v. Weisman,* (1992), at 644). He argues instead that the Constitution "affirmatively mandates accommodation [in the Free Exercise Clause (see below, Question 2)], not merely tolerance of all religions . . . " (*Lamb's Chapel v. Center Moriches School District,* (1993), at 402)

Certainly in some of its decisions such as that upholding prayer at the beginning of legislative sessions, the Court has conveniently ignored the *Lemon* test. But except under circumstances where the Court finds historic practice mandates some limited accommodation of religious practices, the *Lemon* test remains a frequently used guidepost for distinguishing unconstitutional Establishment of Religion from policies promoting secular values which find parallels in religious principles.

**Question 2**   *Are there limits on a person's right to practice his or her religion?*

The meaning of the First Amendment Free Exercise clause has been the subject of only slightly less dispute than of the Establishment clause. Clearly the state cannot make it a crime for anyone to profess any religious belief. But it is one thing to profess, it is quite something else to practice. When the line is crossed between mere expression of belief to actual practice (the performance of some act or the refusal to perform

some action for religious reasons), the consensus within the courts about freedom of religious exercise breaks down.

As was true of the other principal First Amendment freedom, freedom of speech, when there is agreement over the definition of what is encompassed by Free Exercise of Religion, the Court in recent years has been nearly unanimous in denying the government the right to restrict that freedom except for some narrowly defined "compelling state interest." But some on the Court argue that free exercise protects only the right to believe or profess while others argue it includes the right to practice.

In 1963 in *Sherbert v. Verner*, the Supreme Court seemed to extend to the right to practice religion its most stringent protection. In that case a member of the Seventh Day Adventist religion was denied unemployment benefits because she had refused a job which would have required her to work on Saturday, her sabbath. By a 7 to 2 vote the Supreme Court ruled that the denial of benefits amounted to an unconstitutional abridgement of her right to exercise her religion freely. In other words the Court ruled that the state had impermissibly conditioned her right to a benefit upon her agreement to ignore a central tenet of her religious beliefs.

Even though the unemployment compensation regulations placed no explicit or direct limitation on the free exercise of religion, Justice Brennan, writing for the Court majority argued that

> Sherbert's ineligibility for benefits derive[d] solely from the practice of her religion . . . , [and] the pressure upon her to forego that practice . . . [was] unmistakable. The ruling forces her to choose between following the precepts of her religion and forfeiting benefits, on the one hand, and abandoning one of the precepts of her religion in order to accept work, on the other hand. Governmental imposition of such a choice puts the same kind of burden upon the free exercise of religion as would a fine imposed against appellant for her Saturday worship" (at 737–38).

Because of the Court's ruling Ms. Sherbert would receive unemployment benefits even though she had in effect refused work. In his dissenting opinion Justice Harlan argued that this in effect amounted to requiring the state to show preference for those asserting religious reasons for refusing work over other reasons for refusing to accept a job. A single mother who refused a job because she could not find a babysitter would be denied benefits by the state, but a woman who refused work because of religious scruples would receive benefits. In Justice John Harlan's words as a result of the majority's ruling, "[t]he state . . . must *single out* for financial assistance those whose behavior is religiously motivated, even though it denies such assistance to others whose identical behavior (in this case inability to work on Saturdays) is not religiously motivated." As Justice Potter Stewart asserted in his separate concurring opinion, such preference for religion runs counter to the Court's precedents interpreting the Establishment clause. Stewart himself was not troubled by that conflict because he felt the Court had gone too far in mandating strict separation of church and state. He believed that "the guarantee of religious liberty embodied in the free exercise clause affirmatively requires government to create an atmosphere of hospitality and accommodation to individual religious belief or disbelief" (at 740).

*Sherbert v. Verner* demonstrates that sometimes there is a tension between the Establishment clause and the Free Exercise clause. Sometimes treating everyone the same will penalize those whose religions require that they act differently from the majority. But to provide exceptions to rules applicable to all for those motivated by religious principles can be interpreted as giving special privileges to those belonging to certain religions. If the state gives special treatment to the religious, isn't it guilty of violating the Establishment clause?

The majority opinion written by Justice Brennan had in effect held that only a "compelling state interest" could justify the government's refusal to carve out exceptions to generally applicable law when applying a law to a particular individual would compel him to act in a way contrary to his religion. This decision gives special status to religious beliefs over other interests and beliefs, but the Court majority in *Sherbert* felt such special treatment is required by the Free Exercise clause.

In a subsequent case in 1990, *Employment Division, Department of Human Resources of Oregon v. Smith,* (1989), a narrow Supreme Court majority appears to have abandoned Justice Brennan's approach to free exercise challenges to laws which do not single out religion for special discriminatory treatment but which nonetheless have the effect of penalizing action motivated by religion. This case involved the denial of unemployment benefits to two native Americans who had been fired from a privately operated drug rehabilitation program because they had smoked peyote. Ingesting peyote was an integral part of their particular native American religious ceremonies, but peyote is an illegal drug. Because they were fired for cause, they were denied unemployment benefits as would other workers who were fired for misbehavior. Because the behavior for which they were fired was required by their religion, however, they claimed that to penalize them by denying unemployment benefits would amount to a state punishment of them for freely exercising their religion.

The principal conflict within the Supreme Court over this case concerned the applicable standard by which the Court should judge government conduct under the Free Exercise clause. In his Opinion of the Court, Justice Anton Scalia in effect rejected the compelling state interest test applied by Justice William Brennan in *Sherbert v. Verner.* To Justice Scalia, "[t]he free exercise of religion means, first and foremost, the right to believe and profess whatever religious doctrine one desires"(*Employment Division v. Smith,* at 877). But it does not immunize religiously motivated conduct from generally applicable laws which apply equally to the religious and nonreligious. Unless the law singles out a religious practice for special punishment, there is no basis for a free exercise challenge and no need for the government to show some compelling state interest to justify applying the law even to those who raise a religious objection. To challenge the application of a law to you as a violation of your free exercise of religion, you must first show that the government treated you differently from others who do not share your religious conviction.

An example of a government policy that could not survive even the less sweeping approach of Justice Anton Scalia arose in the case of the *Church of the Lukumi Babalu Aye v. City of Hialeah* (1993). In response to the announced plans of believers in Santeria, a church that believed in and engaged in ritual animal sacrifice, to build a church in Hialeah, Florida, the Hialeah City Council passed an ordinance which among other things banned the killing of animals for ritual sacrifice when the killing was not for "the primary purpose of food consumption" (at 527).

While under the *Smith* test a law banning killing of animals could no doubt survive constitutional challenge even if it did serve to ban religious ceremonies involving animal sacrifice, to survive constitutional challenge the law could not single out religious sacrificial killings for special prohibition. According to the Court in *Church of Lukumi*, this is precisely what the law did. In his Opinion of the Court, Justice Anthony Kennedy acknowledged that even though the law referred directly to "sacrifice" and "ritual," this alone did not suffice to find that it singled out religious killing for special prohibition because such terms can have secular applications. Taken as a whole, however, in light of the history surrounding the law's enactment, it was clear that the law was designed to target the practices of a disfavored religion. The city council resolution accompanying the enactment of the statute referred to the practices of "certain religious groups . . . " (at 534, 535).

Significantly, according to Justice Kennedy's opinion, the city defended its ordinance in court as designed to protect public health and to prevent cruelty to animals. If such were indeed the goals, however according to Justice Kennedy, the ordinance was "under inclusive," in that "[t]hey fail to prohibit non-religious conduct that endangers these interests to similar or greater degree than Santaria sacrifice does" (at 543). He noted that both fishing and extermination of mice and rats are permitted by the statute. In addition "[t]he health risks posed by the improper disposal of animal carcasses are the same whether Santaria sacrifice or some nonreligious killing preceded it. The city does not, however, prohibit hunters from bringing animal kill to their houses, nor does it regulate disposal after their activity" (at 544).

In sum it appears clear that it was the religious motivation for animal destruction that offended the majority of the community and not the destruction of animals itself. For this reason the Court concluded that the ordinance in question was one that targeted a religion for discriminatory treatment.

The controversy within the Court over the appropriate constitutional standard for protecting the free exercise of religion has been extended to Capitol Hill. Religious leaders of many denominations were troubled by the threat potentially posed to free exercise of religion by the Court's approach announced in *Employment Division . . . v. Smith*, 1989. An odd coalition of liberal and conservative clergy and civil libertarians succeeded in persuading Congress in 1993 to pass the Religious Freedom Restoration Act of 1993 (RFRA) which was designed to restore the constitutional protections for minority religions provided by *Sherbert v. Verner*. Because Section 5 of the Fourteenth Amendment gives to Congress the power to "enforce through appropriate legislation. . . ." the provisions of the amendment, Congress asserted that it could advance the free exercise of religion by restoring "the compelling state interest test" from *Sherbert* in challenges to even generally applicable or "neutral" government actions which "substantially burden religious exercise" (*City of Boerne v. Flores*, 1997, at 515). Although in the area of "affirmative action" in race and gender discrimination cases there was precedent for Congress to define rights and liberties more broadly than the Court felt the constitution required (see *Fullilove v. Klutznick*, 1980), the Court in *City of Boerne v. Flores* (1997) argued that the power to enforce is different from the power to define a right or liberty. "Legislation which alters the meaning of the Free Exercise clause cannot be said to be enforcing the clause. Congress does not enforce a constitutional right by changing what that right is. It has been given the power 'to enforce, not the power to determine what constitutes a constitutional violation'" (at 519).

Although the Court in effect focused not on the definition of Free Exercise but rather on the limits of Congressional power to revise constitutional interpretations announced by the Court, the effect of the *City of Boerne* case was to leave in place for now at least the interpretation of the Free Exercise clause adopted in *Employment Division . . . v. Smith*. One's right to exercise freely one's religion is largely confined to the right to believe as one pleases and to be free from discriminatory treatment by government because of one's religious beliefs. Society is free, however, to make it difficult for those in minority religions to practice what they believe as long as the restrictions on conduct apply in the same way to all believers and nonbelievers. Whether this provides enough protection for those of us whose beliefs dictate ways of living different from those approved by society in general will no doubt continue to be debated within the U.S. Supreme Court and beyond.

**Question 3** *Doesn't banning "voluntary prayer" in public schools interfere with children's freedom of religion?*

Images of religious persecution and sectarian violence throughout the world seem to many Americans far removed from the simple innocent act of little children invoking God's blessings on their activities as they embark on their school day. Many, perhaps most of us, find little danger in a child being exposed to a simple prayer. Many believe such an act of quiet reverence, as long as it is not coerced, can set a tone of respect and reflection for young children. If nothing else it can quiet them down and ready them to learn. For these reasons many find it very difficult to understand why prayer is not permitted in public schools. Indeed, many find the absence of prayer to be an affront to their deeply held religious convictions.

In 1962 in *Engel v. Vitale*, however, the U.S. Supreme Court in one of its more controversial decisions declared even formally voluntary prayer in the public schools to be a violation of the Establishment clause of the First Amendment. This Court decision has provoked much debate and repeated efforts to amend the Constitution in order to overturn the Court's decision and restore "voluntary prayer" to the public schools.

*Engel* overturned a "non-denominational prayer" written by the state Board of Regents for use at the beginning of the school day in all the public school classrooms in New York. The prayer was a simple one: "Almighty God, we acknowledge our dependence upon Thee, and we beg Thy blessings upon us, our parents, our teachers and our country" (at 422).

Although this prayer may seen innocuous to most, it was the contention of Steven Engel and other parents of children in a New York school district, that the state policy requiring or permitting use of the Regent's prayer "must be struck down as a violation of the Establishment clause because that prayer was composed by government officials as a part of a governmental program to further religious beliefs" (at 425). Justice Hugo Black writing for the Court majority agreed because under the Establishment clause "it is no part of the business of government to compose official prayers for any group of the American people to recite as a part of a religious program carried on by government" (at 425).

Justice Black recited the history of religious persecution in England and its continuation in early America as the previous victims of persecution used their new power here to impose their religious beliefs on others. It was in part that history, he contended, that led to the First Amendment

Establishment and Free Exercise clauses. The First Amendment religion clauses state that "Congress shall make no laws respecting the establishment of religion, nor prohibiting the free exercise thereof."

Because the New York school prayer law in question had been limited by the New York Court of Appeals to requiring recitation of the prayer only by "voluntary" participants, Justice Black acknowledged the possibility that it did not run afoul of the Free Exercise clause of the First Amendment applied to the states through the Due Process clause of the Fourteenth Amendment. He asserted, however, that even so-called "voluntary" public school prayer clearly violated the Establishment clause of the First Amendment.

> The Establishment Clause, unlike the Free Exercise Clause, does not depend upon a showing of direct governmental compulsion and is violated by enactment of laws which establish an official religion whether those laws operate directly to coerce nonbelieving individuals or not. . . . The purposes underlying the Establishment Clause go much further than that. Its first and most immediate purpose rested on a belief that a union of government and religion tends to destroy government and to degrade religion (at 431).

To understand Justice Black's contention that a union between religion and government tends to degrade religion, consider how many Americans feel about public officials. Is it really good for religion to be closely associated with them? At a more serious level Justice Black contended that in both England and in America "whenever government had allied itself with one particular form of religion, the inevitable result had been that it incurred the hatred, disrespect and even contempt of those who held contrary beliefs" (at 431).

Although Justice Black's opinion noted that the prayer was in the strictest sense voluntary and therefore not violative of the Free Exercise clause of the First Amendment, he nonetheless questioned whether any school prayer can be truly voluntary. "When the power, prestige and financial support of government is placed behind a particular religious belief, the indirect coercive pressure upon religious minorities to conform to the prevailing officially approved religion is plain" (at 431). While one might doubt the significance of that pressure on adults, a point made by the Court in its decision permitting prayers in legislative chambers (see *Marsh v. Chambers,* 1983), pressure on children not to appear "different," and, even more so, pressure not to offend their teachers, could well prove overwhelming.

It was the coercive nature of such indirect pressure that led in part to the Supreme Court's decision striking down a public school graduation prayer in *Lee v. Weisman,* (1992). Distinguishing the circumstances of a public school graduation from a prayer at a legislative session, Justice Kennedy wrote:

> The atmosphere at the opening of a session of a state legislature where adults are free to enter and leave with little comment and for any number of reasons cannot compare with the constraining potential of the one school event [graduation] most important for the student to attend. The influence and force of a formal exercise in a school graduation are far greater than the prayer exercise we condoned in *Marsh*. . . . At a high school graduation, teachers and principals must and do maintain a high degree of control over the precise contents of the program, the speeches, the timing, the movements, the dress, and the decorum of the students. In this atmosphere the state imposed character of an invocation and benediction by clergy selected by the school combine to make the prayer a state-sanctioned religious exercise in which the student was left with no alternative but to submit . . . (at 597).

Justice Scalia's dissent vigorously challenges this notion of coercion as a basis for rejecting the constitutionality of school-sponsored voluntary prayer. Since no one in *Lee* is being forced to actually recite the prayer, he sees no coercion. All, in fact, students are required to do is maintain a respectful silence while those who choose to pray, do so.

> The Court's notion that a student who simply sits in "respectful silence" during the invocation and benediction (when all others are standing) has somehow joined—or would somehow be perceived as having joined is nothing short of ludicrous. We indeed live in a vulgar age. But surely "our social conventions," have not coarsened to the point that anyone who does not stand on his chair and shout obscenities can reasonably be deemed to have assented to everything said in his presence. Since the court does not dispute that students exposed to prayer at graduation ceremonies retain (despite "subtle coercive pressures") the free will to sit, there is absolutely no basis for the Court's decision (at 637).

Others in the Court majority placed less emphasis on coercion than did Justice Kennedy. They emphasized rather the need for the state to maintain neutrality on religious matters. For the state to sponsor prayer at public events, is for the state to send a message favoring or endorsing religion. To the nonreligious or to religious minorities, such sponsorship lessens their relative standing or status in the community.

Because the Court in its school prayer cases has emphasized government authorship, endorsement, and even coercion in support of particular prayers, some have sought to blunt this argument by proposing that students themselves be permitted to initiate, select, or compose prayers for school use. Rather than the state mandating a prayer or prayers, which is viewed by many as "establishment" of religion, if students themselves compose and lead the prayers, this could be viewed as their engaging in the "free exercise" of religion. To prevent students from voluntarily praying as they please is viewed by some as suppressing religious belief and expression.

One can, however, anticipate a host of possible problems with this approach. Who, for example, would decide who is to lead others in prayer? What if the student composing the prayer would choose to pray in a manner profoundly offensive to others? Some Christians might want to pray for the conversion of Jews. Some Islamic students might pray for victory in a "holy war." Might not some atheistic students reasonably demand "equal time" and offend the deeply held religious convictions of some of their classmates?

To the argument that not permitting organized prayer interferes with the free exercise of the religious convictions of a majority of students, supporters of the Court's school prayer decisions sometimes respond that all are free to pray whenever they please quietly to themselves. To those desiring public devotion and dedication to God, this enforced silence concerning what they view as the most important part of their lives is an affront.

In its decisions concerning religious exercises in the public schools, the Court has not contended that the public schools must be blind to the role of religion in American society and in the people's lives. Just one year after its decision in *Engel v. Vitale* the Court applied the same reasoning to strike down a Pennsylvania law mandating that verses of the Bible be read in the public schools, without comment by teachers or administrators, at the opening of each school day (at 205).

In rejecting a claim that forbidding Bible reading at the beginning of the school day or the recitation of a prayer establishes "a religion of secularism," Justice Clark wrote:

> We agree of course that the State may not establish a "religion of secularism" in the sense of affirmatively opposing or showing hostility to religion, thus "preferring those who believe in no religion over those who believe. . . ." We do not agree, however, that this decision in any sense has that effect. In addition, it might well be said that one's education is not complete without a study of comparative religion or the history of religion and its relationship to the advancement of civilization. It certainly may be said that the Bible is worthy of study for its literary and historic qualities. Nothing we have said here indicates that such study of the Bible or of religion, when presented objectively

as part of a secular program of education, may not be effected consistently with the First Amendment (at 225).

The Court has made it clear that the Establishment clause does not permit government to sponsor religious devotions in the public schools. It has, however, left the door open to public schools educating students concerning the role played by religion in our society and history. To the devotely religious this walling off of an important part of their children's day from public devotion to God may be deeply troubling. Although the Free Exercise clause permits them to educate their children in a religious environment, the Establishment clause forbids the state to provide such an environment for them.

**Question 4**  *If secular groups are allowed access to the schools, shouldn't religious groups have the same rights?*

When the United States Supreme Court decided that the Constitution forbids government-sponsored prayer in the schools, it did so in part because of the particular vulnerability of children to pressure to conform from both peers and school authority figures, such as teachers. When on the other hand the Court found no constitutional impediment to prayer at the beginning of legislative sessions, it emphasized the fact that adults are not forced to participate and indeed are free to absent themselves from the chamber during the brief prayer.

Among the issues that must be considered as we look at religious use of public schools is the question of whether the Constitutional prohibition of an "establishment of religion" actually places religions at a disadvantage compared to other private groups when it comes to access to public facilities. Are religious viewpoints actually discriminated against in public debate? Does barring religious groups from public expression in public schools or other government facilities violate the free speech rights of such groups? On the other hand does the Free Exercise clause, which guarantees the right of all to their religious beliefs without fear of persecution by government, place religions and religious expression in a privileged position relative to other viewpoints in society?

In 1984 Congress passed the Equal Access Act, which was designed in particular to prohibit discrimination against religious groups who seek to hold meetings and form clubs within public schools when such opportunity was open to other "noncurriculum related" groups. According to the Act,

It shall be unlawful for any public secondary school which receives Federal financial assistance and which has a limited

open forum to deny equal access or a fair opportunity to, or discriminate against, any students who wish to conduct a meeting
within the limited open forum on the basis of religious, political,
philosophical, or other content of speech at such meetings. (*Westside Community Board of Education v. Mergens,* at 235) (1989).

Under the Act's provisions, "a limited open forum" exists whenever
a public secondary school "grants an offering or opportunity for one or
more non-curriculum related student groups to meet on school premises
during non-instructional time. . . "(at 235).

This Act of Congress had the effect of extending to secondary
schools the results of a Supreme Court decision in *Widmar v. Vincent,*
(1981) which on free speech grounds invalidated a state university policy
excluding "student use of facilities 'for purposes of religious worship or
religious teaching' " (*Widmar* at 235). School policies both here and in
*Widmar,* were no doubt designed to avoid running afoul of the Supreme
Court's Establishment clause rulings which in the school area in particular had been concerned with the need of avoiding any union between government and religion. In considering a challenge to the *exclusion* of
religion from the schools on free speech grounds, the Court was careful to
be sure that the establishment of religion line was not crossed. In pressing in the university setting what the Court in *Widmar* itself termed an
"equal access policy," the Court found no violation of the Establishment
clause, but it noted that "[u]niversity students are, of course, young
adults. They are less impressionable than younger students and should
be able to appreciate that the University's policy is one of neutrality
toward religion" (*Widmar,* at 274, n. 14).

In judging the application of the Equal Access Act to a public high
school, the Court had to consider whether Congress was correct in
assuming that permitting religious groups to use public school facilities
would not be misunderstood by high school students as amounting to a
government "endorsement" of religion or of particular religious beliefs. In
part to assure that this misunderstanding would not occur, the Equal
Access Act specifically forbade school authorities or teachers from "promoting, leading or participating in a [religious] meeting." Their involvement had to be confined to merely a "custodial role" (*Widmar,* at 237). By
merely permitting religious groups, like other groups, to take advantage
of the "limited public forum" provided by after-school activities, the
Equal Access Act, in the Court's view, does not endorse religion in violation of the Establishment clause. As Justice Sandra Day O'Connor wrote
in her Opinion of the Court,

There is a crucial difference between *government* speech
endorsing religion, which the Establishment Clause forbids,

and *private* speech endorsing religion, which the Free Speech and Free Exercise clauses protect. We think that secondary school students are mature enough and are likely to understand that a school does not endorse or support student speech that it merely permits on a nondiscriminatory basis.

. . . Under the Act, a school with a limited open forum may not lawfully deny access to a Jewish students' club, a Young Democrats club, or a philosophy club devoted to the study of Nietzsche. To the extent that a religious club is merely one of many different student-initiated voluntary clubs, students should perceive no message of government endorsement of religion (at 253).

The Equal Access Act, however, does not tell us what the Constitution requires. In upholding the application of the Equal Access Act, the Court of necessity had to interpret the Act itself. In deciding whether it conforms to the Constitution, they had to interpret the Constitution.

In his dissenting opinion, Justice John Paul Stevens expressed concern that the Court majority misconstrued the Equal Access Act as requiring opening of schools to religious and controversial groups whenever it permits noncourse-related clubs to exist on campus. Justice Stevens argued that there is a fundamental difference between a chess club, for example, and a Young Republican or Young Socialist club. Congress, he contended, did not mean that the presence of a chess club or a scuba diving club would trigger the requirement that virtually all groups, however controversial would be permitted. On the other hand, to permit a religious club to form in a setting, such as the one before the Court, where the religious organization in question would be the only "advocacy" group actually on campus, could impermissably lead to the perception of endorsement of its religious message by students. Precisely because there were not in fact a broad array of advocacy groups and clubs at Westside High School, forcing this school to permit a Christian club to form might well send a message of state endorsement and support of particular religious beliefs.

More recently in *Lamb's Chapel v. Center Moriches Union Free School District,* (1993) the Court again addressed the question of when or if religious viewpoints can be banned from schools and other public institutions. This case squarely addressed the Constitutional issue and, unlike *Board of Education v. Mergens*, did not require interpretation of the Equal Access Act. The question in this case was, when may government forbid use of school facilities after school by a religious organization? In this case a religious group sought to use the public school during after-school hours to show a film series on family values and child rearing. Under New York State law school facilities can be used by private groups for ten different purposes, which do not include religious purposes. Discussion by private groups of child rearing and other family issues would be permitted, but because the school district viewed the proposed film series as church related, it was barred. The issue according to the Court was whether this restriction on the use of the facilities to express a religious viewpoint on a subject matter for which the school facility may be used violated the free speech clause of the First Amendment.

Although the Court argued that government may decide that certain subject matter are not suitable topics for discussion in fora that are not fully open to the public, ". . . access to a nonpublic forum can be based on subject matter and speaker identity [only] so long as the distinctions drawn are reasonable in light of the purposes served by the forum and are viewpoint neutral (citations omitted)", (*Lamb's Chapel*). Although the Court acknowledged that under New York State policy all religions and religious views are treated alike, this does not answer the question ". . . whether it discriminates on the basis of viewpoint to permit school property to be used for the presentation of all views about family issues and child rearing except those dealing with the subject matter from a religious standpoint" (at 394).

In other words in opening the schools to a discussion of family values in after-school hours when students were no longer required to attend, could the state bar the expression of religious perspectives? To the Court the answer was no. According to Justice O'Connor's Opinion for the Court, "[t]he principle that has emerged from our cases 'is that the First Amendment forbids the government to regulate speech in ways that favor some viewpoints or ideas at the expense of others.' " (*City Council of Los Angeles v. Taxpayers for Vincent,* at 495).

Unlike the State of New York, the Court was not concerned that opening the school during after-school hours to this expression of a religious viewpoint might amount to an unconstitutional establishment of religion. The position adopted by the Court was one of neutrality. The school would be available to all points of view concerning relevant subject matters. To open the schools in this context to church groups, as well as others, could not be seen as government "endorsement" of religion.

So long as government itself does not advance a religious perspective, it appears that the Constitutional requirement of separation of church and state permits access to public facilities by church groups on the same basis as other groups to express their points of view. So long as government permits private groups to use public facilities to express their point of view, it appears that the Constitutional protection of freedom of speech requires access be given to religious as well as secular groups.

Providing "equal access" to religious groups to noninstructional after-class fora, however, requires that access also be provided to nonreligious groups as well. Gay, lesbian, bisexual, transsexual and other groups have points of view on family values and childrearing as well as religious groups. Nazi groups can have views on the meaning of patriotism as well as the Boy Scouts. What both the Equal Access Act passed by Congress and upheld as constitutional by the Court and Court decisions interpreting the Free Speech and Free Exercise clauses of the First Amendment themselves now mean is that no group with a point of view on issues open for discussion after hours in our public schools or other public fora may be barred. In theory at least, it may well be that in seeking an audience for religious messages in the public schools religious groups and their supporters in government may have opened the door to less popular groups as well. On the other hand, because in many communities religious perspectives dominate, we have to wonder whether equal access can turn into special privilege with the public forum becoming dominated by religious expression. If religious advocacy does come to dominate the after-school activities within our public schools, have we jeopardized the separation of church and state?

## Question 5    *Doesn't teaching evolution in the schools amount to the establishment of secular religion?*

The Scopes Trial, the subject of a popular movie, *Inherit the Wind,* made in 1960, pitted two giants of American history, William Jennings Bryan and Clarence Darrow, in a courtroom battle over science and religion in America. On one side were those who accepted conventional scientific teaching concerning evolution of the human species; on the other were those who believed in a literal interpretation of the story of Genesis in the Bible. To those who revere the Bible as literal historical truth, Darwin's theory of evolution is blasphemous in that it denies that the story of Adam and Eve in Genesis actually describes the origins of the human species. Because such teaching challenges the deeply held religious convictions of many, state legislatures in some states have banned the teaching of evolution in science classes.

Even in the last decade of the twentieth century many felt so strongly that evolution was antireligious that they succeeded in persuading some textbook publishers to omit discussion of evolution in scientific textbooks and in the state of Kansas succeeded in removing discussion of evolution from the state-mandated science curriculum. Although legislative efforts to actually ban teaching evolution in the schools were rejected by the U.S. Supreme Court in *Epperson v. Arkansas* (1968), efforts to influence school scientific curriculum to better conform to "fundamentalist" religious teaching did not stop.

From a constitutional law perspective, cases involving conflicts between science and religion present difficult problems. To the person having a deeply held religious conviction that evolution is not true and contrary to God's law, having the state nonetheless teach this in the school can be seen as a threat to their religious freedom. Are not their children being indoctrinated by government command in a belief system that attacks fundamental religious principles? On the other hand, to the scientist or the student of science, isn't omitting the dominant scientific explanation for human origins and biological development from science classes, because it conflicts with religious beliefs, the same as an unconstitutional establishment of religion?

*Epperson v. Arkansas* concerned a constitutional challenge to an Arkansas law passed in 1928 which ". . . [made] it unlawful for a teacher in any state-supported school or university 'to teach the theory or doctrine that mankind ascended or descended from a lower order of animals,' or 'to adopt or use in any such institution a textbook that teaches' this theory" (at 99). Despite the fact that there was no record of any person actually being prosecuted for offending the statute in question, the Court accepted a case from a teacher who felt under the threat of prosecution because she assigned a text which included a discussion of evolution.

The Supreme Court decided that the state ban on teaching evolution ran afoul of the First Amendment. In the words of Justice Abe Fortas in the Opinion of the Court,

> . . . the law must be stricken because of its conflict with the constitutional prohibition of state laws respecting an establishment of religion or prohibiting the free exercise thereof. The overriding fact is that Arkansas' law selects from the body of knowledge a particular segment which it proscribes for the sole reason that it is deemed to conflict with a particular religious doctrine; that is, with a particular interpretation of the Book of Genesis by a particular religious group" (at 103).

Having failed to ban completely the teaching of evolution in the public schools, those who were deeply troubled on religious and perhaps other grounds sought other means to lessen the threat they perceived coming from teaching children evolution. In 1987 the Supreme Court, in *Edwards v. Aguillard* (1987) heard a challenge to the Balanced Treatment for Creation-Science and Evolution-Science in Public School Instruction Act passed by the Louisiana legislature in 1982. According to Justice Brennan's opinion of the Court, "[t]he Creationism Act . . . [forbade] the teaching of the theory of evolution in the public schools unless accompanied by instruction in 'creation science.'" The Act did not require the teaching of either evolution or so-called creation science. It did, however, require "[i]f either is taught . . . the other must also be taught . . . " (at 581).

In a sense this Balanced-Treatment Act responded to the Court's decision in *Epperson*. Rather than banning evolution outright from the classroom, this new law merely required that so-called "creation science" receive equal attention. This case placed the Court in the difficult position of judging what is and what is not a legitimate scientific theory. It also placed the Court in the position of challenging the stated rationale of the legislation before it. The legislature could claim that they were merely responding to genuine controversy within the community by requiring that both sides be heard. The legislature in fact asserted that its purpose was to advance "academic freedom."

In deciding whether or not the Act violated the Establishment clause of the First Amendment, the Court majority applied what has come to be called the *Lemon* test. Although the *Lemon* Test is discussed at greater length above (see Question 1), we must briefly look at it now to see how it was applied in this case. According to Chief Justice Burger's opinion in *Lemon v. Kurtzman,* (1971),

> Every Analysis . . . [applying the Establishment Clause] must begin with consideration of the cumulative criteria developed by the Court over many years. Three such tests may be learned from our cases. First, the statute must have a secular legislative purpose; second, its principal or primary effect must be one that neither advances nor inhibits religion; finally, the statute must not foster 'an excessive government Entanglement with religion (at 612–613).

In *Edwards* Justice Brennan applied the so-called "purpose prong" of the *Lemon* test to invalidate the Louisiana Balanced Treatment statute. Under this test the Court asks whether there is a secular legislative purpose or whether the purpose of the statute is to advance religion in general or some particular religious belief. In Justice Brennan's words,

> In this case, the purpose of the Creationism Act was to restructure the scientific curriculum to conform with a particular religious view point. Out of the many possible science subjects taught in the public schools, the legislature chose to affect the teaching of the one scientific theory that historically has been opposed by certain religious sects. . . . [T]he Creationism Act is designed *either* to promote the theory of creation science which embodies a particular religious tenet by requiring that creation science be taught whenever evolution is taught *or* to prohibit

the teaching of a scientific theory disfavored by certain religious sects by forbidding the teaching of evolution when creation science is not also taught. The Establishment Clause, however, "forbids *alike* the preference of a religious doctrine *or* the prohibition of theory which is deemed antagonistic to a particular dogma." (Citing *Epperson*, at 106–07, in *Edwards*, at 593.)

Justice Brennan rejected the State's contention that its purpose was to promote "academic freedom" by exposing students to both sides of the evolution debate. He noted that the Balanced Treatment Act provided funding for the development of curriculum guides for "creation science" without providing comparable guides for evolution (at 588). Further the Act specifically forbids school authorities from discriminating ". . .against anyone who 'chooses to be a creation-scientist,' but fails to protect those who choose to teach evolution. . . ."(at 588). In further support of his rejection of the "academic freedom" purpose advanced by the state, Justice Brennan cited evidence from the legislative history, including statements by leading advocates of creation science, that their religious views must be included in the curriculum.

If advancing academic freedom had been the real purpose behind the Act, then Brennan argued it would ". . . enhanc[e] the freedom of teachers to teach what they will" (at 586). Instead the act forbids teachers to teach evolution unless they also teach "creation science." In so doing it restricts the freedom of teachers rather than enhances it.

Although Justice Brennan's view of academic freedom more closely conforms to conventional understanding of the term than does the state's emphasis on "balanced" presentation of contending viewpoints, the position of the state cannot simply be dismissed as wholly without merit. Would a law requiring that students be exposed to both Northern and Southern perspectives concerning the causes of the Civil War be consistent with academic freedom? It would restrict a teacher's freedom to teach what he or she pleases, but wouldn't such a law be better than simply allowing teachers who hold a purely regional perspective to "indoctrinate" students? Are not all teachers restricted in what they can teach by course descriptions or in lower grades by school board or administration imposed "lesson plans"?

From the religious perspective the banning of their understanding of the origins of human beings amounts to the adoption of an alien and purely secular orthodoxy. Many now contend that the courts have imposed a quasireligion, "secular humanism," on the schools. But if public institutions are permitted to teach religiously founded perspectives, the Court majority in effect asks, how are we to maintain the separation of church and state mandated by the First Amendment? According to the

Court's decisions, public schools may teach science, but the Constitution requires that the teaching of beliefs based on faith be left to others.

### Question 6　*Is the separation of Church and state breaking down?*

During the summer of 1999 Congress, in response to school shootings debated various measures designed to control youth violence. In the midst of vigorous debate concerning gun control, a proposal was introduced in the House of Representatives to require the posting of the Ten Commandments in classrooms throughout America. Advocates no doubt felt that a decline in values had at least in part led to the violence affecting American society. At the same time the then leading contenders for both the Democratic and Republican nominations for president of the United States argued for the increased use of religious organizations in the distribution of government benefits to the poor. These proposals serve as examples of the ongoing controversy concerning the separation of church and state. They reflect as well the belief of many that America has gone too far in separating religious expression from our public life.

On the Supreme Court itself the 1980s brought movement away from the relatively simple concept of a "wall of separation" between church and state. More conservative justices on the Court argued that accommodation between church and state does not violate the Establishment clause. On the other hand in applying the Free Exercise clause, these same justices, in many instances, made it more difficult for citizens successfully to assert a constitutional exemption from laws when compliance would conflict with religious principles.

While the prohibition against an "establishment of religion" primarily restrains any attempt by the the majority to use government power to advance its purely religious values, the protection for free exercise primarily protects religious minorities from state oppression and coercion. The potential threat to separation of church and state presented by trends in the judicial interpretation of the religion clauses of the First Amendment during the 1980s and 1990s may be one of increased links between religion and government and possibly decreased need to accommodate those whose religious beliefs (or disbeliefs) deviate far from the views of the mainstream of American society. Of course, as we saw above in Question 2, a willingness to accommodate religious beliefs by giving people the right to disregard certain laws which may conflict with their religions can, itself, be viewed as unconstitutional preferential treatment of religion.

It is important, however, to remember that insistence on a strict separation is a relatively recent development in American constitutional interpretation. The first case cited in Question 1 of this chapter calling for a "wall of separation," *Everson v. Board of Education*(1947), actually permitted a very limited program of state support for student transportation to religious schools. The case probably most frequently cited in the popular press as a sign of the rigid separation of church and state, *Engel v. Vitale*, which forbade state-sponsored prayer in public schools, still holds today and was reinforced by *Wallace v. Jaffree* (1985), which forbade a state-sponsored moment for silent prayer in the schools and *Lee v. Weisman* (1992) which banned state-sponsored prayer at public high school graduation ceremonies.

While the school prayer decisions and many others serve as symbols of the separation of church and state, there have been many other decisions particularly in recent years, that have permitted state assistance to religious institutions when the primary purpose and effect of that assistance has been considered by the Court to advance a secular purpose. In 1988, for example, in *Bowen v. Kendrick*, the Supreme Court upheld the expenditure of public funds to aid churches and other private institutions counseling against premarital sex. Earlier in *Meek v. Pittenger,* (1973) the Court had upheld the loan of secular textbooks to parochial schools. In *Mueller v. Allen* (1983) the Court upheld an annual tax deduction for parents of children attending religious schools to help defray the costs of private education. In *Zobrest v. Catalina Foothills School District,* (1993) the Court upheld a publicly funded sign language interpreter for a deaf child attending a religious school, even though the interpreter would inevitably be conveying religious messages. And in 1997 in *Agostino v. Felton,* the Supreme Court reversed itself and overturned its prior ruling in *Aguilar v. Felton* (1985), which had declared unconstitutional a federal program that paid to send public school teachers into parochial schools to provide remedial educational assistance to poor and disadvantaged students. As a result of *Aguilar* it had been necessary for states to provide such educational assistance in separate buildings or portable classrooms physically removed from the religious institution. The Court had feared that sending public school teachers into religious schools would require such careful supervision of their work to assure that they were not participating in religious instruction as to require "an excessive entanglement" between church and state. In 1997, however, the Court in effect argued that its concern about "excessive entanglement" had itself been excessive. Now the Court was willing to trust publicly funded teachers not to engage in religious education; so very close monitoring of what happened within the confines of the church school was no longer necessary. If close monitoring of what goes on in the remedial education classes is not necessary, then any entanglement between church and state associated with such monitoring need not be "excessive."

The Court's ruling in *Agostino V. Felton*, then, can serve as a symbol of the somewhat relaxed concern for strict maintenance of the separation of church and state. Together this and many other accommodations to religion and religious institutions approved by the Court have taken us far beyond the "wall of separation" encouraged by Jefferson and cited approvingly by the late Justice Hugo Black in the *Everson* decision.

There is, however, no question that today the Supreme Court remains sharply divided over church-state issues. On the one hand there are justices who largely remain faithful to the so-called *Lemon* test discussed several times earlier in this chapter. On the other hand, there are justices who largely ridicule that standard or who believe it goes much farther than the framers intended in insisting on isolating the state from religion and vice versa.

The most controversial element of the so-called *Lemon* test is the requirement that any government statute in any way affecting religion must first have " a secular legislative purpose." In *Edwards v. Aguilard,* Justice Anton Scalia resorted to ridicule in his dissent:

> Our cases interpreting and applying the purpose test have made such a maze of the Establishment Clause that even the most conscientious governmental officials can only guess what motives will be held unconstitutional. We have said essentially the following: Government may not act with the purpose of advancing religion except when forced to do so by the Free Exercise Clause (which is now and then); or when eliminating existing governmental hostility to religion (which exists sometimes); or even when accommodating governmentally uninhibited religious practices, except that at some point (it is unclear where) intentional accommodation results in the fostering of religion, which is of course unconstitutional. . . .
>
> But the difficulty of knowing what vitiating purpose one is looking for is as nothing compared with the difficulty of knowing how or where to find it. For while it is possible to discern the objective "purpose" of a statute (i.e., the public good at which its provision appear to be directed), or even the formal motivation for a statute where that is explicitly set forth . . . , discerning the subjective motivation of those enacting the statute is, to be honest, almost always an impossible task. The number of possible motivations, to begin with, is not binary, or indeed even finite. In the present case, for example, a particular legislator need not have voted for the Act either because he wanted to foster religion or because he wanted to improve education. He may have thought the bill would provide jobs for his district, or he may have wanted to make amends with a faction of his party he had alienated on another vote, or he may

have hoped the Governor would appreciate his vote and make a fund raising appearance for him . . . . [O]r he may have been mad at his wife who opposed the bill, or he may have been intoxicated and utterly *un*motivated when the vote was called, or he may have accidentally voted "yes" instead of "no," or, of course, he may have had (and very likely did have) a combination of some of the above and many other motivations. To look for *the sole purpose* of even a single legislator is probably to look for something that does not exist (at 637).

This problem is compounded further by the question of whose purpose or motivation is relevant. Should one legislator's impermissible motivation be sufficient to condemn a statute? Must the majority who voted for the statute share the impermissible purpose? If Justice Scalia is correct that it is impossible to know even the complete motivation of one legislator, how he asks, are we to know the collective purpose of the entire legislature?

Although Justice Scalia's attack on the *Lemon* test has not yet succeeded in getting it fully rejected, today despite that standard, a Court majority finds no constitutional problem with far-ranging support by government for nonreligious educational programs within religious schools. Whether then the separation of church and state is threatened by recent developments depends in good measure on whether one believes the Court in some of its rulings has taken this separation too far. We began our discussion of religion by citing Justice Black's opinion for the Court in the *Everson* case. That opinion itself has been criticized for its reliance upon Jefferson's metaphor of a "wall of separation between church and state." In his dissenting opinion in *Wallace v. Jaffree,* (1984) then Associate Justice Rehnquist roundly criticized the *Everson* decision as being inconsistent with the history of the First Amendment and of the intent of its framers. According to Justice Rehnquist,

> The framers intended the Establishment Clause to prohibit the designation of any church as a "national" one. The Clause also was designed to stop the Federal Government from asserting a preference for one religious denomination or sect over others. Given the "incorporation" of the Establishment Clause as against the States via the Fourteenth Amendment in *Everson*, States are prohibited as well from establishing a religion or discriminating between sects. As its history abundantly shows, however, nothing in the Establishment Clause requires government to be strictly neutral between religion and irreligion, nor does that Clause prohibit Congress or the States from pursuing legitimate secular ends through nondiscriminatory sectarian means (at 113).

In light of such cited historical practices as the proclamation of a day of national Thanksgiving by almost all of our presidents at the behest of Congress, Justice Rehnquist concludes that the Court's overturning of a moment of silence in Alabama schools because the state wished to "characterize prayer as a favored practice" would come as a "shock to those who drafted the Bill of Rights . . ." (at 113).

If one agrees with now Chief Justice Rehnquist, the separation of church and state most certainly is not breaking down. On the contrary the separation of church *from* state and state *from* church has gone much too far. Nonetheless there is little doubt that the changing personnel on the Court over the last 20 years has eroded somewhat the vision of a strict separation envisioned in the *Everson* decision. At least as of today, however, there appears to be little threat that persecution of religious minorities or of those having no religion will result from the very limited "accommodations" of religion sanctioned by the Court. Nor is there much threat that the power of government will be wielded in support of any particular religion. But there appears to be a real possibility that religions and religious institutions could play a larger role in our public life. Whether this actually threatens the values behind the First Amendment is a judgment we will all need to make for ourselves.

## REFERENCES

*Agostino v. Felton* 521 U.S. 203, 1997 (1997).

*Aguilar v. Felton*, 473 U.S. 402.

*Bowen v. Kendrick*, 487 U.S. 589.

*Church of the Lukumi Babalu Aye v. City of Hialieh*, 508 U.S. 520 (1993).

*City Council of Los Angeles v. Tax Payers for Vincent*, 446 U.S. 789 (1984).

*City of Boerne v. Flores*, 521 U.S. 507 (1987).

*Edwards v. Aguillard*, 482 U.S. 578 (1984).

*Employment Division of Department of Human Resources of Oregon v. Smith*, 494 U.S. 872 (1989).

*Engel v. Vitale*, 370 U.S. 421 (1962).

*Epperson v. Arkansas*, 393 U.S. 97 (1968).

*Everson v. Board of Education*, 330 U.S. 1 (1947).

*Fullilove v. Klutznick*, 448 U.S. 448 (1980).

*Lamb's Chapel v. Center Moriches Union Free School District*, 508 U.S. 398 (1993).

*Larkin v. Grendel's Den, Inc.*, 459 U.S. 116 (1982).

*Lee v. Weisman*, 505 U.S. 577 (1992).

*Lemon v. Kurtzman*, 402 U.S. 602 (1971).

*Lynch v. Donnelly*, 465 U.S. 668 (1984).

*Marsh v. Chambers*, 463 U.S. 783 (1983).

*McGowan v. Maryland*, 366 U.S. 420 (1961).

*Meek v. Pittenger*, 413 U.S. 349 (1973).

*Mueller v. Allen*, 463 U.S. 388 (1985).

*Sherbert v. Verner*, 374 U.S. 398 (1963).

*Stone v. Graham*, 449 U.S. 39 (1980).

*Wallace v. Jaffree*, 472 U.S. 38 (1985).

*Westside Community Board of Education v. Mergens*, 496 U.S. 226 (1989).

*Widmar v. Vincent*, 454 U.S. 263 (1981).

*Zobrest v. Catalina Foothills School District*, 113 S. Ct. 2463 (1993).

### CHAPTER 4

# Equality Under the Constitution

## INTRODUCTION

In the Declaration of Independence the founders of the United States proclaimed their belief that "all men are created equal." While Americans from the beginning have consistently rejected the notion of a hereditary nobility and today assert their fidelity to equality of opportunity, many of us celebrate the wealthy and vigorously oppose any attempts to limit through taxation wealth we can leave our children. Most incongruous in light of our proclaimed belief in the equality of all people has been our tragic history of racial oppression. The author of the Declaration of Independence "owned" slaves. For most of our history we have struggled with slavery and its legacy.

In order to understand equality under the Constitution we must understand the Equal Protection clause of the Fourteenth Amendment. Question 1 asks: *How does the Constitution make us equal?* This section begins by noting that the Constitution provides for "equality" in only the limited sense of "equal protection of the laws." It then proceeds to look at various applications of the Equal Protection clause of the Fourteenth Amendment and the justification for applying different standards in cases of racial, gender, and other forms of discrimination.

The most obvious manifestation of inequality in America has been its treatment of African-Americans even after the abolition of slavery. Question 2, therefore asks: *If the Constitution commands "equal protection of the laws," why was racial segregation permitted?* This section discusses *Plessy* v. *Ferguson* and the rise of the "separate but equal doctrine"; and, finally, the relationship between societal trends and values and constitutional standards concerning race.

Once our society began to take the command of the Equal Protection clause seriously in the twentieth century, it had to confront how practically to undo the effects of racial discrimination. Question 3: *Why did the courts order "forced busing"?* discusses the difficulties encountered in removing the effects of past discrimination and the role of school "busing." It first, however, reviews *Brown* v. *Board of Education*, 1954, the Court decision that declared segregation unconstitutional and the evolution of the remedies for school segregation.

Today probably the most controversial issue relating to equality under the law is "affirmative action" because affirmative action is broadly perceived as permitting preferential treatment of those who had been victims of racial or gender discrimination, Question 4 asks: *Isn't "affirmative action" just another form of racial or sexual discrimination?* This section reviews the controversy surrounding affirmative action. Special attention is paid to the arguments of proponents and opponents of affirmative action concerning when it is necessary for government to take race or gender into account in decision making. In reviewing recent Supreme Court decisions it shows how the Court has moved away from affirmative action and toward a "colorblind" approach to equal protection. In doing so, however, the Court has in effect placed limits on the capacity of Congress and the state legislatures to use their powers to regulate the economy to advance the interests of Americans who may have been left behind. As was noted in Chapter 1, Civil Rights laws have sometimes been used to broaden the promise of equality promised by post-Civil War amendments to the Constitution. These Civil Rights laws, themselves, are subject to the restraints in the Constitution when, in the Court's view, advancing the interests of disadvantaged minority groups might be perceived as coming at the expense of equal treatment for members on the majority racial group.

While to many the struggle for an Equal Rights Amendment to the Constitution may appear to be a fading memory of the distant past, Question 5 asks: *Do we still need a new Equal Rights Amendment (ERA) to secure gender equality?* Although the Court has used the Fourteenth Amendment to attack gender discrimination in the twentieth century, it has not interpreted it to ban gender discrimination to the degree that it bans race discrimination. If we had the ERA, however, the Constitution would treat race discrimination and sex discrimination alike. With a review of the Court's most recent decisions relating to gender discrimination, this section should assist the reader in deciding for him or herself whether an Equal Rights Amendment is in fact needed.

Finally, having reviewed the Court's varying interpretations of the Equal Protection clause, this chapter concludes by asking the question: *How do you know if you are a victim of unconstitutional discrimination?* This section discusses the so-called "intent" requirement in both racial and gender discrimination cases. It covers the reasons why the Court demands evidence of intentional discrimination and will not accept evidence of unequal results alone as sufficient to prove a violation of the Fourteenth Amendment requirement of Equal Protection of the laws. It also discusses the Court's shifting interpretation of the "intent standard," itself as demonstrated in the Court's decision in *McCleskey v. Kemp,* 1987, the race and capital punishment case. Together this discussion should allow the reader to come to some judgments concerning equality under the constitution.

## Question 1   *How does the Constitution make us equal?*

A visit to any large American city should quickly demonstrate the limits of America's commitment to equality. In New York City, for example, garish displays of wealth exist side by side with signs of extreme poverty. If the guards are not looking, homeless people might pass through the lobby of Trump Tower, but none can hope to afford even temporary shelter in the floors above.

Such stark reminders of inequality exist despite the Fourteenth Amendment's command that "No State shall . . . deny to any person within its jurisdiction the equal protection of the laws." Although this important constitutional command does provide us with some protection from some kinds of state-imposed inequality, it leaves untouched inequalities which are not directly attributable to government policies.

"Equal protection of the laws" does not even require that the state treat all people alike. Tax laws, regulatory policies, laws designed to protect the health, safety, and welfare of people all make distinctions among people. Laws permitted under the Fourteenth Amendment routinely place us in different classifications based on our income, age, education and/or demonstrated qualifications without serious constitutional challenge. Laws or government policies which make distinctions among people based on race, ethnicity, and gender, however, lead to serious constitutional disputes. Why are some classifications of people permitted by the sweeping language of the Equal Protection clause while others are forbidden? To answer this question we must look beyond the language of the Fourteenth amendment to its history.

The Fourteenth amendment, like the Thirteenth and Fifteenth, was a product of the Civil War. As the Supreme Court in its early decisions interpreting the scope of the Fourteenth Amendment Equal Protection clause made clear, all of these amendments together were designed with the "common purpose . . . [of] securing to a race recently emancipated [all] the civil rights" that whites enjoyed. (*Strauder v. West Virginia*) (1880). The Court majority in the *Slaughterhouse cases* (1873), only five years following the adoption of the Fourteenth Amendment, stated: "We doubt very much whether any action of a State not directed by way of discrimination against Negroes as a class, or on account of their race, will ever be held to come within the purview of the . . . [Equal Protection Clause]" (at 81).

That the original intent behind the Equal Protection clause of the Fourteenth Amendment was to protect the African-American population that had been denied the most basic rights cannot be disputed. But since its adoption the Amendment has gradually through judicial interpretation been given broader scope. While the Constitution implicitly argues that differences of race cannot justify different government treatment of peoples, other differences may justify and even demand different treatment. In deciding when the Constitution tolerates classifying people in order to provide different treatment, the Court has often used this society's treatment of African-Americans as a yardstick. It has sometimes attempted to compare the situation of a population group claiming to be disadvantaged by some distinction written into law with the historic condition of blacks. In deciding whether to treat "discrimination" against a particular population group in the same way as discrimination against blacks under the Equal Protection clause, the Court has often inquired whether the group in question is " 'a discrete and insular minority' requiring extraordinary protection from the majoritarian political process." (*Caroline Products,* n. 4 in *Bakke,* at 288 ). The "majoritarian political process," of course, refers to the power to elect and remove government officials according to how well they protect a group's interests. This power is of little use to a group that, because of its minority status (relatively small numbers), lacks the voting power to elect people representing its interests.

It did not take the Court long to extend the reach of the Fourteenth Amendment Equal Protection clause to other racial and ethnic minorities. In *Strauder v. West Virginia* (1879), the case in which the Court found that exclusion of blacks from jury service violated the Equal Protection clause, the Court noted that the exclusion of "naturalized Celtic Irishmen," for example, would also be inconsistent "with the spirit of the Amendment." Other cases that followed extending the protection of the Amendment to Chinese and Mexican-Americans rested on similar foundations, that is, discrimination against minorities who had historically been victims of discrimination and who were unable to protect themselves through the ballot box.

In recognizing that the abolition of racial discrimination was the primary purpose behind the Fourteenth Amendment, the Court nonetheless has recognized that sometimes considerations of race may be permissible under the Constitution. In light of the history of the grossest forms of racial oppression in the United States, however, the Court has decided not to trust government claims that the use of racial criteria or classifications in the law is justifiable.

In *Korematsu v. United States* (1944) the Court provided the standard still used today to judge government policies which treat people of different races differently. *Korematsu* was one of a series of cases that came to the Court challenging various restrictions, ranging from curfews to confinement in concentration camps, placed upon Americans of Japanese ancestry living on the West Coast following the start of World War II. In his opinion for the Court Justice Black declared that "all legal restrictions which curtail the civil rights of a single racial group are *immediately* suspect. That is not to say that all such restrictions are unconstitutional. It is to say that courts must subject them to the *most rigid scrutiny*. Pressing public necessity may sometimes justify the existence of such restrictions; racial antagonism never can [emphasis added]" (at 216).

Despite applying what has now come to be called "strict scrutiny," the Court found that the fear of the military authorities that an invasion of the West Coast was imminent and that there was no time to judge the loyalty of individual Japanese living there, justified the "exclusion" and confinement of people on the basis of their race. Although this result today is almost universally condemned, and in 1988 Congress authorized reparations to Japanese Americans who were victimized, the "strict scrutiny" standard applied to *suspect classifications* survives. Since *Korematsu* legislation or government action that subjects racial and ethnic minorities to discriminatory treatment has generally been struck down by the Court. Except for the limited area in which racial classifications are used to overcome past racial discrimination against minorities (see Question 4 below), the strict scrutiny standard has presented a barrier in the way of legislation based on racial classifications that legislatures have been unable to surmount.

Racial classifications are only upheld in Court if the Government can prove some "compelling state interest"—some "pressing public necessity"—that cannot be accomplished without drawing racial distinctions.

Although "strict scrutiny" is the standard by which the Court judges racial and ethnic classifications, other types of classifications in the law are generally not subject to such rigorous review by the courts. Although no one can seriously doubt that sex discrimination has historically been a part of our society and of government policy, government policies that discriminate on the basis of sex have not generally been seen as impossible to justify under the Constitution.

On the surface this lesser concern for sex discrimination might seem puzzling. The words of the Fourteenth Amendment after all refer to "persons" and not simply to men. It is clear, however, that the male framers of the Fourteenth Amendment and the male legislators who ratified it had no interest in abolishing or restricting sex discrimination. Despite this clear record, the Supreme Court has gradually read "women's rights," or more broadly, gender equality, into the Fourteenth Amendment. The Court has done this in part by recognizing the odious history of sex discrimination in American history and by seeing similarities between our society's treatment of all women and its treatment of black men and women.

These parallel patterns of discrimination led four justices on the Supreme Court to argue in *Frontiero v. Richardson* (1973) that for purposes of constitutional adjudication "classifications based upon sex, like classifications based upon race, alienage, and national origin, are inherently suspect and must therefore be subjected to close judicial scrutiny" (at 682). Justice Brennan supported this conclusion by citing our nation's

> . . . long and unfortunate history of sex discrimination. Traditionally, such discrimination was rationalized by an attitude of "romantic paternalism" which, in practical effect, put women, not on a pedestal, but in a cage. As a result of notions such as these, our statute books gradually became laden with gross, stereotyped distinctions between the sexes and, indeed, throughout much of the 19th century the position of women in our society was, in many respects, comparable to that of blacks under the pre-Civil War slave codes. Neither slaves nor women could hold office, serve on juries, or bring suit in their own names, and married women traditionally were denied the legal capacity to hold and convey property or to serve as legal guardians of their own children (at 685).

Despite the logic of Justice Brennan's argument the Court as a whole has not been willing to go quite so far. In his concurring opinion in *Frontiero* Justice Powell argued that the Court should not on its own treat sex discrimination as a "suspect classification" subject to "strict scrutiny." At the time of *Frontiero* the proposed Equal Rights Amendment was before the country (see discussion of Question 5 below). If it were to be approved, sex discrimination would be given the same status as race discrimination under the Constitution. In its absence, however, treating sex discrimination exactly as race would have amounted to a "judicial amendment" to the Constitution.

If sex classifications are not to be subject to "strict scrutiny," then how should they be treated? Generally, classifications in the law based on criteria other than race or ethnicity have been subjected to "deferential analysis." Under this approach the actions of a legislature will be upheld so long as "[t]he distinctions drawn by a challenged statute bear some rational relationship to a legitimate state end and will be set aside as violative of the Equal Protection clause only if based on reasons totally unrelated to the pursuit of that goal" (*McDonald v. Board of Election Commissioners,* at 809, 1969). Under this rational basis test the Court will not use its own judgment for what is fair or wise policy. It defers to legislative judgments as long as they are not clearly arbitrary or capricious. When, for example, states set 16 as the minimum age requirement for a driver's license, they clearly classify people according to age. Reasonable people might argue the wisdom of that particular age classification, but few could argue that setting such an age limit has no rational basis. According to the Court, classifications of this sort do not offend the Equal Protection clause of the Fourteenth Amendment even though they deny to 15-year-olds privileges granted to 16-year-olds. Clearly the two age groups are not treated equally, but abolishing such unequal treatment was not the purpose of the Equal Protection clause.

Although for much of our history sex discrimination was subjected to this "rationality test," the Court today has developed what has been called an "intermediate" level of review for sex discrimination cases. Although sex discrimination cases are not treated precisely the same as race cases, such cases are no longer subjected to only the rational basis test. While not subjecting sex classifications to "strict scrutiny," the Court has devised a new test, sometimes referred to as "heightened scrutiny," to be applied in sex discrimination cases. Under this test "classifications by gender must serve important governmental objectives and must be substantially related to achievement of those objectives." (*Craig v. Boren,* 429 at 197, 1976).

Although we generally think of women as the victims of sex discrimination, *Craig v. Boren,* the case in which the Supreme Court adopted the "heightened scrutiny" standard, concerned a claim of discrimination against men. Under Oklahoma law, 3.2 percent beer could not be sold to men until the age of 21; women, on the other hand, could purchase such beer at the age of 18. The state justified this "discrimination" on the basis of evidence that young men had significantly more alcohol-related driving accidents and arrests for "driving under the influence" than did young women. In the interests of traffic safety, therefore, young men were denied access to beer which could be purchased by women of similar age.

Although the evidence in question would probably have been significant enough to survive scrutiny by the Court under "deferential analysis," using the the rational basis test, it was not considered sufficient proof that the gender-based distinction was "substantially related to the achievement" of the admittedly "important objective " of assuring highway safety (at 204). In sum because a small but admittedly larger proportion of men than women drink and drive, you cannot discriminate against all men.

Under the Fourteenth Amendment's Equal Protection clause we do not all have to be treated alike in all things. The Court recognizes that the Fourteenth Amendment was added to the Constitution primarily to prevent the states from continuing to oppress African-Americans after the formal institution of slavery was abolished. Discrimination based on race was the principal target of the Amendment, and the Court in adopting the "strict scrutiny" standard for cases involving racial and ethnic classifications has today made it extremely difficult for government to treat people differently because of their race, something over which the individual has no control. Because sex, like race, is an "immutable characteristic" (*Frontiero*, at 686), the Court has come to see sex classifications, too, as difficult to justify under the Fourteenth Amendment. No doubt in large part because of the Court's recognition that the Fourteenth Amendment was not initially intended to abolish legal distinctions based on sex, the "heightened" scrutiny standard makes it somewhat easier for government to justify treating men and women differently. After all there are real differences based on gender; there are few, if any, real natural differences between people based on race. For a law or policy to survive "strict scrutiny" in a race case, the government must show a "compelling state interest." To survive "heightened scrutiny" in a sex discrimination case, the government must show that the policy is justified by some "important governmental objective." The difference is one of degree.

Generally, when the government classifies people for purposes unrelated to such "immutable characteristics" as race, ethnicity, or sex, all that the Fourteenth Amendment requires is that similarly situated people be treated alike. Whether it is a good idea to tax people of different incomes differently or to set any particular age as a qualification for a driver's license or for some other "privilege" or benefit is left to legislative discretion. All the Fourteenth Amendment requires is that the classification in question not be clearly arbitrary.

**Question 2**    *If the Constitution commands "equal protection of the laws," why was racial segregation permitted for so long?*

Prior to the late 1960s and early 1970s Americans throughout the South and some border states were rigidly segregated (separated) in schools and places of public accommodation on the basis of race. Although segregation affected all facets of life, it was most obviously present in the public schools. Black children were forbidden by law from attending school with white children. Therefore, Southern communities had "dual school systems," separate schools for black and white children.

Before the Civil War, when African-Americans lived in slavery, laws generally forbade blacks from becoming educated at all. Whites recognized that education, the ability to read and write, would make it easier for blacks to communicate and organize to resist the slave system. Following the Civil War attempts were made to keep blacks in subservient positions. One reason for the approval of the Fourteenth Amendment was to forbid the emerging pattern of legal discrimination against those who had been slaves.

Despite the Fourteenth Amendment, segregation, both privately practiced and legally enforced, continued to exist following the Civil War. The Fourteenth Amendment, however, provided a tool to use to challenge the continuing forced racial separation and exclusion of African-Americans. Segregation, however, raised a somewhat different issue from other forms of discrimination. On the surface at least, segregation treated blacks and whites alike. Each was kept apart from the other.

In *Plessy v. Ferguson* (1896), the Supreme Court faced the question of whether the Equal Protection clause of the Fourteenth Amendment permitted state-enforced racial separation. *Plessy* involved a challenge to an 1890 Louisiana law that required "equal but separate accommodations" for white and black railroad passengers. Although the Court recognized that "[t]he object of the Fourteenth Amendment was undoubtedly to enforce the absolute equality of the two races before the law," it nonetheless argued that "it could not have been intended to abolish distinctions based upon race."

The Court contended that segregation of blacks from whites was permitted by the Fourteenth Amendment because it did not deny the equality of blacks. In effect the Court said that if blacks chose to interpret segregation laws as branding them as inferior, that was their problem. Nothing in the law declared them to be inferior.

In accepting this particular form of segregation, however, the Court denied that it would be ". . . authorizing . . . [state legislatures, if they chose, to require separate railway cars for] people whose hair is a certain color, or who are aliens, or who belong to certain nationalities, or to enact laws requiring . . . [blacks] to walk upon one side of the street, and white people upon the other, or requiring white men's houses to be painted white, and . . . [black] men's black, or their vehicles or business signs to be of different colors, upon the theory that one side of the street is as good as the other, or that a house of one color is as good as another color." Rather the Court argued that only "reasonable" laws would be upheld. Only practices that conformed to the "established usages, customs, and traditions of the people, and with a view to the promotion of their comfort, and the preservation of the public peace and good order"(at 549–550) would be permitted.

In deciding that the segregation of blacks from whites met these criteria the Court referred to the existence of racially segregated schools in Massachusetts, a state that had banned slavery long before the Civil War, for support. In citing a Massachusetts court decision upholding such segregation in 1850, the Court failed to note, however, that this decision came nearly 20 years before the Fourteenth Amendment was added to the U.S. Constitution. The 1850 Massachusetts court that upheld segregation did not have to enforce the Equal Protection clause, because it did not yet exist.

Clearly the established "customs" upon which the Court relied to justify segregation in the post-Civil War period were products of the very institutions and practices that the Thirteenth, Fourteenth and Fifteenth Amendments were designed to overturn. What the Court reflected in *Plessy* was the climate of racism that had marked American society from the beginning.

Only Justice Harlan dissented from the *Plessy* decision. He knew that the so-called "separate but equal" doctrine which emerged from this case was a sham that would fool no one. He wrote that everyone understood that the true purpose behind the segregation was ". . . not so much to exclude white persons from railroad cars occupied by blacks, as to exclude colored people from coaches [assigned] to white persons" (at 557). Harlan recognized the harm that would flow from such a policy of exclusion. Because "the destinies of the two races [are] indissolubly linked together, . . . the interests of both require that the common government of all shall not permit the seeds of race hate to be planted under the sanction of law" (at 560).

It did not take long for the mask of "equality" that might have obscured the true significance of the so-called "separate but equal doctrine" to fall away. In *Cumming v. County Board of Education* (1899) only a few years after *Plessy,* the Supreme Court decided unanimously that the "separate but equal" doctrine did not require a Southern community to provide a public high school to educate black children even though it provided one for white children. So much for equality.

These Court decisions can be explained only through an understanding of racism. People who had for hundreds of years held others in slavery had to convince themselves that their actions were justified by their natural superiority. Rather than admit that they pursued their personal profit through the total oppression of others like themselves, they denied the full humanity of those whom they had enslaved. Although the Civil War could wipe out the formal institution of slavery, it could not so quickly banish the attitudes of white supremacy that had served as the foundation for African slavery in North America for centuries.

Although for a brief time following the Civil War blacks obtained some political power and social privileges in the South, most of these advances quickly vanished once the Southern white majority regained control of their affairs from federal authorities. *Plessy v. Ferguson* did not cause segregation, but it did provide the "legal" justification for it. In words that proved prophetic, the lone dissenter in *Plessy,* Justice Harlan warned that the Court's decision would "in time, prove to be quite as pernicious as the decision made . . ." in *Dred Scott,* the decision that had declared that Congress lacked the power to even restrict the expansion of slavery under the pre-Civil War Constitution (at 559). In assessing the separate but equal doctrine, Harlan correctly observed that "[t]he thin disguise of 'equal accommodations' [will] not mislead any one, nor atone for the wrong this day done" (at 562).

**Question 3**   *Why did the courts order "forced busing"?*

Under the system of segregation, black children were educated separately from white children throughout the Southern and border states. This system of segregation was kept in place through the force of law. While today most Americans condemn the system of segregation known as "apartheid" which until recently was practiced in South Africa, many of us forget that only a generation ago America had its own version of apartheid. Despite the clear command of the Fourteenth Amendment requiring "equal protection of the laws," children were classified according to their race and forcibly separated into separate educational systems. Despite the so-called "separate but equal doctrine" announced in the *Plessy v. Ferguson* decision (see Question 2 above), few seriously argued that the education given black children was equal to what whites, using their dominant position in government, provided for themselves.

Despite the Supreme Court's 8 to 1 endorsement of segregation in *Plessy v. Ferguson*, the leadership of the black community did not abandon efforts to get government to enforce the Equal Protection clause of the Fourteenth Amendment. The NAACP (National Association for the Advancement of Colored People) Legal Defense Fund financed and led a series of court cases designed to eat away at the foundations of segregated education. Because it is difficult to get the Supreme Court directly to overturn its own prior decisions, the NAACP at first attempted to get the Court not to reject the "separate but equal" doctrine but rather to enforce it. If states forced blacks to attend separate educational facilities, then they must assure that such facilities are equal.

Although segregation had its greatest impact in the public school system, the legal assault on segregation in schools began at the professional school level. Every state provided at least some public education to black children, but many states provided no places for blacks in their graduate and professional schools. In a series of cases beginning in the late 1930s dealing with such schools, the Supreme Court in effect chipped away at the foundations of the "separate but equal" doctrine.

At first its decisions invalidated obviously unequal educational opportunities for blacks and whites seeking graduate and professional school educations. When states requiring segregation began to recognize that the Court would demand equality in professional education, some took rather bizarre steps designed to maintain segregation. Oklahoma, for example, did admit a black to its state graduate school of education, but school regulations required that he be separated by barriers from whites within classrooms as well as in the library and cafeteria. Although such practices made communication between whites and blacks difficult or impossible, it did on the surface provide the black student exposure to the same instructors and facilities as whites.

The Supreme Court, however, decided in effect that segregation itself interferes with equal educational opportunity. In striking down the practices which physically separated black and white students, the Court argued that "such restrictions impair . . . [the student's] ability to study, to engage in discussion and exchange views with other students, and in general, to learn his profession." The Court had in effect rejected "restrictions imposed by the State which prohibited the intellectual commingling of students. . . ." (*McLaurin v. Oklahoma State Board of Regents*, at 641, 1950). In effect the Court had struck down a form of segregation.

Finally, the stage was set for a direct assault on segregated public school education. In 1954 the U.S. Supreme Court heard together appeals from lower court decisions in five separate challenges to segregation of the public schools. This time, however, the NAACP did not focus on the unequal facilities or instruction provided to black children. Instead they challenged the forced separation of minority black children from the dominant majority in the society, whites. For purposes of its decision in *Brown v. Board of Education* (1954), the Court assumed that "tangible factors," such as facilities, teacher salaries, and qualifications, supplies, and so on had been either "equalized or were being equalized" (at 492). The question then presented by the case was: "Does segregation of children in public schools solely on the basis of race, even though the physical facilities and other 'tangible' factors may be equal, deprive the children of the minority group equal educational opportunities?" (at 493).

In deciding that forced racial segregation did deny blacks the equal protection of the laws, the Court considered a number of factors. Probably the most significant influence on the Court, however, was the recognition of the central role played by education in contemporary American society. Attendance at school is after all compelled by the state today, and "education is perhaps the most important [and most expensive] function of state and local governments" (at 493). Education is not simply designed to provide students with skills necessary for future employment, rather it is "a foundation of good citizenship, . . . awakening the child to cultural values, . . . and . . . helping him to adjust normally to his environment" (*Brown,* at 493).

Segregation in education sends to the minority child an unmistakable message that he is excluded from the mainstream of American life. In the words of Chief Justice Warren, "[t]o separate . . . [black children] from others of similar age and qualifications solely because of their race generates a feeling of inferiority *as to their status in the community* [emphasis added] that may affect their hearts and minds in a way unlikely ever to be undone." (at 494).

Although the Court based its decision in part on evidence produced by psychological studies, no amount of social science evidence was required to explain the impact of segregation on those whom it was designed to exclude. Blacks knew that the white majority kept them apart in order to keep them down. Segregation told black children that they had no ". . . status in the community." It took no personal sense of inferiority for an excluded black child to know that his opportunities for success in a society dominated by a group that wanted to exclude him were few indeed.

For reasons such as these, the Supreme Court in *Brown* took the extraordinary step of finally explicitly repudiating its decision in *Plessy v. Ferguson* 58 years earlier. The Court ". . . conclude[d] that in the field of public education the doctrine of 'separate but equal' has no place. Separate educational facilities are inherently unequal" (at 495).

The Court's rejection of state-imposed segregation, although crucial, still left open the question of how desegregation might be accomplished. For decades school systems had been structured on the basis of segregation. School buildings were located and constructed to serve one-race populations. Teachers were hired and assigned on the basis of race. School bus routes were drawn to transport white children to white schools and black children to black schools. To undo what had been built up over generations would not be a simple task. Recognizing these facts, the Court in its first decision implementing its ruling in *Brown,* instructed the lower court at first to rely on the "good faith" efforts of local school authorities to make "a prompt and reasonable start" toward desegregation. The district courts were authorized to issue the orders "as are necessary and proper to admit [the students in whose name *Brown* was brought] to public schools on a racially nondiscriminatory basis *with all deliberate speed* [emphasis added] . . ." *Brown v. Bd. of Education* (II).

During the decade immediately following *Brown* "massive resistance" on the part of whites throughout the South stood in the way of any significant progress toward desegregation. As late as ten years after

*Brown* "only 1.2 percent of the black students in the eleven Southern states attended schools with whites" (*U.S. Commission on Civil Rights*, p. 10). Faced with this record of resistance and defiance the Supreme Court in a 1961 decision proclaimed that "the time for 'deliberate speed' has run out." As Justice Black observed by then "[t]he original [*Brown*] plaintiffs ha[d] doubtless all passed high school age. There ha[d] been entirely too much deliberation and not enough speed in enforcing constitutional rights . . ." (*Griffin v. County School Board of Prince Edward County,* at 229–31, 1961). Despite these words of impatience, however, progress toward desegregation remained slow.

The Court was right in 1955 when it recognized how complex the task would be to do away with a deeply entrenched "dual" school system. Although in 1968 it decided to judge desegregation efforts by the results they produced (*Green v. New Kent County,* 1968), it was not until 1970 that the Court clearly endorsed the only policy capable of ending the separation of black and white children in many school districts where it continued.

When segregation was legal, both black and white children were "bused," often past schools near where they lived to more distant schools assigned to their particular race. In large metropolitan school districts, however, schools were naturally deliberately designed and built to serve the race that predominated in a particular area. Schools intended to serve black children only were built where mostly blacks lived. Schools serving only whites were built in predominantly white areas. If a particular section of a city had only 200 black children living within it, a small school designed to accommodate those students might be built. If a nearby area had 1000 white children, then a larger school was built convenient to that particular concentration of one racial group.

In the years before *Brown* when segregation was legally required the system was designed to accommodate segregation. Once segregation became illegal, however, the system had to be redesigned. School buildings once constructed, however, cannot simply be moved.

In many communities school authorities changed their announced policy of segregation, but the system designed to accommodate segregation kept blacks and whites apart. Instead of requiring that all blacks must attend one school and all whites another, the school boards now said all children will be assigned to "neighborhood schools." But the Supreme Court eventually recognized that a decision to open a school to all regardless of race in a particular area will have little meaning if the school's location was chosen in the first place to serve one race which predominates in the area. "All things being equal, with no history of discrimination, it might, [according to Chief Justice Burger], be desirable to assign pupils to schools nearest to their homes. But all things are not equal in a system that has been deliberately constructed and maintained

to enforce racial segregation" (*Swann v. Charlotte-Mecklenburg Board of Education,* at 28, 1971).

In response to what the Court termed such a "loaded game board" (at 29), students might have to be assigned to schools distant from their homes in order to bring about an end of state imposed segregation. Just as school bus transportation had been used to deliver students to segregated schools, it would now be used to dismantle segregation.

In ordering busing for the purpose of integration, the Court used "a normal and accepted tool of educational policy" (at 29). Transporting students was the only practical means available to produce desegregation in areas where residential segregation was closely associated with school segregation. An unlimited use of "busing" could produce whatever degree of desegregation that the Court might feel was desirable. But the Court recognized that there were practical and legal limits. Although there is much racial isolation throughout the United States, the Court could only order remedies when racial segregation was a product of deliberate government action (see discussion of Question 6 below). In addition, transportation of students would only be ordered as long as it did not risk the health or safety of children or significantly impinge on the education process.

Court-ordered "busing," like desegregation itself, was extremely controversial from the day it began. Many of those who claimed to favor desegregation vigorously opposed "busing." Yet busing was ordered because as a practical matter no other means appeared to be available to undo the effects of generations of decisions imposing segregation. Students throughout suburban and rural America were routinely "bused" to school every day because schools are far away from home. When this routine measure was used to end segregation, however, bus loads of children were sometimes attacked with stones. In the days of legal segregation buses were routinely used to separate children. When they were used to try to end separation, they became controversial. As Jesse Jackson once said: "It ain't the bus, it's us." Opposition to busing had in many instances become a socially acceptable way to oppose integration itself.

## Question 4   *Isn't "affirmative action" just another form of racial or sexual discrimination?*

The term "affirmative action" refers to many different policies, all of which have in common the goals of abolishing the lingering effects of past discrimination and assuring that discrimination does not reoccur. Affirmative action programs range from simple requirements that, for example, open job opportunities be widely advertised so that minorities and women will be alerted to apply, to "preferential hiring policies" designed to assure that a certain minimum percentage of jobs or contracts will actually be filled by minority or women applicants.

Employment discrimination in America has in the past taken many forms. Often certain racial and ethnic groups were openly told that they were not wanted. Most of the better positions in society were routinely reserved for men. Some institutions such as police and fire departments would simply not even allow women to apply. Probably more common than open announced policies of racial discrimination was the simple practice of racial exclusion. If blacks applied, they would simply never be hired. Having gotten the unmistakable message, after a while other members of the excluded racial or ethnic groups would learn there was no point in even applying.

With the passage of the Civil Rights Act of 1964, generally racial and sexual discrimination in most places of private employment became illegal. Lawsuits under the Fourteenth Amendment's Equal Protection clause led to court orders banning discrimination in employment by state and local governments as well. Old habits and attitudes, however, were not easily swept away by words written in a statute book or court decision. To put into practice what had been written into law, legislatures and the courts began to require employers, especially those found to have discriminated against minorities and/or women in the past, to take certain steps to assure that minorities and women would in fact have access to opportunities long denied to them.

To white males who had not been forced to compete with minorities and women for jobs or contracts, affirmative action appeared to limit their opportunities. Sometimes these new programs assaulted the traditionally privileged position of white males, and such sudden loss of what had been theirs produced resentment.

Consider the story of a firefighter in a Massachusetts community. He had been a firefighter all his adult life. He lived in a town that had traditionally given preference in hiring to the sons of firefighters. Now his son was of age and ready to follow in his father's footsteps. There was a problem, however. There had never been a black hired as a firefighter in this community, so naturally there were no black sons who could claim the privilege of following their fathers into the fire department.

When the courts or an Equal Employment Opportunities Commission stepped in to ban the practice of giving preference to the sons of firefighters, the family of this white male firefighter was deeply resentful. Something they had come to expect was no longer theirs. When the position no longer reserved for their son goes to a black applicant, it is easy for the white who has been passed over to blame his fate on affirmative action. If the black applicant obtained the position in open competition with white applicants, however, this was not really affirmative action; it was simple nondiscrimination. The old policy which gave special advantage to the sons of firefighters was not based upon individual merit but rather on accident of birth.

If, however, the black applicant obtained the position over better qualified whites in order to give blacks representation within a fire department in which few or no blacks had served before, then this is a form of affirmative action. It would represent the kind of "preferential hiring" that has produced the most controversy and led to charges of "reverse discrimination," that is, discrimination against the white majority instead of against a minority.

The Supreme Court's view of "affirmative action" programs involving "preferential treatment" of minorities or women has not always been clear. Until its 1995 decision in *Adarand Constructors Inc. v. Pena*, the Court had generally been tolerant of affirmative action programs involving "preferences" which are in effect ordered by Congress under its power to regulate business through it power to "regulate commerce among the states" and through its powers to enforce the provisions of the Fourteenth Amendment against state and local governments. It had, however, generally only approved state-and local government-initiated or court-ordered "preferences" for minorities when they were designed to remedy proven instances of past discrimination against minorities or women. According to Court decisions, removing the lingering effects of past deliberate discrimination is a "compelling state interest" sufficient to overcome the general constitutional prohibition against racial classifications (see Question 1). In effect the Court recognizes that we must sometimes consciously consider race if we are to undo past racial discrimination.

When, however, state governments attempt to use "preferential treatment" or quotas in order to assure some given percentage of minority employment or inclusion in some benefit without having first made a specific finding of actual discrimination against minorities by the agency in question, the Supreme Court has ruled that such racial policies violate the Fourteenth Amendment Equal Protection clause. In effect, under such circumstances the Court has determined that discrimination against whites in the name of benefiting previously disadvantaged minorities is as constitutionally suspect as discrimination against minorities.

In 1989 the U.S. Supreme Court weighed the constitutionality of a Minority Business Utilization Plan developed by the City of Richmond, Virginia in order to assure participation by Minority Business Enterprises (MBEs) in construction contracts awarded by the city. Although the record showed that minority-owned businesses had in the past obtained only a minute portion of the contracts awarded by the city in which blacks constituted approximately 50 percent of the population, "[t]here was no direct evidence of race discrimination on the part of the City in letting contracts." (*City of Richmond v. J. A. Croson Co*, at 485, 1989). Because of the wide gap between the proportion of blacks in the city's population and the share of contracts awarded to blacks and because of evidence elsewhere in the country of widespread discrimination in the construction industry, the city decided that 30 percent of all construction contracts would be awarded to businesses over which minorities had dominant control. This policy, according to the Court, had the effect of excluding whites from competing for "a fixed percentage of public contracts based solely upon race."

The central question for the Court as it considered the constitutionality of such policies was whether it should treat policies designed to benefit groups that had historically been victimized by discrimination throughout our society the same way as it treats policies that discriminate against such groups today. If "discrimination" in favor of blacks is as bad as discrimination against blacks, then "strict scrutiny" must be applied and only policies justified by some "compelling state interest" may be upheld.

The issue of how the Court should view alleged discrimination against members of the majority racial group, whites, had previously been debated on the Court in *Regents of the University of California v Bakke,* (1978). While recognizing that the original purpose behind the Fourteenth Amendment was to protect those who had been enslaved, blacks, from hostile government action, Justice Powell argued that the meaning of the Amendment had evolved over time. For generations beginning with *Plessy v. Ferguson,* 1896 (see Question 2 above), the Fourteenth Amendment's Equal Protection clause had for all intents and purposes been ignored. By the time the Court "rediscovered" the Equal Protection clause, Justice Powell argued, ". . . it was no longer possible to peg the guarantees of the Fourteenth Amendment to the struggle for equality of one racial minority. . . . [By then], the United States had become a nation of minorities . . . most of which can lay claim to a history of prior discrimination at the hands of the State and private individuals" (at 295). In light of this history, Powell concluded that the "guarantee of equal protection cannot mean one thing when applied to one individual and something else when applied to a person of another color" (at 290).

The Court in effect adopted Powell's view when in the *Richmond* case, it, for the first time, unambiguously decided that allegations of unconstitutional discrimination against any racial or ethnic group will be subject to the same level of judicial review. In the view of Justice O'Connor writing for the Court majority:

> Absent searching judicial inquiry into the justification for . . . racially based measures, there is simply no way of determining what classifications are "benign" or "remedial" and what classifications are in fact motivated by illegitimate notions of racial inferiority or simple racial politics. Indeed, the purpose of strict

scrutiny is to "smoke out" illegitimate uses of race by assuring that the legislative body is pursuing a goal important enough to warrant use of a highly suspect tool (at 493).

Resolving what had been an inconsistency in its treatment of racial "set sides" or preferences by states and by the federal government, Justice O'Connor writing for a divided court (5 to 4) in *Adarand v. Pena,* 1995 decided that the standard for judging all racial classifications, without regard for whether they benefit or harm minorities, must be the same. According to O'Connor, ". . . all racial classifications, imposed by whatever federal, state or local actor, must be analyzed by a reviewing court under strict scrutiny. In other words, such classifications are constitutional only if they are narrowly tailored measures that further compelling governmental interests" (at 227). In layman's language, government policies may treat people of different races differently only when such policies are essential to accomplishing some goal of paramount importance, and those policies must be designed so as to affect adversely only those necessary to accomplish that goal.

On the issue of racial set asides or preferences, the Court has been and remains today sharply divided. Most of its decisions which have gone against racial preferences or set asides for minorities whom society has historically discriminated against have produced vigorous dissents. The dissenters, however, have not simply urged blanket approval for affirmative action programs. Their opinions have recognized the possibility that such a program might be abused. They have, however, urged greater tolerance for government efforts to help those whom society has long discriminated against, even when doing so might jeopardize the interests of some members of the majority racial group.

In his dissent in *Adarand*, Justice John Paul Stevens, for example, accused the majority of the Court of

> . . . [assuming] that there is no significant difference between a decision by the majority to impose a special burden on the members of a minority race and a decision by the majority to provide a benefit to certain members of that minority notwithstanding its incidental burden on some members of the majority. In my opinion that assumption is untenable. There is no moral or constitutional equivalence between a policy that is designed to perpetuate a caste system and one that seeks to eradicate racial subordination. Invidious discrimination is an engine of oppression, subjugating a disfavored group to enhance or maintain the power of the majority. Remedial race-based preferences reflect the opposite impulse: a desire to foster equality . . . (at 243).

In support of his argument, Justice Stevens discussed a part-real–part-hypothetical example. Justice Stevens first noted that many Japanese-Americans were subjected to "exclusion" from certain areas on the West Coast during World War II, many being placed in what most would term "concentration camps" solely because of their race, while at the same time other Japanese-Americans were recruited and drafted into the military and "exhibited exceptional heroism." In light of this history, Stevens asked how the Court would treat a hypothetical program designed to "reward that service with a federal program that gave all Japanese-American veterans an extraordinary preference in Government employment." Such a program, he noted, would have been based on the same racial and ethnic characteristics that had led to the discriminatory treatment against Japanese-Americans. Were the Court to follow its insistence on similar treatment for all racial classifications announced in *Adarand*, it would no doubt have condemned the program designed as compensation for victims of discrimination. "The consistency the Court espouses," according to Justice Stevens, however, "would disregard the difference between a 'no trespassing' sign and a welcome mat. It would treat a Dixiecrat Senator's decision to vote against Thurgood Marshall's confirmation in order to keep an African-American off the Supreme Court as on a par with President Johnson' evaluation of his nominees race as a positive factor . . ."(*Adarand*, at 245).

The debate over affirmative action is in many ways a debate over how far our society has come in giving African-Americans, in particular, the same rights and status as is enjoyed by European-Americans. If by simply outlawing discrimination we have succeeded in doing away with discrimination against blacks, then affirmative action, or at least those forms involving racial preference, is probably unnecessary. If, however, blacks and other victims of discrimination continue to suffer the effects of discrimination practiced throughout our society for centuries, then racial preference in employment, in the awarding of contracts, or school admissions might be necessary to assure that they have the opportunities they would have enjoyed except for the long history of discrimination against them.

The differing views in the Supreme Court over the constitutionality of affirmative action programs and how society should deal with the continuing effects of discrimination were most directly expressed in the *Richmond* case in the separate opinions of Justices Thurgood Marshall and Antonin Scalia. In arguing against all programs based on race, except those specifically and narrowly designed to undo a state's own racially discriminatory actions, Justice Scalia wrote:

> It is plainly true that in our society blacks have suffered discrimination immeasurably greater than any directed at other

racial groups. But those who believe that racial preferences can help "even the score" display, and reinforce, a manner of thinking by race that was the source of the injustice and that will, if it endures within our society, be the source of more injustice still . . . (at 527, 28).

To Justice Scalia, then, affirmative action programs designed to assure representation of blacks and others in positions from which they have long been excluded are themselves racially discriminatory. For him the Constitution requires government to be "colorblind."

From the perspective of Justice Marshall, however, the views espoused by Justice Scalia and indeed similar views shared by a majority of the Court are not so much colorblind as they are blind to the

> . . . tragic and indelible fact that discrimination against blacks and other racial minorities . . . has pervaded our nation's history and continues to scar our society. . . . In concluding that . . . [considerations of race designed to remedy past discrimination] warrant no different standard of review under the Constitution than the most brutal and repugnant forms of state-sponsored racism, [Marshall argued,] a majority of . . . [the] Court signals that it regards racial discrimination as largely a phenomenon of the past. . . . In constitutionalizing its wishful thinking, the majority . . .does a grave disservice . . . to those victims of past and present racial discrimination in this nation whom government has sought to assist (at 552).

**Question 5**   *Do we still need a new Equal Rights Amendment (ERA) to secure gender equality?*

During the early 1970s it looked very likely that an Equal Rights Amendment, guaranteeing that "[e]quality of rights under the law shall not be denied or abridged by the United States or by any State on account of sex," would become part of the United States Constitution. The proposed amendment, which easily obtained the necessary two-thirds vote in the United States House of Representatives and Senate, failed to obtain the approval of the legislatures of three-quarters of the states to become part of the Constitution. The reasons for this failure were many. Many religious and other conservatives opposed the notion of gender equality in principal, some believing it contrary to the Bible. Others worried that it would end special privileges and exemptions enjoyed by women, such as exception from compulsory military service when conscription is in place.

Others, felt that it would end all distinctions between men and women, forcing the end of separate restroom facilities in public places, and so forth. Many others, however, felt that the Supreme Court's decisions relating to the Fourteenth Amendment had already provided sufficient protections for the rights of women, the gender presumed to require protection from discrimination.

Clearly whether we need or want an Equal Rights Amendment in the Constitution depends in part on the accuracy of some of the fears expressed by opponents to the amendment and in part on your position on many of these disputed questions.

Although in Question 1 we have already briefly addressed contemporary Supreme Court treatment of gender discrimination under the Fourteenth Amendment, it is best to begin with a somewhat more detailed analysis of the current legal status of gender discrimination under the Constitution. As was noted above under Question 1, current judicial interpretation of the Fourteenth Amendment gives government somewhat more leeway in drawing legal distinctions between men and women than is permitted between and among racial and ethnic groups. Partly because of the fact that the Fourteenth Amendment was initially clearly intended to outlaw state government discrimination based on race and was silent on the question of gender, a Supreme Court majority has never held that gender distinctions in the law are constitutionally impermissible unless justified by some compelling state interest (the standard in race discrimination cases). Rather the Court has evolved a standard for judging gender discrimination that falls somewhat short of the "strict scrutiny" stand it has adopted for judging the constitutionality of racial classifications.

First in *Craig v. Boren* (1976), and consistently since, the Court unambiguously elevated gender discrimination to a special status under the Fourteenth and Fifth Amendments, a status not quite as suspect as racial distinctions, but still one requiring a "heightened" level of judicial scrutiny. Although until the Court's decision in *Reed v. Reed* (1971), the Court routinely upheld legal distinctions between men and women founded on gender stereotypes and the traditionally subordinate role of women in society and in the marketplace, in *Reed* the Court set the stage for the more explicit rejection of such stereotypes as the foundation for legislation which *Craig* made controlling.

The *Reed* decision struck down an Idaho law which required an automatic male preference in designating executors of estates between equally qualified males and females. Although the Court decision rejected the male preference provision as having no rational foundation, the state contended it served to avoid the necessity and expense of administrative hearings. The Court, however, considered this justification inadequate, contending that the male preference provision was "the very kind of arbitrary legislative choice" (at 76) forbidden by the Fourteenth Amendment.

Following the *Reed* case the Court began to define the special constitutional status of gender discrimination under the Fifth and Fourteenth Amendments. Four Justices in the *Frontiero* case (see above, Question 1) argued that gender discrimination is indistinguishable from race discrimination under the Constitution. According to them only a compelling state interest could justify gender distinctions in the law. The Court majority subsequent to *Frontiero* has with increasing consistency adopted the standard from *Craig*. The settled character of the "heightened scrutiny" standard from *Craig* is evidenced by the fact that in his concurring opinion in *United States v. Virginia* (1996), Chief Justice Rehnquist, the author of a vigorous dissent in *Craig,* himself relies on *Craig*. He wrote: "Two decades ago in *Craig v. Boren . . . ,* we announced that 'to withstand constitutional challenge, . . . classifications by gender must serve important governmental objectives and must be substantially related to the achievement of those objectives.' We have adhered to that standard ever since." (at 2288).

In *United States v. Virginia* the Court majority further amplified the "heightened scrutiny" applied in gender discrimination cases and provided some explanation of why race and gender cases are not treated exactly alike. A review of that decision should aid us in beginning to come to an answer for the question of whether an Equal Rights Amendment promoting gender equality under the Constitution is either necessary or desirable today.

The basic issue in *United States v. Virginia,* was the constitutionality of the exclusion of women from the Virginia Military Institute (VMI). In response to a legal challenge to VMI policy excluding women, a federal appeal court found that a single-gender military training program of the type in existence at VMI was constitutionally permissible if a comparable program were created elsewhere to serve women. If no such program were created, then women would have to be admitted to VMI,

Virginia responded to this Court ruling by creating Virginia Women's Institute for Leadership, an institution that lacked much of the vigorous "adversative" military training found at VMI, emphasizing instead the cultivation of leadership skills among the women cadets.

According to Justice Ruth Baeder Ginsburg's Opinion of the Court, the case as it came to the Supreme Court presented two issues:

> First, does the exclusion of women from the educational opportunities provided by VMI—extraordinary opportunities for military training and civilian leadership development—deny to women "capable of all the individual activities required of VMI cadets," the equal protection of the laws guaranteed by the Fourteenth

Amendment? Second, if VMI's "unique" situation—as Virginia's sole single-sex public institution of higher education—offends the Constitution's equal protection principle, what is the remedial requirement? (at 2274).

According to Justice Ginzburg's Opinion for the Court any defense of a gender-based classification must have an "exceedingly persuasive justification" to survive what she termed the Court's "skeptical scrutiny" (at 2274). Her decision, which repeated the *Craig* requirement that the state must bear the burden of showing that any gender-based classification serves "important government objectives and that the discriminatory means employed are substantially related to the achievement of those objectives," nonetheless refused to go so far as to equate racial discrimination with gender discrimination.

As we consider the question of the need for a new Equal [gender] Rights amendment, this distinction between the Court's treatment of race and gender may be crucial. For as Justice Ginzburg noted under the strict scrutiny standard applied in race cases today, "[s]upposed "inherent differences" are no longer accepted as a ground for race or national origin classifications . . . . Physical differences between men and women, however, are enduring: 'The two sexes are not fungible; a community made up exclusively of one [sex] is different from a community composed of both' " (*Ballard v. United States,* at 2276).

Acknowledging then that all distinctions among men and women in the law and public policy need not necessarily flow from invidious discrimination, but rather reflect natural and inevitable differences, Justice Ginzburg acknowledges that gender will sometimes serve as a legitimate basis for different treatment in the law without offending the Constitution. In applying this principle to the case of Virginia Military Institute, Justice Ginzburg argued that at least some women have shown that they are indeed capable of participating in training as physically rigorous as that of men. At least for such women, then, excluding them from VMI did constitute unconstitutional discrimination.

The implications of this decision for the debate over a new Equal Rights Amendment are not certain. On the one hand, if a new ERA were to become part of the Constitution, then the legal distinction between the treatment of gender and race discrimination would likely disappear. Just as racial classifications are now subject to strict scrutiny and can survive challenge only on a showing that they serve a "compelling state interest and are narrowly tailored to serving that interest," so too would gender classifications. While now under the *Craig* test, gender classifications are not held to quite such a strict test in that the interests that must be advanced by them need be "important" but not quite "compelling," after

ERA gender classifications would have to be justified by the "stricter" standard applied to race if they were to survive challenge.

But Justice Ginzburg's opinion does provide a foundation for gender classifications surviving even after ERA. If the gender classification were in fact based on real differences between men and women, they might then be deemed sufficient under some circumstances to survive strict scrutiny. Today, on the other hand, racial differences are never considered sufficiently real to meet the compelling state interest test. Although it is quite conceivable to imagine legal distinctions meant to protect women of childbearing age, for example, from physical injury affecting their potential children or their ability to reproduce, it is also quite reasonable to treat men differently as a class because they cannot bear children.

Even under the compelling state interest test, real differences justified by such a paramount interest could serve as the basis for different legal treatment. What Justice Ginzburg provides, therefore, is a reasoned foundation for understanding and acting on genuine differences that are more likely to exist in a gender than in a racial context. With such an understanding the application of the "strict scrutiny" standard to gender cases, which would almost certainly follow the adoption of an ERA, would still permit distinctions in law based upon physical distinctions that are real and not merely the reflection of stereotype and/or prejudice.

There is, however, one area where an ERA might have what people concerned about women's rights might view as a detrimental effect on women's interests. In the area of affirmative action, programs designed to compensate women and minorities for past discrimination against them as groups, an ERA might serve to remove a current advantage which women enjoy over racial and ethnic minorities. Today the Supreme Court treats all racial classifications in the law the same. Even so-called "benign discrimination"—discrimination designed to benefit previously disadvantaged racial groups is subjected to "strict scrutiny" and is therefore very difficult to defend against constitutional challenge. Only programs designed to make up for proven instances of deliberate racial discrimination against specific individuals and identifiable groups have survived application of strict scrutiny in the racial context. The Court has rejected making up for general societal discrimination against African-Americans, for example, as sufficient justification for different treatment of whites and blacks to be considered a "compelling" state interest. Today because there is no ERA and gender discrimination is subjected to the lessor standard of "heightened scrutiny," different treatment of men and women is more easily defended if the purpose is to compensate women generally for historic discrimination against all women. As Justice Ginzburg noted in her opinion in *United States v. Virginia*, today still "[s]ex classifications may be used to compensate women 'for particular economic disabilities [they have] suffered" *Califano v. Webster,* at 313 (1977) . . . to promote equal employment opportunity . . ." (at 2276). Under current Supreme Court application of the strict scrutiny test to *all* racial classifications, however, such amorphous justifications would not be sufficient to justify a racial classification. To the degree an ERA would lead to equal treatment of racial and gender classifications under the law, women might lose an advantage they now have as society confronts its history of both racial and gender discrimination.

As Justice John Paul Stevens noted in his dissent in the *Adarand* case, it is indeed ironic that the Fourteenth Amendment, which was designed to undo our legacy of racial oppression, has now been used to make it more difficult for government to take steps to make up for past societal discrimination, while on the other hand, this same Fourteenth Amendment which ignored gender discrimination now permits such steps to make up for society's history of past gender discrimination.

Without an ERA, of course, it is always possible for courts to return to their past tolerance of vast gender discrimination against women. With women now constituting a majority of the electorate and a very substantial portion of the work force and even the professions, it seems unlikely that legislatures will again pass discriminatory legislation against women. Discrimination in favor of women, however, such as in the exemption from military service, still survives in some areas. Perhaps men would benefit more from an ERA than would women.

---

**Question 6**   *How do you know if you are a victim of unconstitutional discrimination?*

You visit a community and observe that a neighborhood is entirely white while another is entirely black. You see a schoolyard filled with children all of the same race. You visit a state medical school and find that 98 percent of those enrolled are white or you watch a fire and see that all of the firefighters are men. We look at the death rows across America and find a much higher percentage of blacks there than we find in the population as a whole. We all know that this list could go on indefinitely. Whether we focus on race or sex, we can see that one race or sex often receives an apparently disproportionate share of society's benefits while another carries a disproportionate share of the burdens. Many of us are led to ask: If this isn't proof of discrimination, what is?

The Constitution commands that "no State shall . . . deny to any person . . . the equal protection of the laws." Although the examples cited above illustrate differences in our society's treatment of people on the basis of race or sex, they may not all represent unconstitutional denials of equal protection. Before condemning all of these illustrations as signs of unconstitutional discrimination, we must first ask: Who is responsible for the apparent differences? Are any of the them a reflection of the genuine choices of different people? Are some of them a simple reflection of differences in economic status which many in society believe either is or should be beyond the control of government?

Recognizing in part that the Constitution does not expect uniformity and that Americans expect and even respect differences, the Court has argued that the Constitution prohibits only intentional government-imposed discrimination. Even government policies which themselves have the effect of producing differences among people of different races are not considered unconstitutional unless they were selected with that specific racial purpose in mind.

Consider the Social Security system. Everyone of working age pays into the Social Security trust fund. Once a person reaches 65, he or she collects benefits loosely based on the amount of his or her contribution. Although individual white and black men both pay Social Security taxes, a far smaller proportion of black men live to the age of 65 than do white men. Is the Social Security system discriminatory?

There is no doubt that the system has a discriminatory effect on the black male population as a whole, but individual blacks who live to 65 are treated the same as individual whites. Were the disproportionate burdens the Social Security system places on the overall black population intended by those who designed the system? Is it a reflection of the desires of the Congresses that continue the system?

Were black Americans to challenge the racially discriminatory impact of the Social Security system in court, there is little doubt that the U.S. Supreme Court would find it to be perfectly constitutional. When confronted with a government policy that has a *racially disproportionate effect*, the Court demands evidence that the policy is a result of *discriminatory intent*. When only evidence of a disproportionate racial effect is presented, the Court will presume discriminatory intent only when the effect ". . . is very difficult to explain on non-racial grounds" (*Washington v. Davis*, at 242 (1976).

Since a neutral non-racial justification for the Social Security system, providing income for people who live beyond working years, could be advanced, the Court would find the evidence of discriminatory effect insufficient to establish a constitutional violation. Before finding unconstitutional discrimination, the Court has ruled that proof must be presented that the ". . . decision maker . . . selected or reaffirmed a . . .[policy] at least in part 'because of,' not merely 'in spite of,' its adverse effects upon an identifiable group" *Personnel Administrator v. Feeney*, at 279, 1979). Although Congress should be aware of the differences between the life expectancies of blacks and whites, it seems likely that Congress designed the Social Security system in spite of those differences not because of them.

While in the past racial criteria for government actions were written into statutes and regulations, today few government officials or agencies would be so foolish as to openly admit a discriminatory purpose. To prove discriminatory intent, therefore, we must look into ". . . such circumstantial and direct evidence of intent as may be available." As a start we must look to see whether policies that have had racially disproportionate effects have been singled out by policy makers for special treatment. Have they been handled differently from policies that have no racial impact? More specifically, in his opinion in *Arlington Heights v. Metropolitan Housing Authority* (1977), Justice Lewis Powell suggested review of racially suspect governmental decision making in an attempt to find some deviation from the norm in such aspects as the "specific sequence of events leading up to the challenged decision," "departures from normal procedures," or "substantive departures" (at 266–68).

What the Court looks for in such inquiries are signs that the potential racial impact of a decision has led decision makers to act in some unusual way. If, as is likely, decision makers will not admit that their actions were racially motivated, evidence must be developed by studying their behavior. If, for example, following normal procedures would have led to a result from which blacks might have benefited, but the officials for no apparent reason disregard normal procedures and act in an unusual way resulting in a decision detrimental to black interests, the courts might then be willing to demand some explanation for the decision under challenge. If no neutral (nonracial) explanation is available, then the courts are generally willing to presume that an action which produced a "discriminatory effect" resulted from unconstitutional discriminatory intent.

Although race seems still to make a difference in almost all aspects of life, debate over the role of race in the administration of criminal justice is probably the most intense. Blacks and other minorities often feel the least protected by the forces of law and order and at the same time the most likely to be treated severely by them.

For much of American history there was little doubt that racism influenced decisions concerning the death penalty. Belief that the death penalty was administered in a racially discriminatory manner influenced in part the Supreme Court's decision declaring then existing death penalty laws unconstitutional in 1972 (*Furman v. Georgia*). Today the death penalty is back, and the controversy concerning its racially discriminatory application continues.

In 1987 a challenge to existing death penalty laws was mounted which raised a new question about how race enters into the criminal justice system. A black man, Warren McCleskey, challenged his death sentence claiming in essence that had he and others like him killed black people rather than white people, they would not have been sentenced to death. In support of this argument his lawyers presented a statistical study that showed that persons who were convicted of murdering whites were 11 times more likely to be sentenced to death than were persons who killed blacks. The data they presented reflected not only the apparent impact of race upon the sentencing decisions of juries in the state of Georgia where the study was done, it reflected as well the decision of prosecutors to even request the death penalty. While prosecutors requested death penalties in 70 percent of the cases where the defendant was black and the victim was white, they sought the death penalty in only 15 percent of the cases where the defendant was black and the victim was black (at 286–287).

Recognizing that differences in the specific nature of crimes committed might explain some of the difference in sentencing, the statistical analysis presented to the Court sought to take into account explanations other than race that might have accounted for the skewed result. In the end after extensive analysis of the data, even after accounting for the impact of 39 nonracial variables or explanations, the study concluded that "defendants charged with killing white victims were 4.3 times as likely to receive a death sentence as defendants charged with killing blacks" (at 287).

When the Supreme Court was confronted with these data, it did not dispute their accuracy; it did, however, refuse to accept them as proof of unconstitutional discrimination. Although the Court had ruled in *Washington v. Davis* that when a pattern exists "that is unexplainable on grounds other than race . . ." it would find sufficient proof of discriminatory intent, the Court in *McCleskey* concluded that "[w]here the discretion that is fundamental to our criminal justice system is involved, we decline to assume that what is unexplained is invidious [or discriminatory]" (at 313).

Prosecutors, judges, and juries make choices—exercise discretion—everyday. In deciding on appropriate punishment for crimes within the limits set by law, they are left to their human judgment. Such discretion is designed to adjust the broad impact of the law to individual circumstances. It is considered essential to justice. While the Court majority in the *McCleskey* case apparently believed that sufficient safeguards are built into the criminal justice process to rule out improper motivation in the exercise of discretion, others, including the four justices who dissented, had severe doubts. They believed that racial discrimination is a continuing problem in this society, and they believed that the evidence assembled on *McCleskey's* behalf should have been enough to strike down capital punishment laws that produce such dramatically different results apparently depending upon the race of the victim of the crime.

While the rules of evidence, constraints on the jury selection process and routine appellate court review all make decision making in the criminal justice system different from other kinds of government decision making, the *McCleskey* case raises the question of whether those differences are significant enough to justify treating evidence of racial discrimination differently. The dramatic differences in the application of the death penalty against those killing whites over those killing blacks were not explained by the Court on grounds other than race. Had this been a state employment discrimination case or a school segregation case there is little doubt that the type of statistical evidence presented in McCleskey's behalf would have been sufficient to prove unconstitutional discrimination.

Justice Brennan, one of the four dissenters from the Court's decision upholding McCleskey's death sentence, felt that the Court's decision disregarded the history of race relations in America:

> At the time our Constitution was framed 200 years ago this year, blacks "had for more than a century been regarded as beings of an inferior order, and all together unfit to associate with the white race, either in social or political relations; and as so far inferior, that they had no rights which the white man was bound to respect." *Dred Scott v. Sandford,* (1857). . . .
>
> In more recent times, we have sought to free ourselves from the burden of this history. . . . These have been honorable steps, but we cannot pretend that in three decades we have completely escaped the grip of an historical legacy spanning centuries. Warren McCleskey's evidence confronts us with the subtle and persistent influence of the past. His message is a disturbing one for a society that has formally repudiated racism, and a frustrating one to a Nation accustomed to regarding its destiny as the product of its own will. Nonetheless, we ignore him at our peril, for we remain imprisoned by the past as long as we deny its influence in the present (at 343-44).

While not challenging the fact that blacks often benefit less and suffer more from government actions than do whites, the Court refuses to presume that such measurable differences in results reflect any denial of "equal protection of the laws." Rather than acknowledging that racism may be a routine feature of American life, the Court treats racism as something unusual. No matter how obvious your predicament may seem, you are not a victim of unconstitutional discrimination unless you can satisfy the courts that government has intentionally discriminated against you. The equal protection of the laws does not guarantee that all will equally share in this society's benefits or burdens.

## REFERENCES

*Adarand Constructors, Inc. v. Pena*, 515 U.S. 200.

*Arlington Heights v. Metropolitan Housing Authority*, 429 U.S. 252 (1977).

*Ballard v. United States*, 397 U.S. 187 (1946).

*Brown v. Board of Education*, 347 U.S. 483 (1954).

*Brown v. Board of Education (II)*, 349 U.S. 294 (1955).

*Califano v. Webster*, 430 U.S. 313 (1977).

*City of Richmond v. J. A. Croson Co.*, 488 U.S. 469 (1989).

*Craig v. Boren*, 429 U.S. 190 (1976).

*Cumming v. County Board of Education*, 175 U.S. 528 (1899).

*Dred Scott v. Sandford*, 60 U.S. 393 (1856).

*Frontiero v. Richardson*, 411 U.S. 677 (1973).

*Furman v. Georgia*, 408 U.S. 238 (1972).

*Green v. New Kent County*, 391 U.S. 430 (1968).

*Griffin v. County School Board of Prince Edwards County*, 337 U.S. 218 (1961).

*Korematsu v. United States*, 323 U.S. 214 (1944).

*McCleskey v. Kemp*, 481 U.S. 279 (1987).

*McDonald v. Board of Election Commissioners*, 394 U.S. 802 (1964).

*McLaurin v. Oklahoma State Board of Regents*, 339 U.S. 637 (1950).

*Personnel Adminstrator v. Feeney*, 442 U.S. 256 (1979).

*Plessy v. Ferguson*, 163 U.S. 537 (1896).

*Reed v. Reed*, 402 U.S. 71 (1971).

*Regents of the University of California v. Bakke*, 438 U.S. 268 (1978).

*Strauder v. West Virginia*, 100 U.S. 303 (1880).

*Swann v. Charlotte-Mecklenburg Board of Education*, 402 U.S. 1 (1971).

*The Slaughterhouse Cases*, 83 U.S. 36 (1873).

*United States v. Virginia*, 116 S. Ct 2264 (1996).

U.S. Commission on Civil Rights, *Twenty Years after Brown: Equality of Educational Opportunity*. (Washington, D. C.: Government Printing Office, 1975).

*Washington v. Davis*, 426 U.S. 229 (1976).

### CHAPTER 5

# Privacy and Individual Autonomy

Probably no issue of constitutional rights continues to produce as much controversy as the debate over the right to privacy. To this point we have discussed conflicts within the Court over the precise meaning of liberties and rights protected by the Constitution. With the right to privacy, however, the first debate concerns whether the Constitution includes any such right at all. Question 1 introduces this controversy by asking: *How much privacy do we have a right to expect?* This section discusses the debate over just what aspects of privacy are protected by the Constitution. This discussion focuses on the Supreme Court's decision in *Griswold* in which Justice Douglas argued that privacy finds its roots in the First, Third, Fourth, Fifth, Ninth, and Fourteenth Amendments. Conversely, this section reviews Justice Black's dissenting argument that there is no constitutional right to privacy as such. In discussing the concurring opinions of Justices Harlan and Arthur Goldberg, however, this section lays the foundation for broader discussions that follow concerning how the Court identifies constitutionally protected rights and liberties not specifically mentioned in the Constitution.

The most controversial issue under the heading of the right to privacy has no doubt been a woman's right to choose abortion. Question 2 asks: *How did the "right to privacy" lead to women's right to have an abortion?* This section discusses the U.S. Supreme Court's decision in *Roe v. Wade* and the argument that a woman's control over her body and over the decision to have children flows from the general "right to privacy." *Roe v. Wade* and other cases dealing with competing claims of husbands or a minor girl's parents are discussed.

Much of the controversy over abortion concerns the competing claim of a fetus's "right to life." In light of Supreme Court rulings continuing to uphold a woman's right to choose abortion, Question 3 asks: *Does a fetus's "right to life" ever count more than a woman's right to privacy?* This section discusses the viability standard from *Roe v. Wade* and subsequent cases. It reviews the Court's decision in *Planned Parenthood v. Casey* which gave somewhat greater latitude to government to protect "potential life."

Because early Supreme Court decisions relating to privacy concerned issues relating to intimate associations surrounding family life and reproduction, it was inevitable that other questions relating to sexual intimacy would arise. Question 4 asks: *When may the state regulate private sexual relationships between consenting adults?* This section begins with a discussion of the limits on sexual privacy raised in Justice Harlan's concurring opinion in *Griswold v. Connecticut*. It focuses primarily on the Supreme Courts decision in *Bowers v. Harwick,* the "homosexual sodomy" decision. It explores the deep division that remains on the Supreme Court over the meaning of the right to privacy and the right of the state to regulate personal conduct.

The Court's birth control and abortion decisions in very important ways concern a person's right to control his or her own body and destiny. No issue is more central to such concerns as the decision of when and how we might end our lives. Question 5 asks: *Why doesn't the "right to privacy" include the right to decide to end our lives?* This section reviews the issues surrounding the right to die or the right to assisted suicide. It reviews the Supreme Court's decision upholding state government bans on assisted suicide, even for the terminally ill. It will discuss the debate concerning whether how long each of us lives is itself a profoundly private question that should be beyond society's control.

The questions explored in this chapter concern deeply personal decisions ranging from reproduction and sexual intimacy to circumstances surrounding the end of life itself.

## Question 1   *How much privacy do we have a right to expect?*

To most of us "privacy" means being left alone. When we say, "I wish you would mind your own business," or "Keep out of my personal affairs," we are expressing the expectation that some matters concern no one but ourselves. When we direct such comments to government, we are saying that some things are solely personal concerns and, therefore, of no concern to government or society in general. How we handle such matters concerns only ourselves and those in whom we choose to confide.

The word "privacy" does not appear in the Constitution. When the Court has recognized a "right of privacy," some have argued that it is implicit in other rights which are mentioned. Some elements of privacy, according to the Court, predated the Constitution. They are so obvious that the framers felt no need even to mention them. The fact that certain rights exist which are not explicitly mentioned in the Constitution is recognized in the Ninth Amendment, which states: " The enumeration in the Constitution of certain rights shall not be construed to deny or disparage others retained by the people." In other words, the fact that certain rights are mentioned and explicitly recognized by the Constitution does not mean that these are the only rights we have. Although the Ninth Amendment recognizes the existence of rights beyond those listed, it gives us no help in identifying what those rights might be.

Other sections of the Bill of Rights, however, provide a basis for an expectation of privacy in certain spheres of life. The First Amendment, for example, protects our freedom of association, that is, our freedom to join with others to advance our views and express our opinions. When our opinions, or associations based on them, might cause us embarrassment or worse, the Court has recognized our right to keep such associations private (*NAACP v. Alabama,* 1958).

Probably the most private sphere of all is what goes on in our minds. In striking down a law punishing private possession in one's home of obscene materials, Justice Marshall wrote: "If the First Amendment means anything, it means that a state has no business telling a man, sitting alone in his home, what books he may read or what films he may watch. . . ." In sum, Marshall argued, the First Amendment forbids the state from ". . . controlling a person's private thoughts" (*Stanley v. Georgia,* at 565, 566 (1969).

It was from cases such as these that the right to privacy emerged. In his opinion in *Griswold v. Connecticut* (1965) which upheld the right to privacy and argued it included the right to decide for oneself whether to use birth control devices, Justice Douglas wrote:

> . . . that specific guarantees in the Bill of rights have penumbras, formed by emanations from those guarantees that help give them life and substance. . . . Various guarantees create zones of privacy. The right of association contained in the penumbra of the First Amendment is one. . . . The Third Amendment in its prohibition

against quartering of soldiers "in any house" in time of peace without the consent of the owner is another facet of privacy. The Fourth Amendment explicitly affirms the "right of the people to be secure in their persons, houses, papers, and effects against unreasonable searches and seizures." The Fifth Amendment in its Self-Incrimination Clause enables the citizen to create a zone of privacy which government may not force him to surrender to his detriment. The Ninth Amendment provides: "The enumeration in the constitution, of certain rights, shall not be construed to deny or disparage others retained by the people. (at 479)

When Douglas speaks of "penumbras," he likens the Bill of Rights to the sun. Just as an eclipse reveals a vast array of gasses emanating from the sun not usually visible to the naked eye, close inspection of the provisions of the Bill of Rights seen together reveals zones of privacy. While the First and Fifth Amendments protect us from exposing our private thoughts, when those thoughts could subject us to harm, the Third and Fourth Amendments provide protection for our homes and personal papers. They, in effect, codify the notion that "your home is your castle." Finally, the liberty protected by the Fifth and Fourteenth Amendments has been interpreted at times as protecting us from government intrusion into our "private" affairs.

Although Douglas found the right to privacy to be rooted firmly in the Bill of Rights itself, others in the Court majority emphasized the broad protection of "liberty" in the Due Process clause of the Fourteenth Amendment. The specific issue in *Griswold* concerned the constitutionality of a Connecticut statute that banned the use of birth control devices even by married persons; it also forbade anyone, including physicians, from counseling others in the use of contraceptive devices. According to Justice Goldberg's concurring opinion, this ban on birth control violated rights to liberty rooted in the "traditions and [collective] conscience of our people" (at 493). Goldberg found support in the Ninth Amendment for the notion that some rights and liberties are so fundamental that the framers saw no specific need to mention them directly. Surely the right to marital privacy and control over the decision to have a family rank among such fundamental rights.

As the discussion of incorporation in Chapter 1 demonstrates, giving specific content to the Due Process clause of the Fourteenth Amendment raises difficult issues. "Liberty" can mean different things to different people and certainly to different justices of the U.S. Supreme Court. The justices defending the right of privacy in marital relationships in *Griswold* argued, however, that their decision reflected their reading of history and the established customs and values of society as a whole and not merely their personal predilections.

The idea that the Constitution protects privacy " . . . at certain times and places with respect to certain activities" (Black, J., dissenting, at 508) is not really controversial. Rather, the controversy over privacy arises over the broad sweep given its protection by the Court. Justice Black's dissent argued that the only privacy protected by the Constitution are those elements of privacy covered specifically by the provisions of the Constitution discussed above. He wrote: "I like my privacy as well as the next one, but I am nonetheless compelled to admit that government has a right to invade it unless prohibited by some specific constitutional provision" (at 507). If parts of several amendments to the Constitution provide some element of privacy, Black felt obligated to confine the right of privacy to the sum of those parts. To the majority of the Court, however, the right of privacy implicit in a number of Amendments extends beyond the specifics of those amendments; the whole right of privacy is, therefore, greater than the sum of its parts. To them the right of privacy has provided grounds for limits on government power in a number of spheres, the most controversial of which has been abortion.

**Question 2** *How did the "right to privacy" lead to a woman's right to have an abortion?*

Although in *Griswold v. Connecticut*, 1963 (discussed in Question 1) the Court first explicitly recognized a constitutional right of privacy, that decision did not clearly define its limits. *Griswold*, after all, only directly concerned the right of married persons to use birth control devices. The Supreme Court's decision in *Eisenstadt v. Baird* 405 U.S. 438 (1972), however, extended that right to unmarried persons as well. Because most states at the time of *Griswold* allowed access to contraceptives, it might reasonably be argued that the decision in *Griswold* reflected a broad consensus in society concerning the question of the use of contraceptives; no such consensus existed on the question of access to abortion. In most states until the U.S. Supreme Court decided in *Roe v. Wade* (1973) that the right to privacy "is broad enough to encompass a woman's decision whether or not to terminate her pregnancy," having an abortion was a crime (at 153).

In striking down state laws banning abortion, Justice Blackmun, writing for the majority of the Supreme Court, justified his decision by surveying both the nature of the privacy cases decided to that date and the conflicting historical attitudes concerning abortion. In his decision he noted that the Court had recognized a close link between privacy and

activities relating to marriage, procreation, contraception, family relationships, and child rearing. In effect Blackmun argued that decisions
concerning the size of one's family and control over one's reproductive
function are fundamentally personal. Summing up a woman's interest in
being free to decide with medical advice on abortion, Justice Harry A.
Blackmun wrote:

> The detriment the State would impose upon the pregnant
> woman by denying this choice altogether is apparent. Specific
> and direct harm medically diagnosable even in early preg-
> nancy may be involved. Maternity, or additional offspring,
> may force upon the woman a distressful life and future. Psy-
> chological harm may be imminent. Mental and physical health
> may be taxed by child care. There is also the distress, for all
> concerned, associated with the unwanted child, and there is
> the problem of bringing a child into a family already unable,
> psychologically and otherwise, to care for it. In other cases, as
> in this one, the additional difficulties and continuing stigma of
> unwed motherhood may be involved (at 153).

Against these interests of the mother, the Court weighed the interest in "life" of the fetus. In arguing that a woman does have genuine
interests in being free to terminate a pregnancy, Justice Blackmun recognized that in some instances the state has interests in regulating, and
sometimes prohibiting, abortion as well. The two state interests recognized were protecting the health of the pregnant woman and protecting
the potential human life in her womb. Although the interest in safe-
guarding maternal health presented no great problem for the Court in
confronting the question of abortion, the issue of the rights of potential
human life is at the heart of the abortion debate.

In dealing with abortion as with any other medical procedure the
state has broad latitude to assure through regulation that proper health
and safety standards are followed. The issue in abortion, however, really
is safety for whom? Obviously, if the "safety" of the fetus were the primary concern, abortion would not be permitted at all. If the interests of
the fetus were more important than those of the mother, then every effort
would have to be made to protect the life of the fetus even at the expense
of the mother's life. If, on the other hand, the safety of the mother is
always the primary concern, then abortion would also be permitted when
continued pregnancy jeopardizes the mother's life. Before deciding what
medical regulation of abortion would be permitted, the Court had to
decide the prior question of whether the mother's or the fetus's potential
interests were paramount. Of course, had the Court determined that the

Constitution provided no guidance, this decision could have been left to legislatures.

If the interest in protecting the woman's health is a state's alleged concern, then some regulation of abortion procedures may be appropriate when abortion poses a real risk to the mother's health. This point is reached, according to Justice Blackmun's opinion in *Roe*, when the risk posed by abortion procedures is greater than the risk posed by remaining pregnant. The point where the risk shifts against unregulated abortion was, at least in 1973, at the end of the first trimester of pregnancy. "This is so because of the now established medical fact . . . that until the end of the first trimester mortality in abortion is less than mortality in normal childbirth" (at 163). Simply, a state's claim that it is restricting abortion procedures before this point in order to protect the mother would fall in the face of the medical reality that having an abortion is safer for a pregnant woman than staying pregnant.

In deciding the more difficult question of the competing "claims" of a woman desiring an abortion and of the fetus, Justice Blackmun was forced to address the question of just when life begins. If a developing embryo or later a fetus is recognized as a human life, a person, then it has legal interests which the Court would have to consider. If only an infant after birth is considered a person, then the Court could disregard any "claims" on behalf of the fetus.

For guidance concerning the legal status of the fetus, Justice Blackmun looked to the language of the Constitution and to historic tradition. After citing all references to "persons" in the Constitution, Justice Blackmun observes that the ". . .use of the word is such that it has application only postnatally" (at 157). In general he noted that "[i]n areas other than criminal abortion, the law has been reluctant to endorse any theory that life, as we recognize it, begins before live birth or to accord legal rights to the unborn except in narrowly defined situations and except when the rights are contingent upon birth . . . "(at 161).

On the more difficult question of when human life begins, although Blackmun concludes that the Court "need not resolve the . . . question," he in effect decides that life begins at the point of "viability," that is, the point at which sustaining life independent of the mother outside the womb is possible (albeit with technological assistance.) Before choosing the point of viability over the claim of Texas that life begins at conception, Blackmun reviews the variety of approaches to this question found in religious and philosophical tradition. Although he identifies no clear precise consensus, he does find that the dominant views in religion, philosophy, medicine, and the law tend to focus on some stage of development substantially later than conception. He concludes, therefore, that before the stage when independent life outside the mother's womb is at least technically feasible, the fetus has no legal standing independent of the mother.

### Question 3    *Does a fetus's "right to life" ever count more than a woman's right to privacy?*

The legal status of a fetus in light of the Supreme Court's abortion decisions remains somewhat unclear. Obviously as long as the Court recognizes a woman's right to choose to terminate her pregnancy, it is safe to say that the right to life of a fetus is significantly limited. In *Roe v. Wade* the Court in effect argued that a fetus has no right to life until at least the point of viability, the point at which it can be maintained independent of the mother outside the womb. Since its initial determination of this question in *Roe v Wade,* however, legal recognition of the right to life of the fetus may have increased. What changes have taken place have occurred because of both changes in technology and in the Supreme Court's constitutional interpretation.

The viability standard from *Roe v. Wade* permitted the states to outlaw abortions, if they so chose, once fetal development had reached the stage when independent life outside of the mother's womb could be sustained. At the time when *Roe* was decided technology had advanced to the point that a fetus born prematurely could realistically survive only after the onset of the third trimester of pregnancy. Since then, however, the ability of medicine to sustain a baby born prematurely has begun to move earlier in the pregnancy cycle. If, therefore, fetal viability is the point at which abortion can be banned, then abortion may be banned earlier in the pregnancy today than it could in 1973.

In *Planned Parenthood v. Casey,* (1992) the Supreme Court gave explicit recognition to the changes technological developments have worked on the trimester framework that emerged from *Roe v. Wade.*

> We have seen how time has overtaken some of *Roe's* factual assumptions: advances in maternal health care allow for abortions safe to the mother later in the pregnancy than was true in 1973, and advances in neonatal care have advanced viability to a point somewhat earlier. But these facts go only to the scheme of time limits on the realization of competing interests, and the divergencies from the factual premises of 1973 have no bearing on the validity of *Roe's* central holding, that viability marks the earliest point at which the State's interest in fetal life is constitutionally adequate to justify a legislative ban on nontherapeutic abortions. The soundness of that constitutional judgment in no sense turns on whether viability occurs at approximately 28

weeks, as was usual at the time of *Roe,* at 23 to 24 weeks, as it sometimes does today, or at some moment even slightly earlier in the pregnancy, as it may if fetal respiratory capacity can somehow be enhanced in the future. Whenever it may occur, the attainment of viability may continue to serve as the critical fact, just as it has done since *Roe* was decided . . . (at 860).

The simple answer then to the question of whether the fetus's right to life ever outweighs a mother's right to privacy therefore is yes. According to the Court when a fetus reaches the point of development where a prematurely born infant can be medically sustained, then the mother may legally be prevented from jeopardizing its right to live by terminating her pregnancy. In *Planned Parenthood v. Casey,* however, the Court majority appears to have given the interest of the fetus in life even greater recognition than the evolving viability schedule might imply. That case concerned attempts by the state of Pennsylvania to discourage abortion without directly outlawing it. If because of *Roe* the State could no longer ban abortion outright, could it by lesser means still take steps to advance its asserted interest in protecting "potential" life? If it could advance an interest in "potential life," then how far could it go before the woman's right of privacy becomes paramount?

In the late 1980s Pennsylvania enacted a number of restrictions on women's access to abortions. Together these restrictions appeared designed to discourage women from having abortions and to place impediments in the path of an easy abortion decision. All appeared designed to highlight the state's interest in "potential life," and thus to elevate the independent interest of a fetus in its life. Before an abortion could take place the law required that women (1) be provided with information by doctors on the stage of fetal development; (2) give their consent to the abortion, and if they were minors, obtain parental consent for the abortion; (3) wait at least 24 hours after giving their informed consent before the abortion can actually be performed; and (4) if married, inform their husbands of their intention to have an abortion. Finally, the law imposed various paperwork requirements on doctors performing abortions relating to reporting abortions and public disclosure.

When, in 1992 a challenge to these Pennsylvania restrictions finally reached the U.S. Supreme Court, the Court decided that

[t]hough the woman has the right to choose to terminate her pregnancy before viability, it does not follow that the State is prohibited from taking steps to ensure that this choice is thoughtful and informed. Even in the earliest stages of pregnancy, the State may enact rules and regulations designed to encourage her to know that there are philosophic and social arguments of great weight that can

be brought to bear in favor of continuing the pregnancy to full term and that there are procedures and institutions to allow adoption of unwanted children as well as a certain degree of state assistance if the mother chooses to raise the child herself. (at 872)

In deciding how to measure which state regulations to uphold and which might impermissably interfere with the women's right to choose, the Court applied what it called an "undue burden analysis." According to Justice O'Connor's opinion, "An undue burden exists, and therefore a provision of law is invalid, if its purpose or effect is to place a substantial obstacle in the path of a woman seeking an abortion before the fetus attains viability" (at 878).

To understand what the Court's "undue burden analysis" means in practice, we may see how the Pennsylvania restrictions on abortion fared when subjected to this test. All restrictions, except for the requirement of the husband's notification, survived the Court's scrutiny. The fact that a woman would have to listen to arguments against abortion before exercising her right to an abortion was deemed by the Court not to pose an undue burden. The same was true of the requirement of a 24-hour waiting period, presumably to allow the woman to reflect fully on the consequences of her choice. When confronted with the requirement of spousal notification, however, the Court recognized that for many women this could pose a significant hardship. "There are millions of women in this country who are victims of regular physical and psychological abuse at the hands of their husbands." And as the Court noted, "[s]hould these women become pregnant, they may have very good reasons for not wishing to inform their husbands of their decision to obtain an abortion" (at 893).

In support of the Court majority's conclusion, one can just imagine what the consequences might be for a woman whose pregnancy results from an extramarital relationship, or even from a failure to use contraceptives which an abusive husband might consider to be the woman's responsibility.

On the other hand, many men might view with dismay the Court's refusal to see their stake in their wives pregnancy to be worth even a simple notification that she is considering abortion. Might it not sometimes be true that a wife might incorrectly anticipate her husband's response to a pregnancy? Although the Court's decision recognizes the right of the state to attempt to persuade a woman not to have an abortion, it denies the right of a husband and would-be father.

Whatever one thinks of the particulars of the Court's application of its "undue burden" analysis in *Planned Parenthood v. Casey*, what is clear is that we are left up in the air as to precisely what would constitute an "undue burden." Would, for example a 72-hour waiting period amount to an "undue burden"? Even a 24-hour waiting period could prove burdensome to the less well off. Consider that in many states abortion providers are located in few places. Abortion services may well be far from home. To obtain an abortion one might have to travel hundreds of miles. If required to wait 24 hours from first visit to actual abortion, an overnight stay might be necessary. Hotels can be expensive. If that overnight stay were to stretch to 72 hours, the cost could be even more prohibitive. Would the Court agree that a 72-hour waiting period poses an undue burden? Answers to questions such as these must await further adjudication.

In upholding restrictions on access to abortion that do not actually prohibit abortion, the Court acknowledges what it terms the state's legitimate interest in potential life. This places slightly more weight on the side of the fetus in any balancing of interests between a mother's right to privacy and an asserted fetus's right to life. In assessing the relative weight given to the "interest" in life of the fetus versus the privacy interest of the mother, it is important to remember that nothing in any of the Court's opinions concerning privacy *requires* the government to protect even a viable fetus from abortion. All that the Court has now said is that the state is not forbidden by the Constitution from deciding to ban abortion in order to protect a viable fetus, and as a result of *Planned Parenthood v. Casey* the states *may*, if they choose, place restrictions on abortion as long as those restrictions do not pose an "undue burden." Nothing the Court has said prevents the states from permitting totally unrestricted abortion.

**Question 4**　*When may the state regulate private sexual relationships between consenting adults?*

Widespread public distaste for Independent Counsel Kenneth Starr's investigation of President Bill Clinton's relationship with Monica Lewinsky no doubt in part reflected the view of many that intimate relationships between consenting adults are no one's business but the participants. Although Mr. Starr was not directly investigating the Clinton/Lewinsky relationship, the fact that his inquiry served to bring even its intimate details to public attention caused many to react far more negatively to the investigator than to the conduct of those investigated.

Public revulsion or unease in the face of disclosure of intimate relationships does not, however, insulate private sexual conduct from government scrutiny or even punishment. In 1986 the United States Supreme Court considered a constitutional challenge to a Georgia antisodomy law as applied to consensual homosexual conduct. In a 5 to 4 decision the Supreme Court upheld the right of states to prohibit and punish certain consensual sexual conduct. This Court's decision in *Bowers v. Hardwick*, 1986, brought in sharp relief the limits to the right to privacy that the Court had generally expanded since its decision in *Griswold v. Connecticut* in 1963 (see Questions 1 and 2 above). Although many oppose the Court's decision in *Bowers,* the foundation for this decision had been at least arguably laid in some of the justice's opinions found in *Griswold* itself.

Many states had long had laws forbidding sodomy for both heterosexual and homosexual relationships. Prosecutions for sodomy, at least in the modern era, were, however, exceedingly rare. Even in the case that gave rise to the Supreme Court's decision in *Bowers*, the prosecution was dropped before the case ever went to court. The case came to the Supreme Court because the person against whom the initial charges were made successfully contended that he was always under threat of prosecution because he had no intention of ceasing the forbidden sexual conduct in the future.

The violation of the sodomy statute which led ultimately to Hardwick's challenging Georgia's sodomy law was actually stumbled upon by the police inadvertently. They had gone to Hardwick's apartment to arrest him for another matter, were admitted by a roommate, and directed to Hardwick's room where they observed him engaging in sexual conduct forbidden by the antisodomy statute with another man. The prosecutor subsequently decided against going forward with the prosecution.

When this case ultimately reached the U.S. Supreme Court, the Court had to decide whether its precedents relating to privacy rights justified its striking down state antisodomy statutes. The debate between the Court majority and the dissenters was over the definition and scope of the liberty interests protected by the Due Process clause of the Fourteenth Amendment.

According to Justice White's opinion for the Court, the issue in the *Bowers* case was "whether the Federal Constitution confers a fundamental right upon homosexuals to engage in sodomy" (at 190). Viewed from this perspective, the answer according to Justice White was quite simply no.

When a claim is brought to Court that a state law violated a right protected against the states by the federal Constitution, many on the Court look first to the Bill of Rights to see if that liberty is protected against infringement by Congress. As we saw in Chapter 1, virtually every liberty included in the Bill of Rights has through Supreme Court interpretation been incorporated by the Court into the Due Process clause of the Fourteenth Amendment as among the liberties protected against infringement by the states. When the asserted liberty interest is not among those explicitly recognized by the Constitution, most justices over the years have sought to determine whether the liberty in question is among those fundamental, but unstated, liberties, protected by the Due Process clause. The fact that there are unstated liberties protected by the Constitution is implicit in the Ninth Amendment, which states that '[t]he enumeration in this constitution of certain rights shall not be construed to deny others retained by the people."

Attempts by the Court to identify and give effect to unstated rights, however, as we saw in our discussion of *Griswold* above, have been controversial. In approaching the *Bowers* case, therefore, Justice White discussed how many on the Court have approached this issue:

> Striving to assure itself and the public that announcing rights not readily identifiable in the Constitution's text involves more than the imposition of the Justices' own choice of values upon the States and the Federal Government, the Court sought to identify the nature of the rights qualifying for heightened judicial protection. In *Palko v. Connecticut,* 302 U.S. 319 (1937) it was said that this category includes those fundamental liberties that are "implicit in the concept of ordered liberty," such that "neither liberty nor justice would exist if they were sacrificed." A different description of fundamental liberties appeared in *Moore v. East Cleveland,* 431 U.S. 494 (1977) (opinion of Powell, J.) where they are characterized as those liberties that "are deeply rooted in this nation's history and tradition." . . . (at 194)

Citing the ancient legal and moral condemnations of homosexual conduct, including criminal prohibitions in the original 13 states and in most states today, Justice White asserted that "[a]gainst this background, to claim that a right to engage in such conduct is 'deeply rooted in this Nation's history and tradition' or 'implicit in the concept of ordered liberty' is, at best, factitious" (at 194). Justice White asserted, largely correctly, that most of the Court's precedents relating to the right to privacy concerned marriage, family, and/or procreation, two interests obviously not at issue in homosexual relationships at least at the time the case was decided (the case preceded the as yet largely unsuccessful efforts to win legal recognition for gay marriages).

The Supreme Court in *Bowers* was sharply divided. The division itself was fundamentally over the definition of the controversy before the Court itself. While Justice White asserted that the issue was whether the Constitution conferred on homosexuals a "fundamental right" to engage in sodomy, Justice Blackmun in his dissent saw the issue quite differently. "This case is no more about 'a fundamental right to engage in homosexual sodomy,' as the Court purports to declare, than *Stanley v. Georgia* was about a fundamental right to watch obscene movies, or *Katz v. United States,* (1967) was about a fundamental right to place interstate bets from a telephone booth. Rather, this case is about 'the most comprehensive of rights and the right most valued by civilized men, namely, the right to be left alone' ". *Olmstead v. United States* (1928) (Brandeis, J., dissenting) (*Bowers* at 199).

In making this argument Justice Blackmun asserts that many if not most of the Court's privacy cases do not assert fundamental rights to engage in any specific conduct. Rather they protect areas of personal autonomy, the right of all to decide for themselves how they will conduct certain aspects of their lives and/or certain places or circumstances within which people have a right to be free from government scrutiny or surveillance. He asserts in this instance that ". . . what the Court really has refused to recognize is the fundamental interest all individuals have in controlling the nature of their intimate associations with others" (at 206).

Justice John Paul Stevens also dissented from the Court's decision. His opinion emphasized the discriminatory impact of the Court's decision on homosexuals, discrimination he considered not to be justified by any legitimate state interest. The statute in question, like most other anti-sodomy statutes, did not itself single out homosexual conduct. Instead its definition of prohibited behavior encompassed sexual contact engaged in by many, perhaps most, heterosexual couples as well. Justice Stevens asserted, however, that well-established Court precedents would not permit the enforcement of the statute against heterosexuals. According to Justice Stevens:

> Our prior cases make two propositions abundantly clear. First, the fact that the governing majority in a state has traditionally viewed a particular practice as immoral is not a sufficient reason for upholding a law prohibiting the practice; neither history nor tradition could save a law prohibiting miscegenation (interracial marriage) from constitutional attack. Second, individual decisions by married persons, concerning the intimacies of their physical relationship, even when not intended to produce off-spring, are a form of "liberty" protected by the due process clause of the Fourteenth Amendment . . . (at 216).

Stevens concluded that under existing precedents, the Georgia statute against sodomy could not be enforced against heterosexuals. If it is to be enforced against homosexuals the state needs a justification that rises far above the disapproval or outright hostility of the majority. Unless the state can show that homosexuals have a lesser interest in liberty than heterosexuals or some other interest justifying unequal treatment, he concluded that no such interest existed.

We of course must remember that, as Justice White himself contended, nothing in his decision should be interpreted as a judicial endorsement of the wisdom of the law in question. Nothing in the decision prevents states from legalizing the conduct in question. All that the decision did was assert that nothing in the U.S. Constitution forbids states from prohibiting and punishing homosexual conduct.

Although the dissenters in *Bowers* express views concerning the scope of the right to privacy that many will find attractive, Justice White's opinion was consistent with views held by leading justices at the time the right was first clearly proclaimed in *Griswold v. Connecticut,* (1965). In their concurring opinion in *Griswold* both Justices Arthur Goldberg and Harlan emphasized the limits of their recognition of privacy interests. Quoting from Justice Harlan's dissent in an earlier case, *Poe v. Ullman,* Justice Goldberg repeated, "Adultery, homosexuality and the like are sexual intimacies which the state forbids . . . but the intimacy of husband and wife is necessarily an essential feature of the institution of marriage. . . . It is one thing when the State exerts its power either to forbid extra-marital sexuality . . . or to say who may marry, but it is quite another when, having acknowledged a marriage and the intimacies inherent in it, it undertakes to regulate by means of its criminal law the details of that intimacy" (at 523, 524).

The Court's decision in *Bowers* attracted only a narrow majority, 5 to 4. Following his retirement, Justice Powell, a member of that majority, expressed his unease with the decision. It appears very likely that the Court will revisit the issue before too long.

## Question 5    *Why doesn't the "right to privacy" include the right to decide to end our lives?*

Modern medical care often seems to make it possible to sustain human life long past the point where it seems to many to be meaningful. Diseases such as some cancers and AIDS can take a terrible toll in human suffering sometimes bringing excruciating pain as death approaches. Some linger in such a condition for weeks and months. The prospect of death brings the only promise of relief.

In the 1990s the issue of a "right to die" was brought  most starkly to public consciousness by a physician in Michigan, Jack Kevorkian. Dr. Kevorkian, or "Doctor Death," as he came to be known, assisted dozens of terminally ill patients to hurry their deaths. While Dr. Kevorkian in very public ways asserted the right of patients to end their suffering and hurry their deaths through the active intervention of physicians, others earlier had to fight for the right of the terminally ill to refuse medical intervention which served to prolong life. Physician-assisted suicide involved medical intervention to terminate life more quickly than would occur through natural causes. Withholding treatment or medical intervention is designed to allow nature to take its course.

The Court had long recognized the right of a competent person to refuse medical treatment, even when doing so would hasten death. In his Opinion of the Court in *Cruzon v. Director, Missouri Department of Health* (1990), ". . . the first case in which . . . [the Court] has been squarely presented with the issue of whether the United States Constitution grants what is in common parlance referred to as a "right to die" (at 277), Chief Justice Rehnquist asserted that a person's liberty interest extends so far as to refuse "lifesaving hydration and nutrition" (at 276). Rehnquist based this right in part on the assumption in common law that "even the touching of one person without consent and without legal justification" amounted to a battery. Quoting from *Union Pacific Railroad Company v. Botsford* (1891), Rehnquist argued that "[no] right is held more sacred, or is more carefully guarded, by the common law, than the right of every individual to the possession and control of his own person, free from all restraint or interference of others, unless by clear and unquestionable authority of law" (at 269).

The recognition of an individual's right to refuse treatment in *Cruzon,* however, did not resolve the specific issue in that case. There the right was asserted on Ms. Cruzon's behalf by her parents. Because Ms. Cruzon, as a result of an accident, was in a persistent vegetative state and unable to assert her wishes herself, her parents sought removal of feeding tubes on her behalf. Because, however, Missouri required evidence "by clear and convincing evidence" that the incompetent person would have wished the withdrawal of treatment, evidence unavailable in the instant case, Ms. Cruzon's parents were denied the right to withdraw the feeding tubes and the United States Supreme Court found nothing in the Constitution of the United States that would supersede Missouri's judgment.

The issue then in *Cruzon* was not really the right to die. It was rather what limits the Constitution places on a state's insistence on a clear statement of an incompetent person's wishes. *Cruzon* left in place the rights of a competent person to refuse medical intervention against her will to prolong her life.

The claim of a constitutional right of patients to select the time of their deaths, however, through physician-assisted suicide is considered by the Court to raise different issues. In *Washington v. Glucksberg* (1997) the Supreme Court faced a challenge to the State of Washington's ban on physician-assisted suicide. "The Plaintiffs asserted the existence of a liberty interest protected by the Fourteenth Amendment which extends to a personal choice by a mentally competent, terminally ill adult to commit physician-assisted suicide" (at 708).

Since there was no question of any specific constitutional prohibition on governmental restraint on suicide, the question in this case, as in all other cases asserting a liberty interest under the Fourteenth Amendment, was whether society had long assumed the existence of such a right even though it was not explicitly codified. As Chief Justice Rehnquist wrote in his opinion of the Court: "We begin, as we do in all due-process cases, by examining our nation's history, legal traditions and practices. In almost every state—indeed in almost every western democracy—it is a crime to assist a suicide. The States' assisted suicide bans are not innovations. Rather they are longstanding expressions of the States' commitment to the protection and preservation of all human life . . . (at 710).

Chief Justice Rehnquist recognized that advances in medical technology have had the effect of prolonging both life and the often painful process of death. As he observed, "public concern and democratic action are therefore sharply focused on how best to protect dignity and independence at the end of life" (at 716). But although legislatures have authorized "living wills" and health care proxies to assist citizens in having a say over which medical procedures they may want to refuse to prolong the end of life, they have also almost everywhere rejected proposals to legalize physician-assisted suicide. Were the Court to extend constitutional protection to this newly asserted right to physician-assisted suicide, it would ". . . place the matter outside the arena of public debate and legislative action" (at 720). This, to Chief Justice Rehnquist would be an abuse of judicial authority.

> Here. . . .we are confronted with a consistent and almost universal tradition that has long rejected the asserted right, and continues to reject it today, even for the terminally ill, mentally competent adults. To hold for respondents, we would have to reverse centuries of legal doctrine and practice, and strike down the considered policy choice of almost every State . . . (at 723).

Even as he rejected the notion that physician-assisted suicide was a fundamental right protected by the Fourteenth Amendment from infringement from the state, he still had to consider whether a restriction on the practice was "rationally related to legitimate government interests" (at 728). The Court interprets the Due Process clause of the Fourteenth Amendment to require that any restaints placed on individual liberty or autonomy be at minimum supportable by some understandable justification. The state's chosen policy need not be considered the best, it need only be one supportable by some reasonable arguments.

When using this lenient and permissive standard as a measure, the Court found little difficulty discovering legitimate concerns that might prompt government decision makers to opt to forbid physician-assisted suicide. The first asserted state interest recognized as reasonable by Rehnquist was the state's general interest in preserving human life. Although abortion rights were not specifically mentioned by Rehnquist, the state's interest in protecting human life was recognized even in the Court's most recent decision upholding abortion rights. While in the abortion decision this interest had to give way to the "fundamental right" of privacy, the foundation for abortion rights (see Question 2 above), in this case the Court found no such fundamental right to physician-assisted suicide.

In considering the state's generalized interest in human life, Chief Justice Rehnquist noted the prevalence of mental health disorders, especially depression, in people attempting suicide and the state's strong interest in protecting such vulnerable groups from themselves. The chief justice noted that "[r]esearch indicates . . . many people who request physician-assisted suicide withdraw that request if their depression and pain are treated." Because physicians and others often do not respond adequately to seriously ill patients' needs, however, the State has a legitimate interest in stepping in to protect such patients from their "suicidal impulses" (at 730).

This concern for vulnerable citizens extends further than concern for those suffering from depression or other mental or emotional illnesses. The "poor, elderly, and disabled" may need state protection from abuse and neglect. Among the fears of those opposing physician-assisted suicide is the possibility that financial pressures on individuals, concern for the impact of the costs of lengthy medical treatments on families, including concern that one's estate will be eaten away by the high costs of medical care, could induce a terminally ill person to opt for suicide because of either a misplaced sense of guilt about being a burden or even to pressures being placed on the terminally ill to move on, and save their families the expense and continued emotional distress potentially caused by a loved one's serious illness.

To these concerns the Chief Justice added: "The State's interest here goes beyond protecting the vulnerable from coercion; it extends to protecting disabled and terminally ill people from prejudice, negative and inaccurate stereotypes, and 'societal indifference.' The state's assisted-suicide ban reflects and reinforces its policy that the lives of terminally ill, disabled and elderly people must be no less valued than the lives of the young and healthy, and that a seriously disabled person's suicidal impulses should be interpreted and treated the same way as anyone else's.

Another interest mentioned by Chief Justice Rehnquist, which arguably is advanced by state bans on physician-assisted suicide, is protecting individuals and society from both voluntary and potentially coerced euthanasia. Although not mentioned by Rehnquist, at a time when managed care has assumed an ever larger role in medicine, it is not difficult to imagine heath insurance providers openly encouraging physician-assisted suicide as a cost-saving measure. Many health plans, including Medicare, already pay the costs of "hospice care," designed as relatively inexpensive end of life care for those rejecting more extraordinary measures to temporarily extend life (or the process of dying.) Physician-assisted suicide could become another, even much less costly, way to manage and lessen the costs of death and dying. One can imagine a health plan waiving deductibles and/or co-pays for the costs of physician-assisted suicide as an incentive. Certainly many would think the state would have a rational interest in closing off such options.

Finally, Chief Justice Rehnquist asserted that the state has a legitimate interest in ". . . protecting the integrity and ethics of the medical profession." His decision took note of the expressed opposition to physician-assisted suicide of the American Medical Society, which views the practice as ". . . fundamentally incompatible with the physician's role as healer" (at 731).

Although the chief justice's opinion can be read as total rejection of physician-assisted suicide, all it did in practice is refuse to declare a constitutional restraint on the states as they consider the issue. His opinion and the Constitution as interpreted by him leave open the option for the states to authorize the practice if they choose.

The Court in *Washington v. Glucksberg* was unanimous in its decision that nothing in the Constitution precluded the states from banning physician-assisted suicide, at least under the circumstances of the case before them, but five justices wrote concurring opinions which may in varying degrees have signaled that the Court may not have spoken its last word on the issue.

Justice O'Connor and Justice Stephen Breyer, in their separate concurring opinions, stressed that nothing in the Court's opinion prevents physicians from taking steps to alleviate the pain of dying patients even when a secondary effect might actually be to speed the dying process. In the cases before the Court the states in question did not attempt to limit a physician's latitude in alleviating pain. If they had, Justice O'Connor's concurrence clearly implies that the Court might view the issue differently. Overall she expresses confidence that the delicate concerns involved can and will be addressed through the democratic political process. Nothing in the decision in this case, nor in the opinion of the Court, precludes the states from addressing the concerns of the dying while protecting the vulnerable among us from abuse. If the states were, however, to address this issue by denying even palliative care that alleviates excruciating pain but might hasten death, then she together with Justice Breyer indicates the Court might be forced to revisit this issue.

Recognizing that individuals do have a "liberty interest" that in some instances ". . . may outweigh the state's interest in preserving life at all costs," Justice Stevens argued that "[t]he liberty interest at stake in a case like this differs from, and is stronger than, both the common-law right to refuse medical treatment and the unbridled interest in deciding whether to live or die. It is an interest in determining how, rather than whether a critical threshold shall be crossed . . ." (at 745). In recognizing that the individual has a stake in determining the circumstances of his death, Justice Steven's leaves open the question of how far the state may go to advance its interest in limiting suicide.

Clearly, despite its clear rejection of a constitutionally imposed restraint on the states' ability to forbid physician-assisted suicide, the issue of the right to die has not been left entirely to the changing passions of popular majorities. While rejecting an unfettered interest of individuals to determine the time and circumstances of their deaths, the Court has made it clear individuals may refuse medical treatments and even necessary nourishment to prolong the life of those near death. Where the Court will ultimately strike the balance between individual autonomy and the state's traditional opposition to suicide remains to some degree an open question.

## REFERENCES

*Bowers v. Hardwick*, 478 U.S. 186 (1986).

*Cruzon v. Director, Missouri Department of Health*, 497 U.S. 261 (1990).

*Eisenstadt v. Baird*, 405 U.S. 438 (1972).

*Griswold v. Connecticut*, 381 U.S. 479 (1965).

*Katz v. United States*, 389 U.S. 347 (1967).

*Moore v. East Cleveland*, 431 U.S. 494 (1977).

*NAACP v. Alabama*, 354 U.S. 449 (1958).

*Olmstead v. United States*, 227 U.S. 438 (1928).

*Palko v. Connecticut*, 302 U.S. 319 (1937).

*Planned Parenthood v. Casey*, 505 U.S. 833 (1992).

*Poe v. Olman*, 367 U.S. 497 (1961).

*Roe v. Wade*, 410 U.S. 113 (1973).

*Rust v. Sullivan*, 500 U.S. 173 (1991).

*Stanley v. Georgia*, 394 U.S. 557 (1969).

*Union Pacific Railroad Company v. Botsford*, 141 U.S. 250 (1891).

*Washington v. Glucksberg*, 521 U.S. 702 (1997).

*Roe v. Wade*, 410 U.S. 113 (1973).

*Rust v. Sullivan*, 500 U.S. 173 (1991).

*Stanley v. Georgia*, 394 U.S. 557 (1969).

*Union Pacific Railroad Company v. Botsford*, 141 U.S. 250 (1891).

*Washington v. Glucksberg*, 521 U.S. 702 (1997).

### CHAPTER 6

# Contemporary Issue of Equality and Freedom

## INTRODUCTION

Civil liberties may be of little value to those struggling for mere survival. If one cannot find food, the liberties protected by the Constitution may appear empty promises. Certainly the relative value of rights and liberties to individuals may be dependent at least in part on their capacity to enjoy them, and that capacity is at least in part related to economic well-being. This chapter explores a few questions concerning constitutional liberties where contemporary developments bring into sharp relief the relationship of equality to freedom. While the Supreme Court justices have in some instances attempted to grapple with these questions, their answers to date may appear inadequate to many of us. These questions in particular remain open for further debate as we judge the adequacy of our constitutional rights and liberties.

Our first question asks: *What good are rights and liberties if you lack the resources to take advantage of them?* This section opens with a discussion of the most visible recent controversy concerning the relationship of wealth and rights, that concerning the refusal of government to provide Medicaid funding for abortions. Then it explores the broader question by explaining the grounds used by the Supreme Court to justify requiring government to provide counsel and psychiatrists for poor people accused of crime while failing generally to fund the exercise of other rights and liberties. In the end the answer to this question is left to the judgment of the reader. The purpose of this section is to engage the reader in the exploration of what will remain a troubling question to many.

In Chapter 2 we explored traditional issues relating to the nature and limits of freedom of expression under the First Amendment. Here we explore the limits of those rights in a society marked by significant economic inequality. Our second question, then, asks: *What use is freedom of speech if no one can hear you?* This section discusses the problems posed for the "free marketplace of ideas" by the contemporary communications environment. Although television amplifies the voices of the powerless who become "newsworthy," it can also drown out the voices of those unable to gain access to it. This section discusses First Amendment issues raised by television and other electronic media of communications, the different treatment given by the courts to the electronic and print media, the potential impact of cable television and the Internet, and the continuing problems caused by the disparity in the ability of different interests to reach the audience.

Our third question focuses on the role of economic inequality in our political contests. The third question asks: *Is it possible for the wealthy few to dominate public debate and stifle the "free marketplace of ideas"?* This section explores the issues surrounding our system for financing our election and referenda campaigns. In effect, it asks "if money talks," is spending money to spread one's ideas constitutionally protected free speech? Must the value of viewpoints in the marketplace of ideas be inevitably linked to the financial resources mobilized behind them?

Finally, Question 4 focuses on the capacity of private actors to restrict our freedom. It asks: *Does the Constitution protect us from private institutions which interfere with our liberties and rights?* This section explores whether private corporations and others can restrict our freedom. It discusses whether employers limit our freedom of speech and invade our privacy. Because the Court interprets the Constitution as protecting us only from government infringement of our liberties and rights (State Action Doctrine), even protection against private race and sex discrimination is not mandated by the Constitution. The civil rights protections that we do enjoy result from legislation passed by Congress or state legislatures; as such, they are always vulnerable to changing public sentiment. This section discusses the reasons why our rights and liberties are subject to private attack.

## Question 1   *What use are rights and liberties if you lack the resources to take advantage of them?*

Although the Constitution places limits on the power of government to interfere with many of our choices, it does not generally require the government to provide us with the means or opportunities necessary to act on our choices. No one familiar with the First Amendment could seriously argue that government can stop you from printing an article critical of the president. If you lack the resources to purchase a printing press, however, that right may well appear meaningless to you. Similarly, the government cannot stop you from sending your children to a church school, but government need not (and, indeed, may be forbidden to) pay your child's tuition.

Controversy over the question of when government should aid citizens in the exercise of their liberties has recently focused on the question of access to abortion. In a case challenging the government's failure to provide Medicaid funding for poor women seeking abortions, Justice Stewart, writing for the Supreme Court majority, argued that "although government may not place obstacles in the path of a woman's exercise of her freedom of choice, it need not remove those not of its own creation" (*Harris v. McCrae*, at 317, 1980). The state need not help a poor woman exercise her right to choose an abortion even if without such help access to safe abortion is unavailable to a poor woman.

The abortion funding controversy sharply divided the Supreme Court not only because poverty makes exercise of a right impossible for some, but also because government policy concerning Medicaid funding provides an inducement for women to give up their freedom of choice. Although government will not fund abortion, it will pay the costs of childbirth. To Justice Brennan, a dissenter on the Court in the abortion funding cases, the state's paying for childbirth but not for abortion "clearly operates to coerce indigent pregnant women to bear children they would not otherwise choose to have, and just as clearly, this coercion can only operate upon the poor" (*Maher v. Roe*, 1977 at 483). The core of the majority's argument in the abortion funding cases, however, is that it is the woman's poverty and not some state regulation that has narrowed a woman's choice. The state's policy imposes "no restriction on access to abortion that was not already there" (at 482).

This basic rejection by the Court of any government obligation to fund the exercise of rights was reaffirmed its 1991 decision in *Rust v. Sullivan*. In *Rust* the Court upheld a Department of Health and Human Services regulation that denied federal funding to any family planning program that advised clients concerning even the availability of abortion as a family planning option. Not only was any family planning agency receiving federal funds forbidden to perform abortions; they were also forbidden in effect from informing clients of their right to have an abortion.

When confronted with the argument that this regulation forbidding abortion counseling in federally funded family planning programs limited a physician's freedom of speech as well as a woman's freedom of choice, Justice Rehnquist replied that the Constitution does not require the government to pay for the expression of views that it does not like. "When Congress established a National Endowment for Democracy to encourage other countries to adopt democratic principles, it was not constitutionally required to fund a program to encourage competing lines of political philosophy such as Communism or Fascism." (*Rust v. Sullivan,* at 194, 1991).

Clearly, to a poor woman dependent on direct government assistance or on government-financed programs, the right to choose an abortion is no right at all.

Despite the rather bleak picture painted so far of the opportunities for the poor to take advantage of rights and liberties, there are exceptions. When government assistance is necessary to provide the poor a reasonable opportunity to take advantage of constitutional protections afforded to those accused of crimes, the Court recognizes a positive government duty to help.

The Sixth Amendment to the Constitution provides those accused of crimes with a right to counsel, and the Court in *Gideon v. Wainwright* (1963) recognized that the right is meaningless for a poor defendant if the government does not pay for a lawyer. Similarly, where the state allows appellate court review of criminal convictions, it must provide counsel and necessary documents free to those unable to pay; and where a state allows an insanity defense, it must provide the poor with the aid of a psychiatrist.

Clearly in the criminal justice arena, the Court recognizes that rights mean nothing to one who lacks the ability to exercise them. According to Justice Hugo Black, "there can be no equal justice where the kind of trial a man gets depends on the amount of money he has." (*Griffin v. Illinois*, at 19, 1956). In another decision which required that counsel be appointed to assist the poor in preparing a criminal appeal, Justice Douglas wrote: "The indigent, where the record is unclear or the errors are hidden, has only the right of a meaningless ritual, while the rich man has a meaningful appeal" (*Douglas v. California,* at 358, 1963).

There were some on the Supreme Court who dissented from these decisions which required government help for the poor accused of crimes. Their arguments were very similar to those used by the Court majority in the abortion funding cases many years later. Since, they argued, poverty was not imposed by the state, the state is not required to remove or lessen the effects of poverty. As Justice Harlan wrote in his dissent in *Douglas v. California,* the Constitution ". . . does not impose on the states the affirmative duty to lift the handicaps flowing from differences in economic circumstances. To so construe it would be to read into the Constitution a philosophy of leveling that would be foreign to many of our basic concepts of the proper relations between government and society. The

state may have a moral obligation to eliminate the evils of poverty, but it is not required . . . to give to some whatever others can afford" (at 362).

Despite such views, the Court majority requires the state to assist the poor in the exercise of some rights. Although the bases used for distinguishing between those rights requiring government assistance from those which do not is not always clear, two factors appear to be important. First, the Court considers the degree to which the government is responsible for the fate of the person needing help to exercise their rights or take advantage of their liberty. Second, the Court weighs whether the failure to provide assistance will lead to a complete inability to exercise a right or merely an unequal opportunity. Where the deprivation of rights is absolute, the Court is more likely to find a government obligation to help. Where the deprivation is only relative, the Court keeps hands off.

Although the lack of adequate resources may, for example, interfere with the effectiveness of one's free speech or may prevent a woman from obtaining an abortion, neither of those consequences, however serious, is a direct result of a government action. If, however, a person who is accused of a crime cannot obtain a lawyer to properly defend him, he may, as a result, lose his liberty or even his life. What ultimately happens to the poor person accused of a crime will be a direct result of government action taken against him. The government prosecutes, and if found guilty, the government punishes. However serious the consequences faced by a woman with an unwanted pregnancy may be, it was not the government that made her pregnant.

Finally, even though the Court requires counsel and psychiatric help to aid in the defense of indigent persons accused of crimes, it does not require that the counsel provided to the poor be of a quantity or quality equal to those the rich are able to purchase for themselves. Rather, it requires only "adequate counsel" and a "competent psychiatrist." "Adequate" and "competent" do not mean equal.

Clearly, those who are poor are not in the same position to take advantage of their constitutional rights and liberties as those who are rich. For the majority of us who are neither poor nor rich, our rights are also important. Whether they are adequate is a question which we must answer for ourselves.

**Question 2**   *What use is freedom of speech if no one can hear you?*

If anything can be said to be a hallmark as we enter the twenty-first century, it is the explosion of means and opportunities for the communication of ideas. First Amendment freedoms, which were designed to safeguard freedom of thought, conviction, and communication have historically been ranked first among our freedoms as necessary preconditions for the maintenance of other freedoms and the possibility for democracy and majority rule. Traditionally the best safeguard for those freedoms has been a government policy of "hands-off." Faith in an unfettered marketplace for the communication of ideas in the search for truth has probably been even stronger than faith in free economic competition as the best road to economic progress and prosperity.

If we are to understand new challenges to civil liberties in the contemporary era, however, we must first understand what makes the contemporary communications environment different from that known to the framers of the First Amendment and to the Supreme Court throughout much of our history as it has interpreted the meaning of the First Amendment in the face of ongoing challenges.

When the First Amendment was written, the only means of communication available were the unamplified human voice and the printing press. Pamphlets and newspapers were the means used by the framers of the Constitution themselves and by their contemporaries to rally support for American independence and later for the Constitution itself.

Through the nineteenth century newspapers became increasingly important. Control over great newspapers sometimes gave a few the capacity to influence millions, but still the local pamphleteer and even soapbox orator could have some hope to appeal to the consciences and attention of large numbers of citizens. During the twentieth century increasingly electronic means of communications came to supplant newspapers and replace the unamplified human voice as a means of rallying political support and affecting popular attitudes.

At least until the emergence of television and radio whenever the Supreme Court sought to protect the values of the free marketplace of ideas, it simply restrained government and let voices, even "dangerous" voices, be heard. When television and radio emerged as the leading organs of public communication, however, the Court came to accept that regulation of them was sometimes necessary to keep the marketplace open for competition among ideas. Because television and radio as initially developed went over a limited band of communication channels, someone had to decide who would have the privilege of controlling those limited channels.

In *Red Lion Broadcasting Co., Inc. v. Federal Communications Commission*, (1969) the Supreme Court provided its rationale for treating the broadcast media differently from traditional print media. In reply to the broadcast media's contention that it had the same right as the print media to communicate whatever it chose or to refuse to provide access to whomever it chose, Justice Byron White, for a unanimous Court, wrote:

Where there are substantially more individuals who want to broadcast than there are frequencies to allocate, it is idle to posit an unabridgeable First Amendment right to broadcast comparable to the right of every person to speak, write or publish. If 100 persons want broadcast licenses but there are only 10 frequencies to allocate, all of them may have the same right to a license; but if there is to be any effective communication by radio, only a few can be licensed and the rest must be barred from the airwaves . . . .

There is nothing in the First Amendment which prevents the Government from requiring a licensee to share his frequency with others and to conduct himself as a proxy or fiduciary with obligations to present those views and voices which are representative of his community and which would otherwise, by necessity, be barred from the airwaves. . . . Otherwise, station owners and a few networks would have unfettered power to make time available only to the highest bidders, to communicate only their own views on public issues, people and candidates, and to permit on air only those with whom they agreed. There is no sanctuary in the First Amendment for unlimited private censorship operating in a medium not open to all. . . (at 388–392).

In his opinion for the Court Justice White was defending from a First Amendment challenge the fairness doctrine, a Federal Communications Commission's requirement that broadcasters permit individuals air time to reply to personal attacks and to political editorials. A similar requirement was rejected by the Court for the print media in *Miami Herald Publishing Co. v. Tornillo,* (1974) in which the Court found a "right to reply" law unconstitutional on the grounds that it ran ". . .afoul of the elementary First Amendment proposition that government may not force a newspaper to print copy which, in its journalistic discretion, it chooses to leave on the newspaper floor." The differing treatment was justified simply by the differences he outlined between traditional and modern communications methods.

Several years later, however, Congress did away with the fairness doctrine. The advent of cable television with potentially hundreds of competing channels had made the scarcity argument, upon which the special treatment afforded broadcast media was based, largely obsolete. Theoretically, with cable almost everyone could find some outlet for expressing their view.

With the advent of the Internet and World Wide Web, upon which everyone with computer access and a modem can readily find outlets to express their views, it would seem that the need for government intervention to assure an open marketplace of ideas would have evaporated.

But is this so clear? Both cable and the Internet make it possible for virtually anyone to find some niche within which they might be heard. But heard by whom? The very variety of cable channels and Internet "chat rooms" and Web pages of every description, rather than increasing the competition of ideas in a free marketplace of ideas, may instead lead to increasing isolation of people with contending points of view from each other. Instead of being exposed to a variety of conflicting points of view, we are instead drawn to communicate only with those sharing our own prejudices.

In Chapter 2 we learned that one of the principal arguments in support of allowing even those who advocate violence the opportunity to be heard was that airing such views in the public forum would invite vigorous debate and refutation by others. Through such vigorous debate, it was argued, society would learn of the weaknesses in the arguments of those purveyors of hate or other "dangerous ideas," and truth and tolerance would triumph.

In today's increasingly fragmented communications environment, however, isn't it possible that open debate will be replaced by each of us increasingly seeking out only cable channels or Web sites where others who already share our outlook and prejudices can be found? Rather than being confronted with views that make us uncomfortable, might many seek out only views that reinforce their preexisting prejudices? The ideal of a free marketplace of ideas where all views are heard and forced to compete for society's support might be replaced by a smorgasbord of ideas from which we select only those familiar ideas which suit our tastes, leaving unsampled those ideas that seem alien or challenging.

Of course, to a substantial degree in the days when newspapers were the principal means for obtaining news and observing public debate, many, perhaps most of us, read only those newspapers whose editorial outlook we shared. Even then, however, an effort was often made to present the "news" in a neutral way to inform the public. The most influential leading newspapers were often those that kept their most biased presentations on the editorial page.

If the preeminent purpose of free speech is to permit society to govern itself intelligently having witnessed an open exchange of views on important issues, it may be that the contemporary communications environments of cable TV and the Internet detract more than they add. If, however, the principal value we find in free speech is free expression itself, the opportunity for more and more people to vent their rage or advertise their ideas, then we may be entering a golden age of freedom of speech. As with so many other issues before, the reader is invited to draw his or her own conclusions.

**Question 3** *Is it possible for the wealthy few to dominate public debate and stifle the "free marketplace of ideas"?*

In its determination to safeguard free speech in the contemporary era, the Supreme Court has struck down a variety of legislative efforts to lessen the advantages of those with substantial financial resources from dominating our election campaigns. Two Court decisions in the 1970s, *Buckley v. Valeo* (1976) and *First National Bank of Boston v. Bellotti*, (1978) established the limits on government's capacity to level the playing field in political debate.

Following the scandals accompanying the Nixon presidential reelection campaign in 1972, Congress passed sweeping campaign finance legislation designed to diminish the corrupting influence of big money contributions to the electoral political process and designed at least in part to diminish the advantages of wealthy candidates in electoral competition. The Court majority reasoned that the nearly unfettered ability to spend money to spread your point of view to the widest possible audience was an essential element of First Amendment freedoms. In the words of the per curium opinion:

> A restriction on the amount of money a person or group can spend on political communication during a campaign necessarily reduces the quantity of expression by restricting the number of issues discussed, the depth of their exploration, and the size of the audience reached. This is because virtually every means of communicating ideas in today's mass society requires the expenditure of money (at 19).

Attempts by Congress to place limits on a candidate's ability to spend a candidates own money to advertise his/her positions on the issues and to attack their opponents, according to the Court, struck at First Amendment freedoms. As a result the Court invalidated limits on a candidate's campaign expenditures, except for candidates who agreed to accept such limits in exchange for receiving federal matching funds in presidential election campaigns. In doing so, however, the Court rejected the arguments that limits on expenditures were essential to maintain genuine competition in the electoral arena. Unlimited campaign expenditures might enable the wealthy and those supported by the wealthy to dominate the electoral arena, perhaps drowning out in effect the voices of the poorer candidates or candidates unable to accumulate a huge campaign war chest. But the Court's opinion rejected ". . . the concept that government may restrict the speech of some elements of our society in order to enhance the relative voice of others . . .[ as] wholly foreign to the First

Amendment, which was designed 'to secure the widest possible dissemination of information from diverse and antagonistic sources' . . . " (at 49).

Against the Court's view, Justices Marshall and White both argued that removing the advantages of money can enhance the exchange of ideas and thus serve fundamental First Amendment values. In Justice White's words:

> It is critical to obviate or dispel the impression that federal elections are purely and simply a function of money, that federal offices are bought and sold or that political races are reserved for those who have the facility—and the stomach—for doing whatever it takes to bring together those interests, groups, and individuals that can raise or contribute large fortunes in order to prevail at the polls (at 65).

Justice Thurgood Marshall shared this view, arguing that the interest advanced by expenditure limits on campaigns and by individual wealthy candidates is the "interest in promoting the reality and appearance of equal access to the political arena" (at 287).

The Court did, however, permit Congress to place limits on the size of political contributions to candidates' election campaigns. The Court accepted the argument that allowing unlimited contributions to candidates could serve to corrupt the electoral process, allowing wealthy contributors to "buy" candidates through such contributions. Although such contribution limits in the Court's view did close off one potential channel for contributors to express their viewpoints, they did not prevent contributors from expressing their views independently of the candidates' campaign organizations. For example, the contribution limit upheld by the Court prevents someone with the wealth of a Donald Trump from giving unlimited amounts to candidates who support casino gambling. They would not prevent Mr. Trump, however, from producing his own advertisements extolling the benefits of casino gambling and endorsing by name candidates for public office who share his views; nor would they prevent him from spending unlimited amounts of his own money were he to seek public office himself.

The Court then accepted limits on the amount anyone can give directly to a candidate, accepting the argument that direct contributions can be corrupting and that stopping such corruption and the appearance of such corruption is a sufficiently "compelling state interest" to justify the limited infringement on free speech that such contribution limits entail. But the Court rejected limits on how much either a candidate can spend on his own campaign or how much a noncandidate may spend independently of the candidate's campaign organization in support of a particular candidate as not justified. The Court rejected the argument that the expenditure of vast sums of money for one side of a political campaign itself endangers the open competition of ideas. They opted instead to view the right to spend whatever one pleases to advance one's ideas as a core First Amendment freedom. They in effect endorsed the cliché that "money talks."

Similarly, in *First National Bank of Boston v. Bellotti*, (1978) the Court rejected an effort by the state of Massachusetts to forbid corporations from spending corporate funds to pay for campaign advertising in referenda campaigns. Massachusetts had felt that corporations were permitted by law to accumulate vast sums of money, far outstripping the ability of individuals to compete. The state enacted a limit on corporate participation in campaigns in response to large corporate-sponsored advertising to defeat attempts by the state to amend its state constitution to permit a progressive income tax. Such a tax taxes those earning large incomes at a higher rate than those earning low incomes. Presumably corporate executives found such a tax system contrary to their interests, and they therefore used their control over corporate accounts to attempt to defeat it. Those lower-income groups favoring the progressive income tax did not have ready access to such large amounts of money and could, in effect, be drowned out by corporate advertising. Here too, however, the Supreme Court rejected any efforts to place limits on the expenditure of money to advance particular points of view.

Whether these Court decisions, which have stymied legislative efforts to equalize the resources potentially available to contending sides in political debate, actually stifle the competition of ideas is a matter of judgment. The candidate who spends the most does not always win, but the availability of vast amounts of money to one side in a political contest can discourage others from even attempting to compete. As long as the Supreme Court equates the spending of money for the dissemination of ideas with free speech itself, the free marketplace of ideas may be in danger of monopoly control. As long as regulation of campaign expenditures applies equally to all sides in a debate it may be difficult for some of us to understand how such regulations can be seen as suppressing free speech.

**Question 4**   *Does the Constitution protect us from private institutions which interfere with our liberties and rights?*

Among the most common political phrases in every day American speech is "They can't do that to me, that's unconstitutional." Many of us believe that every perceived injustice from whatever source must violate the Constitution. In fact this is very often not true. The Constitution protects us only from certain kinds of abuse and only from abuse that is directly attributable to government. Many threats to our personal autonomy and freedom of action today, however, arise from nongovernmental sources. At a time when corporate power stretches across continents, far beyond the jurisdiction of any government, we can expect to be subject to potentially arbitrary decisions limiting our choices from a variety of actors. It is important, therefore, to understand the limited reach of our constitutional protections.

The protections for rights and liberties included in the United States constitution restrict only government. The Constitution was designed initially to allocate and assign power to the national or federal government and to limit the capacity of that government to oppress citizens. Following the Civil War and the adoption of the Thirteenth, Fourteenth, and Fifteenth Amendments, new restrictions were placed on the state governments (and by necessary implication on local governments which are viewed as subordinate to state governments.) In addition new powers were given to the national government to protect individual rights and liberties from state encroachment. With the exception of the Thirteenth Amendment's prohibition on "involuntary servitude" throughout the United States, nothing in the Constitution limits the capacity of individuals or purely private institutions from practically interfering with our ability to exercise rights or liberties we might assume we have.

For example, what if your private employer were to decide to hire only Republicans as employees? You could be denied employment, in effect punished, for holding a political belief disapproved by your employer. Although today Congress and the states have generally, through civil rights laws, forbidden private employers from discriminating against employees or potential clients on the basis of race or gender, the Constitution itself has not been interpreted by the Supreme Court as forbidding such conduct. In other words the Constitution in permitting Congress to regulate business through its power to regulate commerce among the states has allowed Congress, when it so chooses, to forbid private racial discrimination within and by businesses engaged in interstate commerce. The Constitution did not force Congress or the states to forbid such discrimination. In fact for decades the Supreme Court argued that the Constitution did not permit Congress to interfere with so-called private discrimination. The states were always free in the exercise of their so-called "police powers," their powers to regulate morality and protect public safety and welfare, to outlaw private discrimination, but for most of our nation's history the states chose to do nothing about it.

To understand how, when, and why most private conduct practically interfering with what we might think of as basic liberties and rights remains free from constitutional restraint requires us to review what is known as the state action doctrine.

A review of the Bill of Rights should make it clear that the restrictions involved are directed at government action. The First Amendment, for example, begins with the words: "Congress shall make no laws respecting an establishment of religion or prohibiting the free exercise thereof." Clearly this restriction is addressed to Congress. The Fourteenth Amendment, which was designed principally to assure that those who had been held in slavery would have the same rights as other citizens, begins with the phrase "No state shall . . . "

When, following the Civil War and the adoption of the Fourteenth Amendment, Congress attempted to assure that former slaves and other African-Americans would be free from some manifestations of private discrimination in the use of such "public accommodations" as privately owned hotels, theaters and railroads, the U.S. Supreme Court was called upon to decide whether Section 5 of the Fourteenth Amendment authorized Congress to restrict or punish such privately initiated discrimination.

Section 5 gave to Congress "the power to enforce this article by appropriate legislation." In deciding what this phrase meant, the Supreme Court in the *Civil Rights Cases* of 1883 assessed in detail the actual language of the Fourteenth Amendment.

> The first section of the Fourteenth Amendment . . . after declaring who shall be citizens of the United States and of the several states, is prohibitory in it character, and prohibitory upon the states. . . . It is state action of a particular character that is prohibited. Individual invasion of individual rights is not the subject matter of the amendment. . . . It nullifies and makes void all state legislation, and state action of every kind, which impairs the privileges and immunities of citizens of the United States, or which injures them in life, liberty, or property without due process of law, or which denies to any of them the equal protection of the laws (at 11).

In the words of Justice Joseph P. Bradley, writing for all but one of the justices then on the U.S. Supreme Court, the Amendment then goes on to authorize Congress to enforce its provisions through "appropriate legislation." But, he asks, "[t]o enforce what"? His answer:

> To enforce the prohibition. To adopt appropriate legislation for correcting the effects of such prohibited state law and state acts, and thus to render them effectively null, void and innocuous. . . . And so. . . until some state law has been passed, or some state action through its officers or agents has been taken, adverse to the rights of citizens sought to be protected by the Fourteenth Amendment, no legislation of the United States under said amendment . . . , can be

called into activity, for the prohibitions of the amendment are against state laws and acts done under state authority (at 11–12).

Although in his dissenting opinion Justice Harlan argued that the Court had misread the intent behind the Fourteenth Amendment, the fundamental principle that only actions attributable to government are restricted by the Constitution has remained virtually unchallenged since. There has, however, been considerable dispute within the Court over the years concerning exactly how much state involvement there must be in a challenged action to trigger constitutional protections. In the contemporary world there are very few activities about which it can be said that government has absolutely no role or responsibility. The line between what is "public" and what is purely "private" is often blurred.

In 1948 in *Shelley v. Kraemer* (1948) the Supreme Court showed in an unusual case one way the state action doctrine can work. It was very common in the past for deeds to property to include "racially restricted covenants" which prohibited sale of the property to nonwhites and often to non-Christians as well. When Shelley, a black man, purchased some land in Missouri in 1948, a white neighbor, Kraemar, objected, contending the sale violated a racially restrictive covenant barring sale to members of "the Negro or Mongolian" race. When the case eventually reached the United States Supreme Court, the Court found the covenant itself to be constitutionally unobjectionable. The Fourteenth Amendment, according to the Court "erect[ed] no shield against merely private conduct, however discriminatory or wrongful. . . . [T]herefore . . . the restrictive agreement standing alone cannot be regarded as a violation of any rights guaranteed . . .by the Fourteenth Amendment" (at 13).

Private contracts, however, are not always self-executing. If both parties to the contract follow their obligations, then even racially discriminatory agreements are permitted by the Constitution. If someone seeks to ignore the contract, however, then the usual recourse is to the courts to seek enforcement of the private agreement. When Kraemer went to the state courts to seek enforcement of the racially restrictive covenant, the Supreme Court ruled that "the action of state courts and judicial officers in their official capacities is to be regarded as action of the State within the meaning of the Fourteenth Amendment. . . " (at 14). Through judicial enforcement what had been immune from constitutional challenge had now become unconstitutional. The involvement of the state courts had triggered constitutional protections.

Although many "state action" cases have concerned efforts to overcome racial discrimination through the Equal Protection clause of the Fourteenth Amendment, actually all efforts to enforce constitutional rights, when private persons or institutions are affected, must first face the hurdle of the requirement that some level of "state action" be found.

Today the Supreme Court insists on a high level of state involvement in an actual decision challenged on constitutional grounds before it will rule that constitutional requirements applicable to government must be followed by ostensibly private institutions.

Under the Fourteenth Amendment, whenever a government agency makes a decision depriving you of some benefit or privilege, it must meet elemental requirements of due process. This is because the Due Process clause of the Fourteenth Amendment says that "No state . . . may deprive any person . . . of life, liberty, or property without due process of law." While what is involved in "due process" can vary depending on the circumstances and the nature of the deprivation in question, due process at least requires that the person suffering some loss at the hand of government have an opportunity to be heard before a decision is final and have some opportunity to appeal the decision made against him or her.

When the deprivation in question comes not from government directly but from some private source, the state action doctrine forces the courts to determine first whether the action of some apparently private institution "may be fairly treated as that of the state itself" (*Jackson v. Metropolitan Edison,* at 351, 1974). Many services upon which even life itself may sometimes depend are provided not by government but by private companies, such as electric utilities, which are, however, generally highly regulated by government. Until recently electricity in most communities was provided by government-regulated but privately owned monopolies. The Supreme Court's decision in *Jackson v. Metropolitan Edison* concerned the decision of a Pennsylvania electric power monopoly to terminate electric service to a customer without what she considered to be adequate notice and the opportunity for a hearing. Despite the fact that the specific termination procedures of the company were "allowed by a provision of its general tariff filed with the [Pennsylvania Public Utility] Commission," the Supreme Court held that Metropolitan Edison was not subject to the Fourteenth Amendment due process requirements that would have applied to a state-owned utility. State acceptance of a utility's policies even when accompanied by heavy and detailed state regulation is not enough to trigger constitutional protections. Before applying constitutional restraints the Court asks "whether there is a sufficiently close nexus between the State and the challenged action of the regulated entity so that the action of the latter may be fairly treated as that of the State itself" (at 351). Because the termination of service practices at issue in the case were initiated by the utility and simply accepted by the state rather than initiated by the state, the Court found insufficient connection to attribute the service termination to state action.

Following the *Jackson* decision, a series of other Supreme Court decisions made it increasingly difficult to subject private institutions to constitutional restraints even when those private institutions were implementing government policies and programs at public expense. For example, Medicaid, the government health care program for the poor, requires different levels of care at government expense in privately owned and operated nursing homes. Patients are reassigned to different levels of care according to guidelines issued by the government. Nonetheless, in *Blum v. Yaretsky* (1982) the Supreme Court said private nursing home decisions implementing these guidelines requiring transfer of patients to lower levels of care were not subject to due process requirements.

Because the decision to transfer a specific patient was made by a nursing home committee rather than by a government official, the Court ruled that Fourteenth Amendment due process procedural protections did not apply. Similarly in *Rendell-Baker v. Kohn* (1982) the Court ruled First Amendment free speech protections and Fourteenth Amendment due process requirements did not restrain a privately owned, yet nearly totally publicly funded, school for maladjusted students, which issued diplomas certified by a public school committee, from firing teachers who had publicly criticized the school's administration. According to the Court, "[t]he core issue presented in the case is not whether [the teachers] were discharged because of their speech or without adequate procedural protections, but whether the school's action in discharging them can fairly be seen as state action (at 839)." To put it simply they have no free speech protections against the school administration unless their action is "attributable to the state." And, according to the Court, "the State can be held responsible for a private decision only when it has exercised coercive power or has provided such significant encouragement either overt or covert, that the choice must in law be deemed to be that of the State" itself (at 840).

The lesson then for anyone concerned about the growing power over our lives exercised by nongovernmental institutions is that unless there is direct collusion between a private decision maker and government in a particular decision affecting our liberties, the actions of the private decision maker are not subject to constitutional guidelines. At a time when governments across America are increasingly "privatizing" government services; that is turning over to private institutions decision-making power over who gets services and benefits, the potential for a shrinking of the areas of our lives protected by constitutional rights and liberties is significant.

There has long been one area where it was thought that government could not escape constitutional protections for rights and liberties by giving government authority to private institutions. These are activities covered by what the Court has termed the public functions doctrine.

Some activities are so closely associated with government and the power of the state that they keep their governmental character no matter who carries them out. Because throughout most of the world, and even in parts of the United States, government has been responsible for the provision of electric power, the party suing in *Jackson v. Metropolitan Edison* asserted that electric utilities should be considered public functions under the state action doctrine. In rejecting this argument, Chief Justice Rehnquist limited the category of public functions to the "exercise by a private entity of powers traditionally exclusively reserved to the state" (at 352–353). Applying this reasoning to the *Jackson* case itself, he argued that because electric power production did not involve government authority delegated to Metropolitan Edison by the state "which is traditionally associated with sovereignty, such as eminent domain. . . . [,the power of government to seize private property for public use]," it could not be considered for constitutional purposes a "public function."

Because in America virtually every activity imaginable from the running of schools to prisons has at some point in our history been exercised by private institutions, it is difficult to think of any contemporary activity, except perhaps the running of elections, that has been recognized as both traditionally and exclusively the prerogative of the state. This being the case it is possible for government to lesson the scope of our constitutional protections by turning over to private institutions ever-increasing aspects of our lives. The time could come when government may not be the greatest threat to our liberties. If that happens, then the significance of our Constitutional rights and liberties could significantly erode.

## REFERENCES

*Blum v. Yaretsky,* 457 U.S. 991 (1982).

*Buckley v. Valeo,* 424 U.S. 1 (1976).

*Civil Rights Cases of 1883,* 109 U.S. 3 (1883).

*Douglas v. California,* 372 U.S. 353 (1963).

*First National Bank of Boston v. Bellotti,* 435 U.S. 765 (1978).

*Gideon v. Wainwright,* 372 U.S. 335 (1963).

*Griffin v. Illinios,* 351 U.S. 512 (1956).

*Harris v. McRae,* 448 U.S. 297 (1980).

*Jackson v. Metropolitan Edison*, 419 U.S. 345 (1974).

*Maher v. Roe*, 432 U.S. 464 (1977).

*Miami Herald Publishing Co. v. Tornillo*, 418 U.S. 241 (1974).

*Red Lion Broadcasting Co., Inc. v. Federal Comunications Commission*, 395 U.S. 367 (1969).

*Rendell-Baker v. Kohn*, 447 U.S. 830 (1982).

*Rust v. Sullivan*, 500 U.S. 173 (1991).

*Shelley v. Kraemer*, 334 U.S. 1 (1948).

# Conclusion: What Is the Future of Civil Rights and Civil Liberties in America?

The future of civil rights and liberties is always insecure. Every period in our history has produced new challenges and setbacks, but at the same time much progress has been made in the over two centuries since the Constitution has served as the governing charter of America. The degree to which our liberties are under threat is, like every other question concerning the Constitution, a matter of opinion and differing interpretation. While protections for the freedom of speech and of the press have probably never been as extensive in the past as they are today, the strict "wall of separation" of church and state that emerged from Court rulings from the 1940s through the 1980s appears to be showing some cracks. This slight erosion in separation of church and state can of course be seen as a pulling back by the Court from rulings which some have seen as jeopardizing the freedom of religion and religious expression also guaranteed by the First Amendment. But Court rulings in the 1990s have also limited our ability to challenge successfully government actions that make it difficult for us to follow our consciences.

The right to privacy, first clearly enunciated by the Supreme Court in the *Griswold v. Connecticut* 1963 decision protecting the right of married couples to use birth control without state interference, later led to the right of women to elect to have an abortion. Court rulings related to privacy from the 1980s on have, however, been marked by an increasing reluctance by the U.S. Supreme Court to extend that right of privacy or personal autonomy to other areas, such as protection for homosexual relationships from state regulation to guaranteeing a right to physician-assisted suicide to the terminally ill. At the same time as the Court rejected these claimed new rights, it has also permitted increasing limits on a woman's right to choose, first enunciated in *Roe v. Wade*.

In the area of civil rights the Court has also been moving in the direction of moving away from some of its more expansive rulings of the 1960s through the 1980s. Increasingly the Court has rejected affirmative action programs designed to assist racial minorities in favor of a color-blind approach that subjects any racial classifications to the same strict scrutiny. Today when considering whether a challenged government policy allegedly disadvantages a member of a racial minority or the white majority, the Court generally approaches it with the same level of extreme skepticism. Whether this changed Court view is a step backward in civil rights or is simply a maturing of our understanding of what racial equality requires is for all of us to judge for ourselves. But it is yet another indication that the scope of civil rights and civil liberties protections in America has been changing in recent decades, and that change can be expected to continue.

Because what the Constitution means at any time is determined by the Supreme Court justices who interpret it, the changes we have seen in constitutional interpretation reflect in large part the changes in the personnel on the U.S. Supreme Court. During the period when the Court began to place limits on the expansion of civil rights and civil liberties protections during the 1970s to the present, the Court has been increasingly dominated by justices appointed by Republican presidents. Today there are only two Democrats on the Supreme Court, both of whom were appointed by President Clinton. Should any of the current justices retire or die before the end of President Clinton's term, it appears likely that the Republican-controlled United States Senate, which must confirm presidential nominations to the U.S. Supreme Court, will delay confirmation of any appointment he may make in order to leave the vacancy in place for the next president to fill. Should the next president be a Republican, in all likelihood the trend of the current Court to limit further expansion of civil liberties and civil rights will continue.

Future threats to civil liberties and civil rights may, however, be more profound than just those traditionally caused by the changing political fortunes of the political parties and shifting personnel on the courts. Technological trends and broader cultural trends in how we view government may pose even more fundamental threats to civil liberties and civil rights. As was noted in Chapter 6 the Internet and other technological innovations affecting communication may pose significant challenges to our understanding of how we protect the values protected by the First Amendment freedom of expression. The proliferation of hate groups advocating violence, possibly mobilizing their supporters over the Internet, will tempt many to wonder about the viability of free speech doctrines which permit advocacy of violence. The fact that such groups are noticed only by those who seek them out and stay largely isolated from competing ideas and values can subject the value of the free market-place of ideas to doubt. Today and in the future those advocating danger-ous ideas may not subject themselves to the competition of the marketplace as each of us becomes more isolated from social forces which we elect to avoid.

Traditional safeguards against government oppression may also become less valuable as government itself shrinks because of ideological suspicion of "big government." As government is increasingly replaced by private arrangements and enterprises, constitutional safeguards for pri-vacy, liberty, and even civil rights become inoperable. As we saw in Chapter 6 for constitutional protections to be triggered there must be some state action jeopardizing rights protected by the Constitution from only government infringement. Private retaliation for our exercise of our political or religious freedoms is not restricted by a Constitution which was designed to constrain government tyranny. The less we are depend-ent on government, then, the less we are protected by constitutional con-straints on government. The more dependent we are on the private sector and corporate power, the more our freedom of expression and action can be restrained. Should the move toward privatization lead to a loosening of civil rights laws which regulate business and now protect us from dis-crimination on racial or religious grounds from private employers and service providers, the Constitution, under current Court interpretations of the State Action Doctrine, will provide us no recourse. Such a repeal of civil rights laws seems unlikely, but equally unlikely is an effort to extend to the private sector protections for our liberties which today restrain only government. A government that governs least may indeed threaten our liberties less, but a private sector which grows to fill the power vacuum left by a weakened government can threaten our individ-ual freedoms. An abusive government can be restrained by the Constitu-tion, but an abusive private sector can be restrained only by government. Before we weaken government too much, we should consider how private power centers can themselves threaten liberty free from constitutional restraints.

## REFERENCES

*Griswold v. Connecticut*, 381 U.S. 479 (1965).

*Roe v. Wade*, 410 U.S. 113 (1973).

# The Constitution
# of the
# United States

**THE PREAMBLE**

We the People of the United States, in Order to form a more perfect Union, establish Justice, insure domestic Tranquility, provide for the common defense, promote the general Welfare, and secure the Blessings of Liberty to ourselves and our Posterity, do ordain and establish this Constitution for the United States of America.

**ARTICLE I**

*Section 1* All legislative Powers herein granted shall be vested in a Congress of the United States, which shall consist of a Senate and House of Representatives.

*Section 2* The House of Representatives shall be composed of Members chosen every second Year by the People of the several States, and the Electors in each State shall have the Qualifications requisite for Electors of the most numerous Branch of the State Legislature.

No Person shall be a Representative who shall not have attained to the Age of twenty five Years, and been seven Years a Citizen of the United States, and who shall not, when elected, be an Inhabitant of that State in which he shall be chosen.

Representatives and direct Taxes[1] shall be apportioned among the several States which may be included within this Union, according to their respective Numbers, *which shall be determined by adding to the whole Number of free Persons, including those bound to Service for a Term of Years, and excluding Indians not taxed, three fifths of all other Persons.*[2] The actual Enumeration shall be made within three Years after the first Meeting of the Congress of the United States, and within every subsequent Term of ten Years, in such Manner as they shall by Law direct. The Number of Representatives shall not exceed one for every thirty Thousand, but each State shall have at least one Representative; and until each enumeration shall be made, the State of New Hampshire shall be entitled to chuse three, Massachusetts eight, Rhode-Island and Providence Plantations one, Connecticut five, New-York six, New Jersey four, Pennsylvania eight, Delaware one, Maryland six, Virginia ten, North Carolina five, South Carolina five, and Georgia three.

When vacancies happen in the Representation from any State, the Executive Authority thereof shall issue Writs of Election to fill such Vacancies.

The House of Representatives shall chuse their Speaker and other Officers; and shall have the sole Power of Impeachment.

*Section 3* The Senate of the United States shall be composed of two Senators from each State, *chosen by the Legislature thereof,*[3] for six Years; and each Senator shall have one Vote.

Immediately after they shall be assembled in Consequence of the first Election, they shall be divided as equally as may be into three Classes. The Seats of the Senators of the first Class shall be vacated at the Expiration of the second Year, of the second Class at the Expiration of the fourth Year, and of the third Class at the Expiration of the sixth Year, so that one third may be chosen every second Year; *and if Vacancies happen by Resignation, or otherwise, during the Recess of the Legislature of any State, the Executive thereof may make temporary Appointments until the next Meeting of the Legislature, which shall then fill such Vacancies.*[4]

No person shall be a Senator who shall not have attained to the Age of thirty Years, and been nine Years a Citizen of the United States, and

---

[1]Modified by the 16th Amendment
[2]Replaced by Section 2, 14th Amendment
[3]Repealed by the 17th Amendment
[4]Modified by the 17th Amendment

who shall not, when elected, be an inhabitant of that State for which he shall be chosen.

The Vice President of the United States shall be President of the Senate, but shall have no Vote, unless they be equally divided.

The Senate shall chuse their other Officers, and also a President pro tempore, in the Absence of the Vice President, or when he shall exercise the Office of President of the United States.

The Senate shall have the sole Power to try all Impeachments. When sitting for that Purpose, they shall be on Oath or Affirmation. When the President of the United States is tried, the Chief Justice shall preside: And no Person shall be convicted without the Concurrence of two thirds of the Members present.

Judgment in Cases of Impeachment shall not extend further than to removal from Office, and disqualification to hold and enjoy any Office of honor, Trust or Profit under the United States; but the Party convicted shall nevertheless be liable and subject to Indictment, Trial, Judgment and Punishment, according to law.

*Section 4* The Times, Places and Manner of holding Elections for Senators and Representatives, shall be prescribed in each State by the Legislature thereof; but the Congress may at any time by Law make or alter such Regulations, except as to the Places of chusing Senators.

The Congress shall assemble at least once in every Year, *and such Meeting shall be on the first Monday in December, unless they shall by Law appoint a different Day.*[5]

*Section 5* Each House shall be the Judge of the Elections, Returns and Qualifications of its own Members, and a Majority of each shall constitute a Quorum to do Business; but a smaller Number may adjourn from day to day, and may be authorized to compel the Attendance of absent Members, in such Manner, and under the Penalties as each House may provide.

Each House may determine the Rules of its Proceedings, punish its Members for disorderly Behaviour, and, with the Concurrence of two thirds, expel a Member.

Each House shall keep a Journal of its Proceedings, and from time to time publish the same, excepting such Parts as may in their Judgment require Secrecy; and the Yeas and Nays of the Members of either House on any question shall, at the Desire of one fifth of those Present, be entered on the Journal.

[5]Changed by the 20th Amendment

Neither House, during the Session of Congress, shall, without the Consent of the other, adjourn for more than three days, nor to any other place than that in which the two Houses shall be sitting.

*Section 6* The Senators and Representatives shall receive a Compensation for their Services, to be ascertained by Law, and paid out of the Treasury of the United States. They shall in all Cases, except Treason, Felony and Breach of the Peace, be privileged from Arrest during their Attendance at the Session of their respective Houses, and in going to and returning from the same; and for any Speech or Debate in either House, they shall not be questioned in any other Place.

No Senator or Representative, shall, during the time for which he was elected, be appointed to any civil Office under the Authority of the United States, which shall have been created, or the Emoluments whereof shall have been encreased during such time; and no Person holding any Office under the United States, shall be a Member of either House during his Continuance in Office.

*Section 7* All Bills for raising Revenue shall originate in the House of Representatives; but the Senate may propose or concur with Amendments as on other Bills.

Every Bill which shall have passed the House of Representatives and the Senate, shall, before it becomes a Law, be presented to the President of the United States; if he approve he shall sign it, but if not he shall return it, with his Objections to that House in which it shall have originated, who shall enter the Objections at large on their Journal, and proceed to reconsider it. If after such Reconsideration two thirds of that House shall agree to pass the Bill, it shall be sent, together with the Objections, to the other House, by which it shall likewise be reconsidered, and if approved by two thirds of that House, it shall become a Law. But in all such Cases the Votes of both Houses shall be determined by yeas and Nays, and the Names of the Persons voting for and against the Bill shall be entered on the Journal of each House respectively. If any Bill shall not be returned by the President within ten Days (Sundays excepted) after it shall have been presented to him, the Same shall be a Law, in like Manner as if he had signed it, unless the Congress by their Adjournment prevent its Return, in which Case it shall not be a Law.

Every Order, Resolution, or Vote to which the Concurrence of the Senate and House of Representatives may be necessary (except on a question of Adjournment) shall be presented to the President of the United States; and before the Same shall take Effect, shall be approved by him, or being disapproved by him, shall be repassed by two thirds of the Senate and House of Representatives, according to the Rules and Limitations prescribed in the Case of a Bill.

*Section 8* The Congress shall have Power To lay and collect Taxes, Duties, Imposts and Excises, to pay the Debts and provide for the common Defence and general Welfare of the United States; but all Duties, Imposts and Excises shall be uniform throughout the United States.

To borrow Money on the Credit of the United States;

To regulate Commerce with foreign Nations, and among the several States, and with the Indian Tribes;

To establish an uniform Rule of Naturalization, and uniform Laws on the subject of Bankruptcies throughout the United States;

To coin Money, regulate the Value thereof, and of foreign Coin, and fix the Standard of Weights and Measures;

To provide for the Punishment of counterfeiting the Securities and current Coin of the United States;

To establish Post Offices and post Roads;

To promote the Progress of Science and useful Arts, by securing for limited Times to Authors and Inventors the exclusive Right to their respective Writings and Discoveries;

To constitute Tribunals inferior to the supreme Court;

To define and punish Piracies and Felonies committed on the high Seas, and Offences against the Law of Nations;

To declare War, grant Letters of Marque and Reprisal, and make Rules concerning Captures on Land and Water;

To raise and support Armies, but no Appropriation of Money to that Use shall be for a longer Term than two Years;

To provide and maintain a Navy;

To make Rules for the Government and Regulation of the land and naval Forces;

To provide for calling for the Militia to execute the Laws of the Union, suppress Insurrections and repel Invasions;

To provide for organizing, arming, and disciplining, the Militia, and for governing such Part of them as may be employed in the Service of the United States, reserving to the States respectively, the Appointment of the Officers, and the Authority of training the Militia according to the discipline prescribed by Congress;

To exercise exclusive Legislation in all Cases whatsoever, over such District (not exceeding ten Miles square) as may, by Cession of particular States, and the Acceptance of Congress, become the Seat of the Government of the United States, and to exercise like Authority over all Places purchased by the Consent of the Legislature of the State in which the Same shall be, for the Erection of Forts, Magazines, Arsenals, dock-Yards, and other needful Buildings;—And

To make all Laws which shall be necessary and proper for carrying into Execution the foregoing Powers, and all other Powers vested by this

Constitution in the Government of the United States, or in any Department or Officer thereof.

*Section 9* The Migration Importation of such Persons as any of the States now existing shall think proper to admit, shall not be prohibited by the Congress prior to the Year one thousand eight hundred and eight, but a Tax or Duty may be imposed on such Importation, not exceeding ten dollars for each Person.

The privilege of the Writ of Habeas Corpus shall not be suspended, unless when in Cases of Rebellion or Invasion the public Safety may require it.

No Bill of Attainder or ex post facto Laws shall be passed.

No Capitation, or other direct, Tax shall be laid, unless in Proportion to the Census or Enumeration herein before directed to be taken.[6]

No Tax or Duty shall be laid on Articles exported from any State.

No Preference shall be given by any Regulation of Commerce or Revenue to the Ports of one State over those of another; nor shall Vessels bound to, or from, one State, be obliged to enter, clear, or pay Duties in another.

No Money shall be drawn from the Treasury, but in Consequence of Appropriations made by Law; and a regular Statement and Account of the Receipts and Expenditures of all public Money shall be published from time to time.

No Title of Nobility shall be granted by the United States; And no Person holding any Office of Profit or Trust under them, shall, without the Consent of Congress, accept of any present, Emolument, Office, or Title, of any kind whatever, from any King, Prince, or foreign State.

*Section 10* No State shall enter into any Treaty, Alliance, or Confederation; grant Letters of Marque and Reprisal; coin Money; emit Bills of Credit; make any Thing but gold and silver Coin a Tender in Payment of Debts; pass any Bill of Attainder, ex post facto Law, or Law impairing the Obligation of Contracts, or grant any Title of Nobility.

No State shall, without the Consent of the Congress, lay any Imposts or Duties on Imports or Exports, except what may be absolutely necessary for executing its inspection Laws: and the net Produce of all Duties and Imposts, laid by any State on Imports or Exports, shall be for the Use of the Treasury of the United States; and all such Laws shall be subject to the Revision and Controul of the Congress.

No State shall, without the Consent of Congress, lay any Duty of Tonnage, keep Troops, or Ships of War in time of Peace, enter into any Agreement or Compact with another State, or with a foreign Power, or

[6]Modified by the 16th Amendment

engage in War, unless actually invaded, or in such imminent Danger as will not admit of Delay.

## ARTICLE II

*Section 1* The executive Power shall be vested in a President of the United States of America. He shall hold his Office during the Term of four Years and, together with the Vice President, chosen for the same Term, be elected as follows:

Each State shall appoint, in such Manner as the Legislature thereof may direct, a Number of Electors, equal to the whole Number of Senators and Representatives to which the State may be entitled in the Congress: but no Senator or Representative, or Person holding an Office of Trust or Profit under the United States, shall be appointed an Elector.

The Electors shall meet in their respective States, and vote by Ballot for two Persons, of whom one at least shall not be an Inhabitant of the same State with themselves. And they shall make a List of all the Persons voted for, and of the Number of Votes for each; which List they shall sign and certify, and transmit sealed to the Seat of the Government of the United States, directed to the President of the Senate. The President of the Senate shall, in the Presence of the Senate and House of Representatives, open all the Certificates, and the Votes shall then be counted. The Person having the greatest Number of Votes shall be the President, if such Number be a Majority of the whole Number of Electors appointed; and if there be more than one who have such Majority and have an equal Number of Votes, then the House of Representatives shall immediately chuse by Ballot one of them for President; and if no person have a Majority, then from the five highest on the List the said House shall in like Manner chuse the President. But in chusing the President, the Votes shall be taken by States, the Representation from each State having one Vote; A quorum for this Purpose shall consist of a Member or Members from two thirds of the States, and a Majority of all the States shall be necessary to a Choice. In every Case, after the Choice of the President, the person having the greatest Number of Votes of the Electors shall be the Vice President. But if there should remain two or more who have equal Vote, the Senate shall chuse from them by Ballot the Vice President.[7]

The Congress may determine the Time of chusing the Electors, and the Day on which they shall give their Votes; which Day shall be the same throughout the United States.

---

[7]Changed by the 12th and 20th Amendments

No Person except a natural born Citizen, or a Citizen of the United States, at the time of the Adoption of this Constitution, shall be eligible to the Office of President; neither shall any Person be eligible to that Office who shall not have attained to the Age of thirty five Years, and been fourteen Years a Resident within the United States.

In Case of the Removal of the President from Office, or of his Death, Resignation, or Inability to discharge the Powers and Duties of the said Office, the same shall devolve on the Vice President, and the Congress may by Law provide for the Case of Removal, Death, Resignation, or Inability, both of the President and Vice President, declaring what Officer shall then act as President, and such Officer shall act accordingly, until the Disability be removed, or a President shall be elected.[8]

The President shall, at stated Times, receive for his Services, a Compensation, which shall neither be encreased nor diminished during the Period of which he shall have been elected, and he shall not receive within that Period any other Emolument from the United States, or any of them.

Before he enter on the Execution of his Office, he shall take the following Oath or Affirmation:—"I do solemnly swear (or affirm) that I will faithfully execute the Office of President of the United States, and will to the best of my Ability, preserve, protect and defend the Constitution of the United States."

*Section 2* The President shall be the Commander in Chief of the Army and Navy of the United States, and of the Militia of the several States, when called into the actual Service of the United States, he may require the Opinion, in writing, of the principal Officer in each of the executive Departments, upon any Subject relating to the Duties of their respective Offices, and he shall have the Power to grant Reprieves and Pardons for Offences against the United States, except in Cases of Impeachment.

He shall have Power, by and with the Advice and Consent of the Senate to make Treaties, provided two thirds of the Senators present concur; and he shall nominate, and by and with the Advice and Consent of the Senate, shall appoint Ambassadors, other public Ministers and Consuls, Judges of the supreme Court, and all other Officers of the United States, whose Appointments are not herein otherwise provided for, and which shall be established by Law: but the Congress may by Law vest the Appointment of such inferior Officers, as they think proper, in the President alone, in the Courts of Law, or in the Heads of Departments.

The President shall have Power to fill up all Vacancies that may happen during the Recess of the Senate, by granting Commissions which shall expire at the End of their next Session.

[8]Modified by the 25th Amendment

*Section 3*  He shall from time to time give to the Congress Information of the State of the Union, and recommend to their Consideration such Measures as he shall judge necessary and expedient; he may, on extraordinary Occasions, convene both Houses, or either of them, and in Case of Disagreement between them, with Respect to the Time of Adjournment, he may adjourn them to such Time as he shall think proper; he shall receive Ambassadors and other public Ministers; he shall take Care that the Laws be faithfully executed, and shall Commission all the Officers of the United States.

*Section 4*  The President, Vice President and all civil Officers of the United States, shall be removed from Office on Impeachment for, and Conviction of, Treason, Bribery, or other High Crimes and Misdemeanors.

## ARTICLE III

*Section 1*  The judicial Power of the United States, shall be vested in one supreme Court, and in such inferior Courts as the Congress may from time to time ordain and establish. The Judges, both the supreme and inferior Courts, shall hold their Offices during good Behaviour, and shall, at stated Times, receive for their Services, a Compensation, which shall not be diminished during their Continuance in Office.

*Section 2*  The judicial Power shall extend to all Cases, in Law and Equity, arising under this Constitution, the Laws of the United States, and Treaties made, or which shall be made, under their Authority;—to all Cases affecting Ambassadors, other public Ministers and Consuls;—to all Cases of admiralty and maritime Jurisdiction;—to Controversies to which the United States shall be a Party;—to Controversies between two or more States; *between a State and Citizens of another State;*[9]—between Citizens of different States;—between Citizens of the same State claiming Lands under Grants of different States, and between a State, or the Citizens thereof, and foreign States, Citizens, or Subjects.

In all Cases affecting Ambassadors, other public Ministers and Consuls, and those in which a State shall be Party, the supreme Court shall have original Jurisdiction. In all the other Cases before mentioned, the supreme Court shall have appellate Jurisdiction, both as to Law and Fact, with such Exceptions, and under such Regulations as Congress shall make.

The Trial of all Crimes, except in Cases of Impeachment, shall be by Jury; and such Trial shall be held in the State where the said Crimes

[9]Modified by the 11th Amendment

shall have been committed; but when not committed within any State, the Trial shall be at such Place or Places as the Congress may by Law have directed.

*Section 3* Treason against the United States, shall consist only in levying War against them, or in adhering to their Enemies, giving them Aid and Comfort. No Persons shall be convicted of Treason unless on the Testimony of two Witnesses to the same overt Act, or on Confession in open Court.

The Congress shall have Power to declare the Punishment of Treason, but no Attainder of Treason shall work Corruption of Blood, or Forfeiture except during the Life of the Person attainted.

## ARTICLE IV

*Section 1* Full Faith and Credit shall be given in each State to the public Acts, Records, and judicial Proceedings of every other State. And the Congress may by general Laws prescribe the Manner in which such Acts, Records and Proceedings shall be proved, and the Effect thereof.

*Section 2* The Citizens of each State shall be entitled to all Privileges and Immunities of Citizens in the several States.

A person charged in any State with Treason, Felony or other Crime, who shall flee from Justice, and be found in another State, shall on Demand of the executive Authority of the State from which he fled, be delivered up, to be removed to the State having jurisdiction of the Crime.

*No person held to Service or Labour in one State, under the Laws thereof, escaping into another, shall, in Consequence of any Law or Regulation therein, be discharged from such Service or Labour, but shall be delivered up on Claim of the Party to whom such Service or Labour may be due.*[10]

*Section 3* New States may be admitted by the Congress into this Union; but no new State shall be formed or erected within the Jurisdiction of any other State; nor any State to be formed by the Junction of two or more States, or Parts of States, without the Consent of the Legislatures of the States concerned as well as of the Congress.

The Congress shall have Power to dispose of and make all needful Rules and Regulations respecting the Territory or other Property belonging to the United States; and nothing in this Constitution shall be

---

[10]Repealed by the 13th Amendment

so construed as to Prejudice any Claims of the United States, or of any particular State.

*Section 4* The United States shall guarantee to every State in this Union a Republican Form of Government, and shall protect each of them against Invasion; and on Application of the Legislature, or of the Executive (when the Legislature cannot be convened) against domestic Violence.

## ARTICLE V

The Congress, whenever two thirds of both Houses shall deem it necessary, shall propose Amendments to this Constitution, or, on the Application of the Legislatures of two thirds of several States, shall call a Convention for proposing Amendments, which, in either Case, shall be valid to all Intents and Purposes, as Part of this Constitution, when ratified by the Legislatures of three fourths of the several States, or by Conventions in three fourths thereof, as the one or the other Mode of Ratification may be proposed by the Congress; Provided that no Amendment which may be made prior to the Year One thousand eight hundred and eight shall in any Manner affect the first and fourth Clauses in the Ninth Section of the first Article; and that no State, without its Consent, shall be deprived of its equal Suffrage in the Senate.

## ARTICLE VI

All Debts contracted and Engagements entered into, before the Adoption of this Constitution, shall be as valid against the United States under the Constitution, as under the Confederation.

This Constitution, and the Laws of the United States which shall be made in Pursuance thereof; and all Treaties made, or which shall be made, under the Authority of the United States, shall be the supreme Law of the Land; and the Judges in every State shall be bound thereby, any Thing in the Constitution or Laws of any State to the Contrary notwithstanding.

The Senators and Representatives before mentioned, and the Members of the several State Legislatures, and all executive and judicial Officers, both of the United States and of the several States, shall be bound by Oath or Affirmation, to support this Constitution; but no religious Test shall ever be required as a Qualification to any Office or public Trust under the United States.

## ARTICLE VII

The Ratification of the Conventions of nine States, shall be sufficient for the Establishment of this Constitution between the States so ratifying the Same.

*Done* in Convention by the Unanimous Consent of the States present the Seventeenth Day of September in the Year of our Lord one thousand seven hundred and Eighty seven and of the Independence of the United States of America the Twelfth *In Witness whereof We have hereunto subscribed our Names.*

## AMENDMENTS

### The Bill of Rights

[The first ten amendments were ratified on December 15, 1791, and form what is known as the "Bill of Rights."]

## AMENDMENT 1

Congress shall make no law respecting an establishment of religion, or prohibiting the free exercise thereof; or abridging the freedom of speech, or of the press; or the right of the people peaceably to assemble, and to petition the government for a redress of grievances.

## AMENDMENT 2

A well regulated Militia, being necessary to the security of a free State, the right of the people to keep and bear Arms, shall not be infringed.

## AMENDMENT 3

No Soldier shall, in time of peace be quartered in any house, without the consent of the Owner, nor in time of war, but in manner to be prescribed by law.

## AMENDMENT 4

The right of the people to be secure in their persons, houses, papers, and effects, against unreasonable searches and seizures, shall not be violated, and no Warrants shall issue, but upon probable cause, supported by Oath or affirmation, and particularly describing the place to be searched, and the persons or things to be seized.

## AMENDMENT 5

No person shall be held to answer for a capital, or otherwise infamous crime, unless on a presentment or indictment of a Grand jury, except in cases arising in the land or naval forces, or in the Militia, when in actual service in time of War or public danger; nor shall any person be subject for the same offence to be twice put in jeopardy of life or limb; nor shall be compelled in any criminal case to be a witness against himself, nor be deprived of life, liberty, or property, without due process of law; nor shall private property be taken for public use, without just compensation.

## AMENDMENT 6

In all criminal prosecutions, the accused shall enjoy the right to a speedy and public trial, by an impartial jury of the State and district wherein the crime shall have been committed, which district shall have been previously ascertained by law, and to be informed of the nature and cause of the accusation; to be confronted with the witnesses against him; to have compulsory process for obtaining Witnesses in his favor, and to have the Assistance of Counsel for his defense.

## AMENDMENT 7

In Suits at common law, where the value in controversy shall exceed twenty dollars, the right of trial by jury shall be preserved, and no fact tried by a jury shall be otherwise re-examined in any Court of the United States, than according to the rules of the common law.

## AMENDMENT 8

Excessive bail shall not be required, nor excessive fines imposed, nor cruel and unusual punishments inflicted.

## AMENDMENT 9

The enumeration in the Constitution, of certain rights, shall not be construed to deny or disparage others retained by the people.

## AMENDMENT 10

The powers not delegated to the United States by the Constitution, nor prohibited by it to the States, are reserved to the States respectively, or to the people.

## AMENDMENT 11

[Ratified February 7, 1795]

The Judicial power of the United States shall not be construed to extend to any suit in law or equity, commenced or prosecuted against one of the United States by Citizens of another State, or by Citizens or Subjects of any Foreign State.

## AMENDMENT 12

[Ratified June 15, 1804]

The Electors shall meet in their respective states, and vote by ballot for President and Vice-President, one of whom, at least, shall not be an inhabitant of the same state with themselves; they shall name in their ballots the person voted for as President, and in distinct ballots the person voted for as Vice-President, and they shall make distinct lists of all persons voted for as President, and of all persons voted for as Vice-President, and of the number of votes for each, which lists they shall sign and certify, and transmit sealed to the seat of the government of the United States, directed to the President of the Senate;—The President of the Senate shall, in presence of the Senate and House of Representatives, open all the certificates and the votes shall then be counted;—The person having the greatest number of votes for President, shall be the President, if such number be a majority of the whole number of Electors appointed; and if no person have such majority, then from the persons having the highest numbers not exceeding three on the list of those voted for as President, the House of Representatives shall choose immediately, by ballot, the President. But in choosing the President, the votes shall be taken by states, the representation from each state having one vote; a quorum for this purpose shall consist of a member or members from two-thirds of the states, and a majority of all states shall be necessary to a choice. And if the House of Representatives shall not choose a President whenever the right of choice shall devolve upon them, *before the fourth day of March next following*, then the Vice-President shall act as President, as in the case of the death or other constitutional disability of the President.[11] The person having the greatest number of votes as Vice-President, shall be the Vice-President, if such a number be a majority of the whole numbers of Electors appointed, and if no person have a majority, then from the two highest numbers on the list, the Senate shall choose the Vice-President; a quorum for the purpose shall consist of two-thirds of the whole number of Senators, and a majority of the whole number shall be necessary to a choice. But no person constitutionally ineligible to the office of President shall be eligible to that of Vice-President of the United States.

## AMENDMENT 13

[Ratified December 6, 1865]

*Section 1* Neither slavery nor involuntary servitude, except as a punishment for crime whereof the party shall have been duly convicted, shall exist within the United States, or any place subject to their jurisdiction.

*Section 2* Congress shall have power to enforce this article by appropriate legislation.

## AMENDMENT 14

[Ratified July 9, 1868]

*Section 1* All persons born or naturalized in the United States, and subject to the jurisdiction thereof, are citizens of the United States and of the State wherein they reside. No State shall make or enforce any law which shall abridge the privileges or immunities of citizens of the United States; nor shall any State deprive any person of life, liberty, or property, without due process of law; nor deny to any person within its jurisdiction the equal protection of the laws.

---

[11]Changed by the 20th Amendment

*Section 2*  Representatives shall be apportioned among the several States according to their respective numbers, counting the whole number of persons in each State, excluding Indians not taxed. But when the right to vote at any election for the choice of electors for President and Vice President of the United States, Representatives in Congress, the Executive and Judicial officers of a State, or the members of the Legislature thereof, is denied to any of the male inhabitants of such State, being twenty-one[12] years of age, and citizens of the United States, or in any way abridged, except for participation in rebellion, or other crime, the basis of representation therein shall be reduced in the proportion which the number of such male citizens shall bear to the whole number of male citizens twenty-one years of age in such State.

*Section 3*  No person shall be a Senator or Representative in Congress, or elector of President and Vice President, or hold any office, civil or military, under the United States, or under any State, who, having previously taken an oath, as a member of Congress, or as an officer of the United States, or as a member of any State legislature, or as an executive or judicial officer of any State, to support the Constitution of the United States, shall have engaged in insurrection or rebellion against the same, or given aid or comfort to the enemies thereof. But Congress may by a vote of two-thirds of each House, remove such disability.

*Section 4*  The validity of the public debt of the United States, authorized by law, including debts incurred for payment of pensions and bounties for services in suppressing insurrection or rebellion, shall not be questioned. But neither the United States nor any State shall assume or pay any debt or obligation incurred in aid of insurrection or rebellion against the United States, or any claim for the loss or emancipation of any slave; but all such debts, obligations and claims shall be held illegal and void.

*Section 5*  The Congress shall have power to enforce, by appropriate legislation, the provisions of this article.

### AMENDMENT 15

[Ratified February 3, 1870]

*Section 1*  The right of citizens of the United States to vote shall not be denied or abridged by the United States or by any State on account of race, color, or previous condition of servitude.

---

[12]Changed by the 26th Amendment

*Section 2* The Congress shall have power to enforce this article by appropriate legislation.

## AMENDMENT 16

[Ratified February 3, 1913]

The Congress shall have power to lay and collect taxes on incomes, from whatever source derived, without apportionment among the several States, and without regard to any census or enumeration.

## AMENDMENT 17

[Ratified April 8, 1913]

The Senate of the United States shall be composed of two Senators from each State, elected by the people thereof, for six years; and each Senator shall have one vote. The electors in each State shall have the qualifications requisite for electors of the most numerous branch of the State legislatures.

When vacancies happen in the representation of any State in the Senate, the executive authority of such State shall issue writs of election to fill such vacancies: *Provided*, That the Legislature of any State may empower the executive thereof to make temporary appointment until the people fill the vacancies by election as the legislature may direct.

This amendment shall not be so construed as to affect the election or term of any Senator chosen before it becomes valid as part of the Constitution.

## AMENDMENT 18

[Ratified January 16, 1919. Repealed December 5, 1933 by Amendment 21]

*Section 1* After one year from the ratification of this article the manufacture, sale, or transportation of intoxicating liquors within, the importation thereof into, or the exportation thereof from the United States and all territory subject to the jurisdiction thereof for beverage purposes is hereby prohibited.

*Section 2* The Congress and the several states shall have concurrent power to enforce this article by appropriate legislation.

*Section 3* This article shall be inoperative unless it shall have been ratified as an amendment to the Constitution by the legislatures of the several states, as provided in the Constitution, within seven years from the
date of the submission hereof to the States by the Congress.[13]

## AMENDMENT 19

[Ratified August 18, 1920]

The right of the citizens of the United States to vote shall not be denied or
abridged by the United States or by any State on account of sex.

Congress shall have power, by appropriate legislation, to enforce
the provision of this article.

## AMENDMENT 20

[Ratified January 23, 1933]

*Section 1* The terms of the President and Vice President shall end at
noon on the 20th day of January, and the terms of the Senators and Representatives at noon on the 3rd day of January, of the years in which
such terms would have ended if this article had not been ratified; and the
terms of their successors shall then begin.

*Section 2* The Congress shall assemble at least once in every year, and
such meeting shall begin at noon on the 3rd day of January, unless they
shall by law appoint a different day.

*Section 3* If, at the time fixed for the beginning of the term of the President, the President elect shall have died, the Vice President elect shall
become President. If a President shall not have been chosen before the
time fixed for the beginning of his term, or if the President elect shall
have failed to qualify, then the Vice President elect shall act as President until a President shall have qualified; and the Congress may by law
provide for the case wherein neither a President elect nor a Vice President elect shall have qualified, declaring who shall then act as President, or the manner in which one who is to act shall be selected, and
such person shall act accordingly until a President or Vice President
shall have qualified.

---

[13]Repealed by the 21st Amendment

*Section 4*  The Congress may by law provide for the case of the death of any of the persons from whom the House of Representatives may choose a President whenever the right of choice shall have developed upon them, and for the case of the death of any of the persons from whom the Senate may choose a Vice President whenever the right of choice shall have devolved upon them.

*Section 5*  Sections 1 and 2 shall take effect on the 15th day of October following the ratification of this article.

*Section 6*  This article shall be inoperative unless it shall have been ratified as an amendment to the Constitution by the legislatures of three-fourths of the several States within seven years from the date of its submission.

## AMENDMENT 21

[Ratified December 5, 1933]

*Section 1*  The eighteenth article of amendment to the Constitution of the United States is hereby repealed.

*Section 2*  The transportation or importation into any State, Territory, or Possession of the United States for delivery or use therein of intoxicating liquors, in violation of the laws thereof, is hereby prohibited.

*Section 3*  This article shall be inoperative unless it shall have been ratified as an amendment to the Constitution by conventions in the several States, as provided in the Constitution, within seven years from the date of the submission hereof to the States by the Congress.

## AMENDMENT 22

[Ratified February 27, 1951]

*Section 1*  No person shall be elected to the office of the President more than twice, and no person who has held the office of President, or acted as President, for more than two years of a term to which some other person was elected President shall be elected to the Office of the President more than once. But this Article shall not apply to any person holding the office of President when this article was proposed by the Congress, and shall not prevent any person who may be holding the office of President, or acting as President, during the term within which this Article becomes operative from holding the office of President or acting as President during the remainder of such term.

*Section 2* This Article shall be inoperative unless it shall have been ratified as an amendment to the Constitution by the legislatures of three-fourths of the several states within seven years from the date of its submission to the States by the Congress.

## AMENDMENT 23

[Ratified March 29, 1961]

*Section 1* The District constituting the seat of Government of the United States shall appoint in such manner as the Congress may direct:
   A number of electors of President and Vice President equal to the whole number of Senators and Representatives in Congress to which the District would be entitled if it were a State, but in no event more than the least populous State; they shall be in addition to those appointed by the States, but they shall be considered, for the purposes of the election of President and Vice President, to be electors appointed by a State; and they shall meet in the District and perform such duties as provided by the twelfth article of amendment.

*Section 2* The Congress shall have power to enforce this article by appropriate legislation.

## AMENDMENT 24

[Ratified January 23, 1964]

*Section 1* The right of citizens of the United States to vote in any primary or other election for President or Vice President, for electors for President or Vice President, or for Senator or Representative in Congress, shall not be denied or abridged by the United States or any State by reason of failure to pay any poll tax or other tax.

*Section 2* The Congress shall have power to enforce this article by appropriate legislation.

## AMENDMENT 25

[Ratified February 10, 1967]

*Section 1*  In case of the removal of the President from office or his death or resignation, the Vice President shall become President.

*Section 2*  Whenever there is a vacancy in the office of the Vice President, the President shall nominate a Vice President who shall take the office upon confirmation by a majority vote of both houses of Congress.

*Section 3*  Whenever the President transmits to the President pro tempore of the Senate and the Speaker of the House of Representatives his written declaration that he is unable to discharge the powers and duties of his office, and until he transmits to them a written declaration to the contrary, such powers and duties shall be discharged by the Vice President as Acting President.

*Section 4*  Whenever the Vice-President and a majority of either the principal officers of the executive departments, or of such other body as Congress may by law provide, transmit to the President pro tempore of the Senate and the Speaker of the House of Representatives their written declaration that the President is unable to discharge the powers and duties of his office, the Vice President shall immediately assume the powers and duties of the office as Acting President.

Thereafter, when the President transmits to the President pro tempore of the Senate and the Speaker of the House of Representatives his written declaration that no inability exists, he shall resume the powers and duties of his office unless the Vice President and a majority of either the principal officers of the executive departments, or of such other body as Congress may by law provide, transmit within four days to the President pro tempore of the Senate and the Speaker of the House of Representatives their written declaration that the President is unable to discharge the powers and duties of his office. Thereupon Congress shall decide the issue, assembling within forty-eight hours for that purpose if not in session. If the Congress, within twenty-one days after receipt of the latter written declaration, or, if Congress is not in session, within twenty-one days after Congress is required to assemble, determines by two-thirds vote of both houses that the President is unable to discharge the powers and duties of his office, the Vice President shall continue to discharge the same as Acting President; otherwise, the President shall resume the powers and duties of his office.

## AMENDMENT 26

[Ratified July 1, 1971]

*Section 1* The right of citizens of the United States, who are eighteen years of age, or older, to vote shall not be denied or abridged by the United States or by any State on account of age.

*Section 2* The Congress shall have power to enforce this article by appropriate legislation.

## AMENDMENT 27

[Ratified May 7, 1992]

No law, varying the compensation for the services of the Senators and Representatives, shall take effect, until an election of Representatives shall be intervened.

# Index